I0092180

Movement, Velocity, and Rhythm from a Psychoanalytic Perspective

Movement, Velocity, and Rhythm from a Psychoanalytic Perspective: Variable Speed(s) explores philosophical and psychoanalytic theories, as well as artworks, that show sensible bodily rituals for reviving our social and subjective lives. With a wide range of contributors from interdisciplinary backgrounds, it informs readers on how to find rituals for syncing ourselves with others and world rhythms.

The book is divided into three parts on variability, speed, and slowness, and explores rhythmic rituals of renewal, revolution, and reflection. Each chapter provides unique examples from the applied arts, film, television, and literature to show how different practices of rhythm might aid in creative and deep contemplation and includes philosophical and cultural theories for bodily and rhythmic renewal. Without being limited to a clinical perspective, this book provides wide-ranging discussions of the relation between rhythm, trauma, cultural studies, psychosocial studies, continental philosophy, critical psychology, Lacan, and film, to explore modes of becoming more attuned to each moment, to others, and to our own era.

Movement, Velocity, and Rhythm from a Psychoanalytic Perspective will be essential reading for Lacanian psychoanalysts in practice and in training, as well as anyone interested in rhythm at the intersection of Lacanian psychoanalysis and continental philosophy.

Jessica Datema, PhD, is professor of Literature at Bergen Community College, USA. Dr Datema also received a creative writing certificate for studies accomplished at the University of Cambridge, and she has written and edited two other books.

Angie Voela, PhD, is senior lecturer in Psychosocial Studies at the University of East London, UK. She has published several journal articles, including "We Need to Talk About Family: Essays on Neoliberalism, the Family and Popular Culture" and is the author and editor of two previous books.

Movement, Velocity, and Rhythm from a Psychoanalytic Perspective

Variable Speed(s)

Edited by
Jessica Datema and Angie Voela

Routledge
Taylor & Francis Group

LONDON AND NEW YORK

Cover image: Big Fish Eat Little Fish, Pieter Bruegel the Elder, 1557. Harris Brisbane Dick Fund, 1917; The Met.

First published 2023
by Routledge
4 Park Square, Milton Park, Abingdon, Oxon OX14 4RN

and by Routledge
605 Third Avenue, New York, NY 10158

Routledge is an imprint of the Taylor & Francis Group, an informa business

British Library Cataloguing-in-Publication Data
A catalogue record for this book is available from the British Library

ISBN: 978-1-032-04637-2 (hbk)
ISBN: 978-1-032-04639-6 (pbk)
ISBN: 978-1-003-19403-3 (ebk)

DOI: 10.4324/9781003194033

Typeset in Times New Roman
by codeMantra

This is at the same time our dedication, acknowledgment, and song to: Bookism and its founder, the journal *PCS*, Vanessa Sinclair and everyone at Routledge who helped bring the book to reality. Also, thanks to rhythm as what "separates the succession of the linearity of the sequence or length of time; it bends time to give it to time itself" (Jean Luc Nancy *Listening* 17).

Contents

Contributors

Jessica Datema, PhD, is professor of Literature at Bergen Community College. Recently, Dr Datema also received a creative writing certificate for studies accomplished at the University of Cambridge (2014). Her most recent book is *Revisioning War Trauma in Cinema: Uncoming Communities* (Lexington, 2019), co-authored with Dr Manya Steinkoler.

Jennifer Friedlander, PhD, is the author of *Moving Pictures: Where the Police, the Press, and the Art Image Meet*, in which she explores a set of contemporary British art controversies. Her second book, *Feminine Look: Sexuation, Spectatorship, and Subversion*, develops a psychoanalytically based feminist theory of the visual. Her recent book, *Real Deceptions: The Contemporary Reinvention of Realism* (Oxford University Press, 2017), develops a framework for a contemporary aesthetic politics of realism.

Erica D. Galioto, PhD, is associate professor of English at Shippensburg University where she teaches classes in American literature and psychoanalysis, English education, and writing. Her most recent publications are "Maternal Ambivalence in the Novel and Film *We Need to Talk about Kevin,*" in *Psychoanalysis, Culture & Society*, and a chapter in *Teaching Psychoanalytic Desire in The Age of Innocence* (Palgrave, 2020) titled "We're near each other only if we stay far from each other."

Manya Steinkoler, PhD, is associate professor of English at Borough of Manhattan Community College and a psychoanalyst. With Patricia Gherovici, she has co-edited *Madness Yes You Can't: Lacan on Insanity* (Routledge, 2015) and *Lacan on Comedy* (Cambridge University Press, 2016).

Angie Voela, PhD, is a Reader in Psychosocial Studies at the University of East London, UK. She has published *Psychoanalysis, Philosophy and Myth in Contemporary Culture: After Oedipus* (Palgrave Macmillan, 2017) and has published several books and journal articles, including "We Need to Talk about Family: Essays on Neoliberalism, the Family and Popular Culture."

Eve Watson, PhD, MICP, RegPract APPI, is a psychoanalytic practitioner, clinical supervisor, and academic. She writes on psychoanalysis, sexuality studies, poetics, film, and critical theory. Her recent book (w/Dr Noreen Giffney) is *Clinical Encounters in Sexuality: Psychoanalytic Practice and Queer Theory* (Punctum Books, 2017). She is currently the editor of *Lacunae*, the *APPI International Journal for Psychoanalysis*, a peer-reviewed journal.

Introduction

Rhythmic Transformations

Jessica Datema

Variable Speed(s): Contemplating Movement, Velocity, and Rhythm from a Psychoanalytic Perspective

Rhythm is everywhere. It is harnessed by late capital to make demands of citizens and regulate every social realm of private, public, natural, cultural, virtual, or material life. These demands mostly revolve around profit and the speed of operations. Contrarily, our book searches for rhythmic rites that revitalize humanity through leisure, reflection, creativity, or resistance. As opposed to a rigid devotion to profit, or *pistis*, which Agamben calls the new religion of late capital, our book advocates a creative "resistance . . . that slows down the blind and immediate thrust" (Agamben 19). Each section of *Movement, Velocity, and Rhythm* follows the rhythmic potential that emerges from a slow, fast, or variable engagement of the senses. All chapters in our book explore philosophical and psychoanalytic theories, as well as artworks that show sensible bodily rituals for reviving our social and subjective lives.

As outlining the potential of rhythm, all sections of our book respond to a real need for rituals that supplement the contradictory demands of late capital to carry on and keep calm at the same time. Part I "Variable Measures" takes up the dare of discovering mutable practices of cultural engagement that strike a balance between speed and burnout. Jennifer Friedlander's article on the film *Us* explores how rhythmic bodily practices like resistance through dance or a varying repetition may pave the way for revolution. While rhythm is a residue, this section shows how it is a powerful one that allows us to assess the ways we are coping and find better measures.

Part II of *Movement, Velocity, and Rhythm* entitled "Speed" explores creative practices to curb capitalist acceleration and deregulate the exhausted mind and body. Angie Voela's article on rhythm in *Baby Driver* and *The Beat That My Heart Skipped* follows figures in a ritual relation with music via driving and playing piano that both alleviates and enables a life of

DOI: 10.4324/9781003194033-1

fastmoving thuggery. Chapters in the "Speed" section explore hastening because of cultural demands for productivity and utility that began in the industrial age with the invention of machines and have only magnified with technology and global warming. A chapter by Manya Steinkoler and Jessica Datema on Lee Chang Dong's film *Burning* highlights the rapid pace and spread of fires that are escalating after the globalization of late capital, displaced citizens, and polluting of the environment.

Part III of the book entitled "Slowness" explores rhythmic practices of deceleration and includes an article by Jessica Datema entitled "Richtering Rhythms: *Never Look Away*," which is a film about Gerhard Richter's blurry, smeared, smudged, and transient paintings that variably interrupt imaginary wholeness. The film screens over Richter's method of overpainting, which momentarily renders the rhythm of transience, or what Jacques Lacan calls "a stain of the real." Also in this section is a chapter by Erica Galioto that analyzes Ling Ma's *Severance*, which eerily prefigures the COVID-19 pandemic to consider how the physical illness of Shen Fever metaphorically resembles the Lacanian drive run amok and the psychic severance that is its symptom.

Putting cultural, continental, clinical, and aesthetic philosophical paradigms together, *Movement, Velocity, and Rhythm* explores real measured rhythmic practices that offset a viral culture of oscillating frenzy, burnout, and aggression. Each chapter discusses creative measures of rhythmic coping with late capitalist symptoms like languishing or fever that have only becoming more rampant since the pandemic. The book is divided into three parts on variability, speed, and slowness that explore rhythmic rituals of renewal, revolution, or reflection. These practices are often dismissed and discarded by the discourses of science and capitalism. All sections include examples from the applied arts on how practices of rhythm might aid in creative and deep contemplation. Walter Benjamin decreed "the idleness of the *flâneur* is a demonstration against the division of labor" (Benjamin 427). Idling is a timeworn way of resisting regulatory imbalance through rituals of observation, wandering, and recess. Our book explores similar arrhythmic rituals of creative suspense like what analysts call a "cut" in the psychoanalytic session.

Walter Benjamin's *Arcades Project* also describes idleness as both a cultivation and a break from

> the rhythm of today which . . . which satisfies the deep-seated need of this generation to see the "flow" of development disavowed, and the continuous musical accompaniments. To root out every trace of "development" from the image of history and to represent becoming—through the dialectical rupture between sensation and tradition—as a constellation in being; That is no less the tendency of this project. (Benjamin 845)

Movement, Velocity, and Rhythm contrasts the "project" of late capitalist rhythms that disconnect, disavow, and automate to find rhythms beyond trauma that connect history and becoming sensations.

In the same vein, Blanchot describes the multiplying momentum of midnight as what happens "Slowly during those nights when I sleep without sleeping, I become aware—" (Antelme and Dobbels 55). This sort of attention is not conscious or unconscious but a pause that comes from being between awake and asleep, operative and inoperative. Blanchot suggests midnight has a "rhythm, in all these forms, [it] is the movement of a disappearance, the movement of return at to the heart of disappearance—a faltering beat however, which bit by bit affirms itself" (Blanchot, *The Space of Literature* 114). Midnight, as Blanchot refers to Mallarmé's *Igitur*, is an hour where one realizes the present is inexplicable except as knotted to the past and future. It is an ecstatic instant which is often ignored, even though it recurs every day. Midnight marks the repetitiveness and perpetual displacement of being in time that comes back around never the same as the day before. It is an arrhythmic moment punctuated by repetitiveness, doubling back, and circularity. In this regard, midnight serves as a generative space for doubling back and directionless becoming, the zero hour of circadian rhythms.

Finally, our book traces rhythm as manifest in the applied cultural arts, including film and painting. It foregrounds how unconscious bodily rituals (like dance or play) might activate a conscious rhythmic potential. *Movement, Velocity, and Rhythm from a Psychoanalytic Perspective: Variable Speed(s)* is a rethinking of sublimation, trauma, and the body through assemblages of rhythm. Toward that end, our book analyzes how it is possible to find measured rituals or cadenced formations that reset our social and subjective lives. *Movement, Velocity, and Rhythm* explores modes of becoming more attuned to each moment, to others, to our own era, even as automation, alienation, and acting out abound. It is not a book on burnout or exhaustion, but about surviving and seizing all opportunities to find rituals for syncing ourselves with others and world rhythms.

* * *

Rhythm is nowhere. The origin of rhythm resides in the oscillation of word and image, when an event is given form. Rhythms of the mouth, for example, reside in the repetition compulsions of the Lacanian real, which, after the acquisition of language, become demands of speech. The acceptance of an organizing chain of signifiers is not something we write about to explain the dialectic of rhythm. Rather, our book follows rhythm's beat as an event that involves an opening and closing of being in language, what continental philosophy calls the *es gibt* or *il y a*. Rhythm dwells on the edge of speaking being an indicator of "the possibility of form itself."

Continental philosophers like Heidegger initiate discussion of the world rhythms into which existence is thrown. As Simon Critchley has written,

> Dasein is being-in-the-world. Our everyday existence is characterized by complete immersion in the ways of the world. The world fascinates us and my life is completely caught up in its rhythms and activities. The question Heidegger asks in *Being and Time* Chapter 6 is: how is the being-in-the-world to be disclosed? Is there an experience where the world as such and as a whole is revealed to us? Is there a mood in which we pull back from the world and see it as something distinct from us? Heidegger's claim is that being-in-the-world is disclosed in anxiety and is then defined as care. As such, anxiety has an important methodological function in the argument of Being and Time. (Critchley)

Blanchot's *il y a,* with all its Heideggerian and Levinasian inflections, would evoke being (*es gibt*) as an ontological state, like the influences, where some form of movement is at issue. Rather, Blanchot's "It is" is more what stops movement, an emphatic embrace of the inertia in being (*désouvrement*) as constitutive in-itself (*en-soi*).

This "It is" activates a coordination of the world, otherness, and subjective rhythms, which through anxiety and care, nurtures a cadence or pulse from the chaos. As Lacoue-Labarthe says, rhythm is

> something between beat and figure that . . . implies—at the very edge of what of the subject can appear, manifest, or figure itself—the pre-inscription which, conforming us in advance, . . . [also] sends us back to the chaos that obviously was not schematized by *us* so that we should appear as what we are. In this sense, perhaps, "every soul is a rhythmic knot." We ("we") are rhythmed. (Lacoue-Labarthe 202)

The quote refers to Stéphané Mallarmé, who calls the poetic expression of personhood a rhythmic knot. This knot is a person's key signature, and polyphonic song, which is not reducible to naming.

The line is translated differently as "Every soul is a braid of rhythm—*toute âme est un noeud rhythmique* (Mallarmé et al. 33). In a very famous letter written to Léo d'Orfer in 1886 Mallarmé relates,

> Poetry is the expression, through human language reduced to its essential rhythm *[par le langage humain ramené à son rythme essentiel]*, of the mysterious meaning of the aspects of existence: it thus bestows authenticity on our sojourn and constitutes the only spiritual task. (572)

Rhythm is a non-objective part of human language, experience, and voice. It is indirectly accessed through bodily experiences, art, and poetry, not as a material or verifiable object. It binds immeasurable and mysterious aspects of being to metrical parts of the world, for example, clock time to seasons. Rhythm traverses symbolic, imaginary, and real realms of sleep and waking, spatial dwelling, and departure. It is an immaterial real necessity for a dynamic, creative, intellectual, and spiritually fulfilling human life. Our book is a cultural study of rhythm as the symptomatic and sinthomatic knots that defy description or even naming but hold together appearance and the non-apparent. It broadens the discussion of rhythm by drawing on Jacques Lacan as well as other continental philosophers such as Philippe Lacoue-Labarthe, Jean-Luc Nancy, Gilles Deleuze, and Maurice Blanchot to explore rhythm at a fruitful juncture of speaking being and primordial negation.

An early Marxist philosopher writing on rhythm, Henri Lefebvre (1901–1991) critiques theories of rhythm by pointing out,

> this scandal of philosophers from Plato to Hegel . . . without metaphysics. [is] Nothing inert in the world, no things, very diverse rhythms, slow or lively (in relation to us). (This garden that I have before my eyes appears differently to me now from a moment ago. I have understood the rhythms: trees, flowers, birds and insects. They form a polyrhythmia with the surroundings: the simultaneity of the present (therefore of presence), the apparent immobility that contains one thousand and one movements, etc. . . . (Lefebvre 17)

As a rupture of language not reducible to any "theory," rhythm involves the interplay of time, place, and figuration. French philosophy back to Bergson and Bachelard shows how rhythm plays a crucial role in the realization of temporal existence, duration, and discontinuity.

Prior to Lefebvre in 1790, Kant's *The Critique of Judgment* describes the rhythm of reflective judgment, which is not grounded in representation but involves the play of imagination and reason together in opposition. Reflective judgment is a subjective play of mental powers where "The mind feels set in motion in the representation of the sublime in nature. . . . This movement, especially in its inception, may be compared with a vibration" (Kant 107). In *The Critique of Judgment,* Kant notes how aesthetic judgment involves a rhythmic motion and "vibration" that is not grounded in any external reference. Likewise, the Lacanian drives, or Deleuzean lines of flight involve a headless "rhythmization of perception" after reflective judgment. Rhythm is apprehended aesthetically like the sublime as between material objects and bodily sensations. In Deleuze and Lacan, the sublime is not transcendent, but an arrhythmic suspense found in *emoi* (expressions) of pain and beauty (Lacan, *The Ethics of Psychoanalysis* 249).

Post-structuralist philosophers trace rhythm at the end of theory to a primary negation, which is not reducible to foreclosure. It is born from what

Žižek, following Lacan, calls the "minimal difference," or alienation that occurs after the acquisition of language. It is heard in the birth cry that inaugurates subjective division as the splitting of speaking and pre-symbolic being. This antagonism is described differently by post-structuralists as the reverberation of oppositional drives, or by others as a refrain or line of flight. Deleuze describes rhythm's refrain as the "negative at work in destruction, [which] always manifests itself as the other face of construction (Deleuze, *Masochism* 30). Lacoue-Labarthe sees rhythm as not an analyzable or theorizable process, but as something at "work before the birth and after the death of the subject . . . the death of the subject threated by rhythm is not merely negative. Rather it is a moment of mystical affirmation. And at that affirmative moment, where theory fails, rhythm beings to speak" (Lacoue-Labarthe 201). Jacques Lacan also links rhythms to the real driven pain and pleasure, which underlie "reality as *unterlegt*, [underlying] *untertragen*, which with superb ambiguity of the French language appears to be translated by the same word—*souffrance*" (Lacan, *The Four Fundamental Concepts of Psychoanalysis* 53). Within reality is this underlying real negation or pain (*en souffrance*), which also means in suspense, in abeyance, a pulse awaiting attention.

Moreover, Lacan echoes Mallarmé in his late *Seminar XXIII* on sinthomatic creating as working through the Borromean Knot. This knot is a nod to Mallarmé's rhythmic knot as the not-being and primal negation, which Joyce uses as a limit in creating instead of castration. Lacan describes how discourse is determined by the installation of this knot that intertwines the registers. The later Lacan builds on earlier ideas of the sacrifice of being (*jouissance*) in speaking which Lacan says "the symbol first manifests as the killing of the thing, and this death results in the endless perpetuation of the subject's desire" (Lacan, *Ecrits* 262). In the later Lacan, Joyce infuses the word with *jouissance* through the rhythmic knot that is a residue of the painful rift of the symbolic from the real.

Early Lacan conceives of the rhythmic movement as originating from the dialectic of desire that drives the signifying chain. Within the dialectic, the rhythms of the drive are the loci of pain and pleasure, the body's articulations; they are the thrusts and resistances that undergird and propel speaking being. Rhythm is not reducible to the drives or a state of nature, but an interstice concerning the body and the gaps in language. It appears in experiences of intimacy or anxiety as an echo and a reminder of misrepresentation in signification. In short, continental philosophy does not assume we can directly access rhythm as a natural vibration of the material world but that it is only indirectly accessed through extra-linguistic experiences of art, time, trauma, or bodily rituals.

Lacan, Deleuze, and Blanchot coincide in their mutual eschewal of the dialectic as transcendent insofar as it stands in for a present and positive ontology and nevertheless incorporate a dialectic as an uneasy relation between stillness and movement. If there is a stoppage of physical movement, there is the potential for movement of thought via language, the chain of signification.

For Lacan and Blanchot, there is no movement outside writing. Sections from "The Essential Solitude" illustrate this:

> To write *is* to surrender to the fascination of time's absence. . . . The time of time's absence has no present, no presence…The time of time's absence *is* not dialectical. . . . The reversal which, in time's absence, points us constantly back to the presence of absence. . . . The dead present *is* the impossibility of making any presence real. . . . Here fascination reigns . . . and fascination *is* passion for the image. . . . Fascination *is* solitude's gaze. . . . To write *is* to enter the affirmation of the solitude in which fascination threatens. It is to surrender to the risk of time's absence where eternal starting over reigns. (Blanchot, *The Space of Literature* 30–33)

Fascination is found in writing that infinitely fights the impossibility of ever properly representing real being in language. It is a struggle with the necessary pleasures of symbolization that always accompany its solitude and alienation.

The impossibility of representing the real movement of writing that Blanchot describes is like Lacan's description of infinite turning within the four discourses. *Seminar XX* describes how speaking being is contingent upon the necessity and impossibility of four modalities of discourses that are: *ce qui ne cesse pas de s'écrire* (what does not stop writing itself). This dialectic incorporates the necessary as what "doesn't stop being written," the contingent as what doesn't stop not writing itself and the impossible as "what does not stop not being written," that is, the possible (Lacan, *On Feminine Sexuality: The Limits of Love and Knowledge* 94). Lacan describes subjectivity as caught in this movement as a chain of signification that does not stop writing (*écrits*) itself. He picks up on the necessity within discourse that is first described by Freud in the late essays.

Freud mythically figures an arrhythmic relation of language and necessity at the end of his "The Economic Principle of Masochism." A primary negation associated with the pleasures and pain of symbolization is tied to "the rhythms of unpleasure-pleasure, the *fort/da* game and the traumatic dream . . . as equivalent models not only of the beating fantasy and masochistic perversion but also of symbolization at its most basic level. . . . This conceding could also be called a constitutive non-coinciding of the subject with itself; a differing from itself, which constitutes the rhythm" (Civitarese 907). This relation is not reducible to perversion but tied to the painful *necessity* within *logos* that drives speaking being.

Most readers know that even while Freud renounces religion, he uses mythic figures to describe modalities beyond representation. In addition to

Eros and *Thanatos*, he uses *Ananké* to describe the necessity or fate that determines Oedipal logocentrism. Notably, *Ananké* is a feminine power of accident and birth that Freud mentions as the necessity—not intelligent or intentional design—that compels *Logos*. *Ananké* is a painful modality that accompanies the pleasure of symbolization. She is not reducible to maso-chism, but a figure of the accidental necessity bound up in speaking being.

Freud mentions *Logos* and *Ananké* as a mythic figuration of personhood not reducible to parenthood. *Logos* with *Ananké* does not reference persons but the necessity of being in symbolization. It is an antagonism that emerges from the inevitable realization of contingency. As a modality beyond rep-resentation that rotates discourse, *Ananké* is a person's "impersonal" key signature, their inevitable song struggling to surface beyond:

> The *imagos* they leave behind [that] are then linked on the influences of teacher, authorities of self-chosen models and heroes venerated by soci-ety; these persons need no longer be introjected by the ego, which has not become more resistant. The last figure in the series beginning with the parents is that dark supremacy of Fate, which only the fewest among us are able to conceive of impersonally. Little can be said against the Dutch writer, Multatuli, when he substitutes the divine pair *ananké* and *logos* [my translation from the Greek] for the fates of the Greeks [*Moiré*]; but all those who transfer the guidance of the world to Providence, to God, or to God and Nature, rouse a suspicion that they still look upon these farthest and remotest powers as a parent couple—mythologically—and imagine themselves linked to them by libidinal bonds. In *Das Ich* and *das Es* I have made an attempt to derive the objective fear of death in mankind also from the same sort of parental conception of Fate. It seems to be very difficult to free oneself from it. (Freud 265)

Like the mother-tongue, Fate is given voice as if by destiny, without inten-tional thinking. *Logos* with *Ananké* are one poetic figuration of Mallarmé's "rhythmic knot." Necessity, contingency, and impossibility are the rhythmic "knots" that bind being in discourse. These modalities are the "rhythmic knot" and potential that can help one find a rhythm. Our book illustrates how this potential is cultivated through a rhythmic know-how (*savoir-faire*) of habits that shepherd *jouissance*.

Rhythm is a human potential activated through bodily adaptive ritual practices like architecture, composing, or writing that get better as they are practiced. These rituals can aid in constructing attunement and equilibrium for subjects and society. In contrast with the use of rhythm for autocratic measures, our book turns toward necessity and contingency and away from the danger of cultural entropy manifest in autocratic political, capitalist, and technological rhythms. Rhythmic rituals for self-governing avoid ced-ing agency to sync with institutions, calendars, or a cultural rule. Our book explores rhythmic states of knot-being that activate a bodily potential not externally imposed in a turning toward necessity past trauma.

After Freud, post-structuralists like Blanchot figure this necessity within speaking being and knotted entwining other ways, for example, Orpheus and Eurydice. Fate is not cognitively ascertained but felt as a sensory force that is often painful and tragic, that is, one day my heart will stop. It only appears in arrhythmic moments like midnight which expose the intimate opposition of nothing and being, appearance and the non-apparent. Rhythmic modalities appear only briefly in staged moments that disappear as quickly as they appear. Exposures of rhythm are accomplished in a non-mimetic struggle, act, or staging.

Each of our chapters traces artworks that stage the ritual turning of rhythmic modal knots in discourse. One chapter explores the BBC detective farce entitled *Killing Eve* that is a twist on the hard-boiled genre. *Killing Eve* plays with Deleuze's masochist aesthetic stage to expose the painful necessity and chance accident that compels logocentric detection. Eve Watson's article entitled "Radical Temporalities of Trauma, Melancholia and Disaster" reads Lacan, Blanchot, and Sebald to show how a confrontation with the real of trauma can anxiously lead to what Blanchot calls a "responsible or responsive passivity," that answers the impossible and gives repose (Blanchot, *The Writing of the Disaster* 20).

Inertia as an arrhythmic path of ontology, Blanchot writes, happens in and through literature, the arts, and literary works. He writes that the work of art, the literary work, is never finished and does not speak, rather it engages being as "it is." Here the verb "to be," writes Blanchot "declares being in the unique moment of rupture—those very words: *it is*, the point which the work brilliantly illuminates even while receiving its consuming burst of light—we must also comprehend and feel that this point renders the work impossible, because it never permits arrival at the work. It is a region anterior to the beginning where nothing is made of being and in which nothing is accomplished. It is the depth of being's inertia (*désouvrement*)" (Blanchot, *The Space of Literature* 46). Impossibility activates passive being through literature as a generative form as nothing. The danger and power of literature, Blanchot explains, is its impasse, passivity, and inability to stop movement. It sparks a turning toward inertia and unworking (*désouvrement*) that is an arhythmic potential through *en-soi* or being *in-itself*.

One question we feel our book addresses is why a study of continental philosophy and Jacques Lacan on rhythm but not Alfred North Whitehead? The short answer is that analytic philosophy presumes direct access to rhythm without acknowledging its relation to the structure of language. Whitehead's *Process and Reality* puts forth an organic view that existence is a conglomeration of vibratory movements and a/rhythmic patterns. It presents the metaphysical idea of "nature alive" as a function of vibratory matter, which is the basis of creation. Whitehead like other analytic philosophers erroneously presumes direct apprehension outside language and the unconscious to "explain" rhythm.

Rhythm emerges as an exception, surplus, or cadenced gap within symbolization. Moreover, analytic philosophy doesn't account for those measures, tempos, or rhythmic pulses that are not explained and only sensed. These are bodily engagements with the *Real* in Lacan, the *refrain* in Deleuze, or *turning back* in Blanchot. Rhythm exists outside signification, but it can only be accessed therein, as analytic philosophy ignores. It is marked, mapped, or unearthed indirectly through aesthetic sensation—in artworks, bodily rituals, cycles, or gestures—not directly as metaphysical nature.

Presumptions of analytic philosophy on rhythm are exposed in the continental tradition of Heidegger and continue in the philosophies of Jacques Lacan, Maurice Blanchot, and Gilles Deleuze. These philosophers, unlike Whitehead, assume that rhythm is indirectly apprehended via affective holes or gaps in language. They relate to our experience of rhythm as an affective necessity, contingency, or impossibility that occurs when facing primordial negation, for example, "rhythmic knot-being." Like Whitehead, Hegel's conception of the dialectic as a teleological movement assumes both matter and a metaphysical direction in rhythm. Contrarily, continental philosophy conceives of rhythm as an extra-linguistic exposure to unpredictable modalities that drive speaking being.

Our book explores Lacan with Deleuze and Blanchot to trace "rhythmic knot-being" across theoretical and aesthetic "works" as a potential not reducible to any ideological system. It foregrounds and follows the accidents, repetition, holes, and chance rhythms that propel artistic and cultural movements. Rhythm does not fit into any apparent system but is an organizing anarchic force of appearance itself. Nicolas Abraham notes how "instead of saying a 'perception of rhythm' it would be better to speak of 'rhythmization of perception'" (Abraham and Torok 21). Perception does not explain rhythm but rather engages it as an aesthetic and bodily arrangement.

Rhythm, as our book shows, is not only a "knotting" of discourse and speaking being in Jacques Lacan, but also an immanence in Deleuze's transcendental empiricism. As a philosophy of the event, nomadology is directly concerned with arrhythmic processes of becoming not reducible to material reality. In Deleuze, rhythm emerges from the swerve of life force to image, which is a fundamental part of the ontogenetic process of incessant becoming. Language doesn't represent but is an asymmetrical, counter-conditional expression. Each expression is an event or staging of the movement from lifeworld to image since "contents and expressions do not share a form" (Massumi xviii). Rhythm is a creative potential that lies in the drift between content and expression. Deleuzian rhythm is not exactly like the Lacanian Real, which emerges as an exception within language. Rather, it is an extra-linguistic expression—a refrain, swerve, or conversion—and bodily occurrence that is immanent to language.

Deleuze and Guattari, like Lacan, note how the subject is in a sense spoken by forces of expression which are not material. Rhythm is this extra-linguistic force expressed in unmediated, variable, or circular movements of thought or the body. Here we note how our book is about "rhythmic knots" in being, which relate to both the affective experiences of the Lacanian drives and Deleuze's body without organs. As connected to the immanent body and lifeworld, rhythm is first realized as a strike, blow, or birth that is performativity manifest without being cognitively understood. Moreover, for Deleuze, every act of language is a performative event, a line of flight that involves a rhythmic swerve or conversion of lifeworld to image.

Deleuze's cinema and painting books are relevant as they are a study of rhythm, movement, and time in artworks. In *The Logic of Sensation*, Deleuze explains how "the coexistence of all these movements in the painting . . . is rhythm" (Deleuze, *Francis Bacon* 30). Deleuze describes how Francis Bacon's paintings display their own deformity, or form, contracting, through the body without organs. This body lies beneath the organic bodily frame and foregrounds the paintings' own dis/appearance. In this *ex nihilo* process, a pattern happens after rhythm, as a modal force in representation, wins the battle of appearing; this battle *Le battement de l'apparaître is* what initiates shape in being and artistic creation.

Each chapter in our book analyzes an artwork—such as music, cinema, or painting—which, as both Deleuze and Lacan note, comes after a battle of the senses and appearance. This process of creative becoming involves the muse as rhythmic spark awakening our senses. Jean-Luc Nancy notes that rhythm rarely appears, except in art where we "*see* a kind of original unity of the senses and causes a multisensible figure to appear visually. But this operation is directly plugged into a vital power that exceeds all domains and traverses them. This power is Rhythm" (Nancy 23). Nancy highlights how rhythm is a modality and muse that is sensed in artworks that display the beat of disappearing within their appearance.

Maurice Blanchot describes this muse as Eurydice who, like *Ananké*, affects a "turning back" of Orpheus. This unworking is a necessity within representation figured by the rhythmic movement of Orpheus' "turning back." Orpheus' betrayal is analogous to the movement of writing itself, where the acquisition of meaning requires that the word replaces the thing. Blanchot connects this movement of turning, turning back, turning away, or returning to the origin of representation and movement of writing, as the un-coupling of words and things (Blanchot, *The Space of Literature* 176). It is when Orpheus oversteps, turns back, and gazes at Eurydice, that is, faces death/fate, that the rhythmic refrain is born. The journey back from the underworld shows the origin of speech as a song awakened by rhythm.

Ostensibly, in turning back, Orpheus ruins the work since Eurydice returns to the underworld. Yet in looking back, the truth of midnight is revealed as a potential or plenitude out of nothing. Orpheus' turning is an art of saying, like what Lacan calls *l'art dire* that is not a sublimation, but a singing of negation or the very holes in signifying chain itself. This saying is what Lacan calls when "existence is born; that is where we are. It is the fact of the 'that one say'—it is the saying (*dire*) that is behind all that is said (*dit*) -which is something that arises in historical actuality" (Lacan, "On Psychoanalytic Discourse"). The *sinthome*, like Lacan's Milan lecture, describes an art of saying (*l'art dire*) that is an act of saying (*l'act dire*) which happens through the knotting of discourse. Orpheus' music, like the artwork, reveals how saying is an act/art infused with a negation, which is not nonsense but a rhythmic turn. In turning, Orpheus manages to sing (*dire*) negation and necessity, that is, the muse that is *Ananké/Eurydice*, within discourse. The muse is the nothing that sparks interest in the hole, negation, and mysterious knots of being. She is what compels appearance and speech.

Orpheus' "turning" and betrayal of Eurydice is also the beginning of music, or a kind of saying that does not work through lack but out of abundance. Like what Lacan describes as Joyce's non-representational neologism in *Seminar XXIII*, our book explores non-representational artworks that are an act and art of saying (*l'act, l'art dire*) in film, dance, and music. The chapter on the *Killing Eve* follows the multiple turns that make a *condansation* between Eve, the detective, and Villanelle, the *femme fatale* villain (Lacan, *The Sinthome* 62). These women take turns at trying to kill one another, dance with and around one another, then in the last episode of the last season three, perform an Orphic turn on a bridge. Eve and Villanelle suffer in the maternal realm not to avoid negation, but to confront *Ananké* and side step the logocentric rule of The Twelve.

Correlatively, the "leap" is another figuration of being in thrall to an arrhythmic act. In "The Origin of the Work of Art," Heidegger holds that "a leap [*Sprung*]" is "always a head start, in which everything to come is already leaped over, even if as something disguised" (Heidegger, *Poetry, Language, Thought.* 76). For Heidegger, anticipatory resolution is *Dasein's* way of dealing with being thrown into the world, to leap into temporality. Blanchot is also interested in the nature of "a leap" as a limit experience; "there would be no limit if the limit were not passed, revealed as impassable by being passed" (Blanchot, *The Infinite Conversation* 433). Connecting the muse and the idea of inspiration as a leap, Blanchot elaborates, "One can only write if one arrives at the instant towards which one can only move through space opened up by writing. . . . The essence of writing, the difficulty of experience, and the leap of inspiration also lie within this contradiction" (Blanchot, *The Station Hill Blanchot Reader* 442). The leap is stirred by necessity as arising out of the openings, rifts, separations, or fissures in language. Remarkably, rhythm is not merely theoretical, and it must be traced artistically and philosophically to apprehend its shifty ground.

Finally, our introduction to the book's theoretical positions holds that the idea of "rhythmic knot of being" is what exceeds ontological or even symbolic measures. Blanchot notes:

> Let us recall Hölderlin: "All is rhythm" . . . How is this sentence to be understood? "All" does not mean the cosmic in an already ordered totality which it would be rhythm's job to maintain. Rhythm does not belong to the order of nature, or of language, or even of "art," where it seems to predominate. Rhythm is not the simple alternation of the Yes and No, of "giving -withholding," of presence-absence or of living-dying, producing-destroying. Rhythm, while it disengages the multiple from its missing unity, and while it appears regular and seems to govern according to a rule, threatens the rule. For always it exceeds the rule though a reversal [turn/*Kehre*] whereby, being in play or in operation within measure, it is not measured thereby. The enigma of rhythm—dialectical-nondialectical, no more the one than the other is other—is the extreme danger. (Blanchot, *The Writing of the Disaster* 112–13)

This passage from *Writing of the Disaster* echoes passages on danger from Heidegger's essay "The Turning." This essay was first given in 1949 as part of a series of four lectures entitled "Insight into That Which Is." It considers how the modern "epoch" of technology will affect being/Being and its rhythms. In *Being and Time* what Heidegger calls a "turning-toward death" is an existential state where being becomes anticipatory and resolute about death. This lecture again mentions "turning" but as related to the danger of technology, which can entrap and cause being to forget its "Destining" (Heidegger, "The Turning" 37). Notably, the German translation of "destining" is from the word *Geschick* or *schickung*, which means skill or aptitude at handling fate or destiny ("The Turning" 37). Technology creates new rhythmic cycles of earth and world that beget new forms of attunement. The task of being is finding our key signature or destined rhythm.

For Heidegger, the idea of "turning" is inseparable from that of "saving," which is the ability of being to adapt or turn toward its contingency in language. "Destining" is a modality for rhythmically adapting to the changing directions of culture and technology. Heidegger notes how the greatest "danger" is that being will not change. Change requires turning toward the rhythms of trauma and cultural change that challenge as a danger both without and within. "Destining" is a rhythmic turn with necessity that is a response to this danger. It is a way of activating through the variable rhythm of fate and accident to accommodate cultural shifts.

After Heidegger, Blanchot highlights how "turning" is a confrontation with history and the mystery of "rhythmic knot-being." Turning toward rhythm is a way to negotiate change and activate the movements of necessity, contingency, and impossibility that bind. While the rhythms of turning past trauma in theory, literature, life, art, and the world often feel circular and uncanny as if going astray, they can also be an opening. As seen in the moment of midnight, rhythm offers a way of reflectively turning toward a new day despite ever changing cultural *Zeitgeists*. Our book, following Arianne's thread through the labyrinth, turns toward the danger—as dialectical-nondialectical and immeasurable—to approach the enigma of rhythm and unravel its key signatures.

Works Cited

Abraham, Nicolas, and Maria Torok. *Rhythms: On the Work, Translation, and Psychoanalysis*. Translated by Nicholas T. Rand, Stanford University Press, 1995.

Agamben, Giorgio. *Creation and Anarchy: The Work of Art and the Religion of Capitalism*. Stanford University Press, 2019.

Antelme, Robert, and Daniel Dobbels. *On Robert Antelme's The Human Race: Essays and Commentary*. Marlboro Press/Northwestern, 2003.

Benjamin, Walter. *The Arcades Project*. Translated by Rolf Tiedemann, Belknap Press, 1999.

Blanchot, Maurice. *The Infinite Conversation*. University of Minnesota Press, 1993.

——. *The Space of Literature*. Translated by Ann Smock, University of Nebraska Press, 1982.

——. *The Station Hill Blanchot Reader: Fiction & Literary Essays*. Translated by Paul Auster et al., Station Hill/Barrytown, Ltd, 1999.

——. *The Writing of the Disaster*. Translated by Ann Smock, University of Nebraska Press, 1995.

Civitarese, Giuseppe. "Masochism and Its Rhythm." *Journal of the American Psychoanalytic Association*, vol. 64, no. 5, Oct. 2016, pp. 885–916, https://doi.org/10.1177/0003065116674442.

Critchley, Simon. "Being and Time, Part 5: Anxiety." *The Guardian*, 6 July 2009, https://www.theguardian.com/commentisfree/belief/2009/jul/06/heidegger-philosophy-being.

Deleuze, Gilles. *Francis Bacon: The Logic of Sensation*. University of Minnesota Press, 2004.

——. *Masochism: Coldness and Cruelty*. Zone Books, 1991.

Freud, Sigmund. "The Economic Problem of Masochism." *Collected Papers*, edited by James Strachey, vol. 2, The Hogarth Press, 1950, pp. 255–68.

Heidegger, Martin. *Poetry, Language, Thought*. Harper & Row, 1971.

——. "The Turning." *The Question Concerning Technology, and Other Essays*, translated by William Lovitt, Garland Pub, 1977, pp. 36–49.

Kant, Immanuel. *The Critique of Judgement*. Translated by James Creed Meredith, Clarendon Press, 1952.

Lacan, Jacques. *Ecrits: The First Complete Edition in English*. Translated by Bruce Fink, Norton, 2006.

——. *On Feminine Sexuality: The Limits of Love and Knowledge*. Edited by Jacques Alain Miller, Translated by Bruce Fink, vol. 20, WW Norton, 1999.

——. "On Psychoanalytic Discourse." *La Salmandra*, translated by Jack Stone, 1978, pp. 32–55, https://web.archive.org/web/20140729192754/http://web.missouri.edu/~stonej/t67894312xxxv.html.

——. *The Ethics of Psychoanalysis*. Edited by Jacques-Alain Miller, Translated by Dennis Porter, W. W. Norton, 1997.

——. *The Four Fundamental Concepts of Psychoanalysis*. Edited by Jacques-Alain Miller, Translated by Alan Sheridan, Reiss, Norton, 1998.

——. *The Sinthôme: The Seminar of Jacques Lacan, Book XXIII*. Translated by A. R Price, 1st edition, Polity, 2016.

Lacoue-Labarthe, Philippe. *Typography: Mimesis, Philosophy, Politics*. Edited by Christopher Fynsk, Stanford University Press, 1998.

Lefebvre, Henri. *Rhythmanalysis: Space, Time, and Everyday Life*. Bloomsbury Academic, an imprint of Bloomsbury Publishing Plc, 2017.

Mallarmé, Stéphane, et al. *Mallarmé in prose*. New Directions, 2001.

Massumi, Brian, editor. *A Shock to Thought: Expressions after Deleuze and Guattari*. Routledge, 2002.

Nancy, Jean-Luc. *The Muses*. Stanford University Press, 1996.

Part I

Variable Measures

Chapter 1

Killing Eve

Inflections of Rebirth and Pathogenesis

Jessica Datema and Angie Voela

Killing Eve is a very successful TV series (three seasons as of this writing), and detective drama set in modern-day about post-Cold War Europe, an interminable chase of a contract killer, Villanelle, by her nemesis, and a newly minted detective, Eve Polastri, once a low-level MI5 functionary. If the Cold War gave the impression that opposite sides were clearly set apart, the present affords a different perspective: the good times that KGB and MI5 agents were sharing, including sexual relations, the exchange of information and resources contacted with bonhomie if not a genuine spirit of cooperation continue. Yet, the continuation of these practices differs in that no one is sure who the other works for and whose organization is infiltrated by whom. Now operatives from both sides work for or against organized non-state interests. The series' cosmos where oligarchs rule while political and governing bodies' collapse is not dissimilar to our globalized world. In *Eve*, it is an entity known as The Twelve who preside after law breaks down into rhetoric, having no anchor in truth. Thus, *Killing Eve* lays out a farcical world of dissolving symbolization, gender, intelligence, detection, reality, surveillance, and truth.

In terms of genre and gender, *Killing Eve* contains no stable categories but is full of flopped, flipped, and failed detective cases. Eve and Villanelle constitute the detective-killer pair, which, according to the rules of the genre, must eventually confront one another after missed encounters and near misses. The series mocks and mimics classic tropes of the lesbian detective story as described by Linda Williams after Laura Mulvey and Alison Moore (Williams, *Critical Desire*; A. Moore). Twisting the genre of the classic detective story, or perhaps mirroring the collapse of binaries introduced above, the two women find themselves sexually attracted to one another.

Yet, Eve Polastri does not conform as a classic or hard-boiled detective and only stays officially employed until the end of Season II simply to connect with Villanelle. Eve is not only a defunct symbolic woman but also her heart is not really into being a detective solving crimes. Likewise, Villanelle is ostensibly a figure of surplus femininity, but she does not smoothly conform to the hard-boiled "dame with a past." Officially dead, this Russian

DOI: 10.4324/9781003194033-3

woman-born Oxsana is an untraceable psychopathic contract killer working for The Twelve, an odd *femme fatale*[1] who dresses up as a pretty pig baby or clown before fatally destroying whoever is in her path.

Flaunting conventional categories of the genre, *Killing Eve* twists each detective case by delivering little closure or connection. Each season of *Killing Eve* ends as a cessation without conclusion, after numerous killings without consequence or payoff. Likewise, each of *Killing Eve*'s three season endings are not an end but a suspension within a series that culminates in killing without closure. At the end of Season I, Eve almost kills Villanelle. At the end of the second season, Villanelle almost kills Eve, at the end of the third season, they meet again on a bridge in a standoff where they literally turn their back to one another and go their separate ways. Sexual and social relations are stripped of their usual content. Detection and sexuality are twisted into post-postmodern perverse scenes of sliding signification and seductive sport.

Below, we consider the three seasons from the point of view of two women who attempt to navigate the uncertainties of their inner world alongside the symptomatic articulations of the *Killing Eve* cosmos. The series lays out an unregulated, lethal, aggressive, and duplicitous domain that begins with the double negative disappearance of symbolic womanhood. Yet, there is nothing somber about this show. *Killing Eve* is humorous, witty, and irreverent, intentionally so, as we will see below. It employs wit and humor to strike a precarious balance between the waning of symbolic Law and the necessity of desire. The two women's relationship has been characterized as "an exquisitely choreographed, blood-soaked *pas de deux*" (Gompertz), choreographic variations that sidestep the lethal distortion of their hard-boiled bosses. One could also see them as the dueling refiguration of the classic mythic feminine duality, Eve and Lilith. Only now Eve and Villanelle propel the mythic tale through a *pas de deux* around the failure of Law. The world of *Killing Eve* is not only a play on detective and mythic traditions, but it also presents a mystical version of our world today.

Lacanian theorists argue that contemporary society is characterized by the dislocation of the "Discourse of the Master" into the so-called "Capitalist Discourse" (Lacan, "On Psychoanalytic Discourse"). This Discourse upsets the dialectical tension between truth, knowledge, and desire into an increasingly stilted relationship characterized by lack of dialectical movement, regression, an attempt to deny subjective splitting though commodity fetishism, a crisis of representation, the rejection of negativity, and, above all, the prevalence of a sadomasochistic dynamic articulated on the foreclosure of castration (Tomšič 216–18). What should have happened in contemporary society in Lacanian terms—the cut, acceptance of castration, and lack—does not and is mirrored in the cosmos of *Killing Eve*.

Instead, the show demonstrates the distinctive symptoms of a society ruled by capitalist fifth discourse, which, taken to its limit, creates a circuit of its own. These symptoms, Vanheule notes, result from "a number of obstructions that are inherent to the four discourses [that] are not character-istic of the fifth discourse. We can circulate within the capitalist discourse *like go-carts on a racetrack*" (Vanheule 6). Subsequently, characters in *Killing Eve* move without brakes in a world of inexhaustible drive and aggression.

Killing Eve portrays a globalized world without limits that is primarily ruled only by one dictum: *to kill and be killed.* It runs on,

> *Verwerfung*, which is rejection, rejection outside all fields of the sym-bolic . . . and cultural castration. Within the capitalistic logic, the lack at the heart of subjectivity is not seen as a structural consequence of using signifiers, but an accidental frustration that can be remedied within the market of supply and demand. The assumption that an S1 exists for each discomfort is ingrained in this discourse. (Vanheule 7)

Such discomfort is exhibited when characters engorge themselves in sex or material objects, or when they engage in animalistic acts of the real like killing, sex, or eating. There is a mythic and rhythmic dimension to the *Kill-ing Eve* which emerges in frustrated segments of consumption, time, and killing. This dimension relates to Lacan's later seminars which predict cap-italist discourse crashing like a go-cart going off the rails.

Capitalism, for example, proffers an abundance of fetishistic objects, each of them supposedly capable of plugging a specific desire (Declercq). Inevitably, capitalism fails to satiate lack with this offer of objects. This failure compounds the existential problem specific to *Killing Eve*. It is first glimpsed in Villanelle's attempts to use wealth to assuage her loneliness and to distract herself from the knowledge that she is already "dead," that is, non-represented in the symbolic order and in the desire of the Other. This failure soon manifests again in another spectacular manner, which also reveals the obscene under-belly of the failure of the law: rampant aggression, abundance of death, relentless killing, and, above all, impunity. As contract killer for The Twelve, it is as if Villanelle embodies an exacerbated version of her epoch. She is the *reductio ad absurdum* of the very excess generated by the removal of all obstacles to aggression and death. The total permissive-ness and impunity of the powerful, as seen in the show, is defended against by Villanelle. As projection and screen for The Twelve, she is literally the dirty hand of the wealthy, a figure regularly fantasized and mistaken by many in real life for the rich who is not powerful herself.

Killing Eve works through Eve and Villanelle's accidental encounters, which constitute a dance around the failure of law and the paternal meta-phor. Their painful but inventive performance is an unintentional entwining around "reality as *en souffrance, unterlegt*, [underlying] *untertragen*" (Lacan, *The Four Fundamental Concepts of Psychoanalysis* 55–56). Lacan later adds that the work of sinthomatic invention is creating *ex nihilo*, through staged *jouissance* and rhythm, not intentional representation. It is a writing or art of saying that stages "the body—not a body—but the body as such: that is dance . . . '*condansation*'" (Lacan, *The Sinthome* 62). Villanelle and Eve's lethal *pas-de deux* is a dance through pain (*souffrance*) that circumscribes accident as a generative negation. Their variable encounters activate a rhythmic stride while addressing the equally daunting question of being dead or alive.

We examine the *ex nihilo* inventions of Eve and Villanelle, who might alternatively appear saintly and perverse. In Lacanian terms, *Sinthomatic* invention involves an artist, pervert, or a saint, who, like the analysts, inter-acts with what is an underlying real unconscious or a traumatic primary negation (Vanheule 10). Barring a saintly disposition, however, all other mortals must wade their way through the thick and thin of the tainted sym-bolic, fumbling, tiptoeing or . . . *pas de deux* their way through affairs of desire and power. . . . This investigative duo makes a performative act of dancing past disintegrating Names of the Father.

Serial TV, like film and theater, is one of the more transient and perform-ative arts, which have *ex nihilo* baked into their production. Each season or episode emphasizes the fleeting and includes appearances that culminate in disappearance or death. The show's most concrete objects— like wardrobe, architecture, or sets—are more on the side of the transitory arts, like dance. Backdrops change as rapidly as Villanelle's victims. *Killing Eve* began in vir-tual form as a series of three serial Kindle edition novels that were published between 2014 and 2016. The author who wrote the stories upon which the BBC series is based, Luke Jennings, was trained as a dancer at the Rambert school and became a journalist for *Vanity Fair*, *The New Yorker* and was a dance critic for *The Observer*. Jennings was surprised when it was queried as a TV serial for BBC and he subsequently collaborated with the show's creators. Thus, in its conception and serial adaptation, *Killing Eve* displays *condansation* around the material exaltation and disappointment of capi-talist discourse. As variations on fifth discourse sadomasochism, Eve and Villanelle's circuitous dance around law shapes and makes each season of *Killing Eve* an unending serialized performance.

Through shocking or amusing scenes not meant to be interpreted, the series adopts an aesthetic, performative, and arrhythmic approach to the *sexuelle* and symbolic non-rapport inherent within desire. As a theoretical concept that plays out in praxis, rhythm suggests itself through the richness of its connotations in the psychoanalytic field: from the pulsation of life and death which grounds being to matter and the repetition of the *fort/da*, to the grammatical inflections inherent in the vicissitudes of the instinct in sadomasochism, to the punctuation of the signifying chain in the analytic session, to the symbolic cut(s) characteristic of castration. Each episode of *Killing Eve* features a revolving stage whose rhythms fuse the three seasons as epochal and the personal: if the capitalist world has turned decidedly sadomasochistic, rhythm is a modulator of temporalities and pulsions that may be a viable way of coping with or converting a sadomasochism world into one's own stride.

To fully grasp what sadomasochism "looks like" or "practically means" in the context of late capitalism, the series must be understood as it plays out. Each season of *Killing Eve* is a performative staging of rotating rhythms, for example, masochist suspension by Eve and sadistic speed by Villanelle. These rhythms are less representational than performative, and thus can only be appreciated in action. *Killing Eve* stages an absurd excess of death, the unhinged invincibility of a prolific killer who can terminate anyone, including her own mother, and a world very much removed of obstructions to aggression and *thanatos*. If the "traditional" way of living within the symbolic starts with the acceptance of castration as the foundation of one's desire, the epochal and personal challenge underpinning *Killing Eve* is how to negotiate the impossibilities created by the removal of limits and the unleashing of *thanatos*.

In that sense, *Killing Eve* stages and dramatizes the masochistic suspension of symbolic detection and womanhood through Eve on the one hand, and sadistic acceleration of *femme fatale* aggression and *jouissance* through Villanelle on the other. Together, their encounters make a serially suspended performance that turns over detective and sexual genres. Eventually, Eve and Villanelle use this *pas de deux* to prevent their go-cart from going off the track and swerve away from capitalist enslavement to The Twelve. Instead of being caught up in the wheel of capital, Eve and Villanelle dance alongside a political system of tyranny which believes itself to be "above the law." They circumscribe how The Twelve, as 5th Column highly global and professional white collar "bosses," are the truly politically powerful and felonious criminals. Moreover, Eve and Villanelle's interaction is a performative guide to how citizens might r/evolve within globalized late capital.

As we shall see below, the serial form of *Killing Eve* stages many seasons of Eve and Villanelle's contractual *pas de deux*. We are using the term "contract" as an agreement besides the law which evokes the assassin's professional arrangement with their employer, the symbolic "unwritten" bond between the detective and the assassin, and the Deleuzian term for the agreement between two parties entering into masochistic play (Deleuze and Sacher-Masoch 76). The contract, we argue, creates a formal bridge for something else to come into being, just as the detective-assassin relationship spills over into Eve and Villanelle's humorous *condansation* and address to the other to not simply heed one's desire but also assist one back to life. A new myth is born, a modern instantiation of rebirth and parthenogenesis (94). We draw it out using both Deleuze and myth in the Lacanian sense, as: ultimately consisting of facing an impossible situation through the successive articulation of all the forms of the impossibility of the solution. In this sense, mythic creation responds to a question. It runs through the complete circle of what presents itself at the same time as a possible opening and as an opening that is impossible to take. The circuit thus accomplished, something is realized, which means that the subject has put itself on the level of the question (Leader).

From Theory to Performative Praxis

"If you made her can you kill her."
Gertrude Stein, Lu*cretia Borgia. A Play*, 119

The theoretical conceptualization of this chapter explores and advances the affinities between the sadomasochistic tendencies of the discourse of the capitalist and Deleuze's discussion of masochism. Masochism, in Freud as well as in Deleuze is a performative political relation of serial suspense. As such, a study like *Coldness and Cruelty* (Deleuze and Sacher-Masoch 35) alongside psychoanalysis is useful, illuminating, and necessary in relation to sadomasochistic trends of late capitalism. Deleuze argues that masochism operates on many levels simultaneously, including a perverse stage of invention out of negation. It originates from "The aesthetic and dramatic suspense of Masoch that contrasts with the mechanical cumulative repetition [and acceleration of] Sade" (34) He unpacks the power of masochism as performative praxis of de-territorialization and freedom from sexual/symbolic essentialism expedited primarily by the relationship between the contract and the law.

Unlike earlier tendencies to maximize the differences between Lacan and Deleuze, recent attempts to re-appreciate the common ground between the two thinkers focus "not on the ruin of the ethical figure of the Law, but the ruin called subject whose meaning comes though the Other as guarantee of Law existed—Father, God, State, Nature, Destiny" (Desutter 36). While the Lacanian assumption that fifth discourse is primarily sadomasochistic (Tomšič) is valid, its articulation on the abstract level of discourse does not do justice to the subtle negotiation of the performative experience. Deleuze, on the other hand, advises focusing on praxis, the specific and the particular. In this context, masochism can be understood as flipping the law to such an extent as to reveal *jouissance*, and humiliation qua desire animating it (Desutter 37). This latter formulation, de Sutter argues, is also espoused by Lacan in the revision of his initial thesis on masochism upon reading Deleuze (38) and his comment that humor is situated on the side of the masochist (37).

Killing Eve exemplifies the Deleuzean masochist aesthetic, which is less about perversion than politics through the arrhythmia of

> waiting and suspense [which] are the essential characters of the masochist experience (Deleuze and Sacher-Masoch 71). Formally speaking, Deleuze argues, masochism is a state of waiting [divided into two

currents] . . . a rhythmic division of time into two streams, [which] should be "filled" by the particular combination of pleasure and pain. (71)

Caught within the two streams of pleasure and pain, Eve and Villanelle side-step, dodge, and dance their way through the deferment of gender and law. They use serial suspense and an unofficial contract to navigate non-relations in a society that has gone beyond lawless into sadomasochism.

Three specific points of contact between Lacan and Deleuze form the conceptual background of the present reading and our emphasis on praxis. The first point of contact is the "weak symbolic and its relation to gender." The second point is that of humor and play as a technique for dealing with collapsed paternal metaphors. Finally, the third point of contact between Lacan and Deleuze as it informs our reading of *Killing Eve* has to do with the mother as a mythically generative figure.

Both Lacan and Deleuze turn to the ambiguous face of obscenity and Masoch to arrive at the ruin of the law and a desire with no other structure but of a collapsed convention. The narrative fabric and the negotiation of sexuality in *Killing Eve* support this approach. In fact, it is quite easy to be taken in by the pervasive presence of regressive sadomasochism and consider *Killing Eve*'s portrayal of Eve and Villanelle as a perfect example of defeated womanhood in capitalist discourse, for example, woman as bogged down in eternal repetition and essentially non-sexual. However, this is a totalizing and homogenizing view, with "woman" being devoured by modern capitalism as it were. *Killing Eve*'s depiction of gender is less about disappearance or defeat than the oscillating freedom of resistance and the end of paternal mastery.

In *Killing Eve*, desire is enigmatic, without guarantee and guarantor. It unfolds in the enigmatic singularity of the collapse (un-grounding of its guarantee and its guarantor) (Desutter 39). While this is generally the case, the humorous-cruel-aggressive play between contract and law, woman and woman, Eve and Villanelle's hybridized masochist stage makes its own concrete and specific performance.

In abdicating what Lacan calls the "Name of the Father" or mastery, femininity is redoubled as a generative negation besides God and man. *Killing Eve* invokes and mocks traditional binaries of femininity in creation accounts as: "Eve, good, symbolic womanhood, slow" and "Lilith, bad, figure of surplus *jouissance*, fast." It displays both women as uncategorizable, and eventually falling into the sadomasochistic wheel of a global unregulated society. Yet, Villanelle and Eve's *condansations* are not reducible to perversion and unearth an arrhythmic stage driven by feminine *jouissance*. This supplemental stage is a response to post-postmodernism and, of course, the era of post-truth.

In symbolic terms, there is no clear difference between detective and villain, enemy and friend, ending or beginning in *Killing Eve*. Mastery and mystery are subsumed in serially suspended forms, even in The Twelve, a conglomeration of international oligarchs, originally Russian, and former intelligence officers who lack affiliations, borders, nationhood, and limits. The Twelve are the ringleaders of acceleration in this lawless society that lacks limits, castration, or constraints. Carolyn Martens, the spymaster of MI5 and Konstantin, the Russian agent, are 5th Columnists, members of The Twelve who act as if they are not. As a religious reference, The Twelve reveals how late capital has become a religion, with the primary belief being in "money, the new *pistis* [faith]" (Agamben 70). As Apostles, The Twelve are figures who accelerate the lawless global 1% contingent, or belief that money and power makes them all exceed law.

The second point of contact can be called "the re-invention of humor." If the Other is now only a practical joke (Desutter 38) and one is aware of the *jouissance* of the Other (obscene according to Žižek), humor counters the fear of facing how alone we are in constructing our desire (38). As Deleuze mentions, "We have to consider the humorous contribution of Masoch and his conception of the contract and the law in the context of the 1848 Revolution . . . where the law can no longer be grounded on the superior principle of the Good" (Deleuze and Sacher-Masoch 81–83). What is at play in this intense farce? De Sutter argues that something has to hold de Sutter (Desutter 39)—apposite when the injunction to get oneself outside the logic of mastery, or the master as "good." Making sense of the prevailing political and personal senselessness, *Killing Eve* uses humor and farce as performative techniques for handling the failure of law.

What Deleuze calls the masochistic aesthetic of cruel suspense can be playful. It provides a performative way out of the dead ends of capitalist modernity, a non-exist (non-exit) strategy which turns the tables on the existing sadomasochistic order. Like an inept detective, it does not solve any crime and does not reach any truth but works through suspense. This is not failure necessarily. We would even go as far as to say that this is what Deleuze calls re-sexualization as playful resistance to the establishment of sadomasochism and inequity in the 21st century.

Incorporating the formal techniques of detective suspense, *Killing Eve* is a serial TV show that uses farce to stage the failure of law, traditional sexuality, and detection. Episodes are propelled by scenes full of fantastic costumes and amazing backdrops rather than meaningful dialogue or plot. Indeed, the series makes a charade of cruel performances that mock the detective genre and serial TV. *Killing Eve*'s crew filmed at different locations that featured lush scenery, to make the series addictive, like what Lacan calls the "image as taken as real, without a stain" (Lacan, *The Four Fundamental Concepts of Psychoanalysis*). The series mirrors our world where symbolic reality is reduced to the virtual and "the imagery." Everyone in the show—except legit or decent people who are killed—hate reality and use their jobs (as spies, detectives, or assassins) to collapse the real with fantasy.

This is a disavowal of lack and any stain in seeing or understanding that is duplicated in our global world today, where Fear of Missing Out (FOMO) and fantasy magnify as more people take the *virtual* as reality.

Killing Eve exposes the *reductio ad absurdum* of our world as split between the two extremes of speed and suspense. It mirrors our world where capital is accelerated into overdrive, crashing, and/or over invested while contrarily, the imaginary rules without lack or castration. This results in a turn to the simulacra, virtual reality, and acting out in the face of unlimited surveillance. This disavowal of lack is a substitute for "good enough" reality that leads to war, conflicts, and much violence. *Killing Eve* shows this anesthetized world where murders seem unreal, uproarious, funny, and near farcical, as, for example: In a Ms. Piggy mask, Villanelle quarters, ties, and guts a man in the window of an Amsterdam red light district sex shop window while onlookers (like us) laugh and look on. In Berlin, Eve's boss Simon is knifed by Villanelle at a nightclub, where everyone ignores the murder and keeps dancing to the music at top volume. At the end of Season II, Eve is droll to her "co-worker" Hugo who she has sex with then abandons after he is abruptly killed. In Season III before Villanelle kills her mother, she says "what are you doing to do? Take me to an orphanage. . . . Don't pretend you were an angel. . . . Don't pretend you were a mother." These killings are amusing and exemplary of what Baudrillard calls the "seduction simulacra" where desensitization due to cyber stimulation and violent aggressivity multiplies. As our world becomes increasingly virtual and intolerant of lack, it seems that this supposedly kooky cosmos of *Killing Eve* is not so different from our own globalized world.

The final point of contact between Deleuze and Lacan transcends both. Lacanian psychoanalysis remains averse to the figure of the mother, the very figure Deleuze, with a nod to Klein, introduces in the re-configuration of desire in the ruins of the Law. The mother that interests Deleuze is neither the symbolic one that colludes with the Father, nor the primordial "swampy" (bodily) one of imaginary oneness (Deleuze and Sacher-Masoch 55). It is the oral mother, who is generative (95). Ultimately, what interests Deleuze is her multiplicative or (re)birthing potential within the configuration of the masochistic play. We will discuss the potential of the oral mother in detailed ways which might exceed the formal description of the adult masochistic contract in Deleuze in subsequent sections. There we will only introduce the relation of mother to life and death, *eros* and *thanatos*, and some attributes of "the child," including play that invents a bridge for life after the breakdown of law.

Important for opening up a perspective or dimension of myth beyond the ruin(s) of the Father is what we are calling "the mother of myth and *ananké*." The idea that *Killing Eve* portrays the imaginary aggression or psychotic foreclosure of characters is too simple a solution to the open question of being or non-being. Examining the "logic" of masochism, Deleuze alerts us to the fact that clinical perversion, especially when it comes to the Freudian conceptualization of sadism and masochism as pathological, does not address the pain of negation as an opportunity for mythic reinvention. The latter is an important dimension of the masochistic stage in *Killing Eve*.

Killing Eve shows that applying the sadomasochistic argument as clinical perversion, or even psychosis, is not adequate to address the characters' experience. The pathological view does not account for the generative interplay of eros and thanatos, and, more importantly, the rhythmic nature of the case. Deleuze's *Coldness and Cruelty* explores masochism as a mode of transformation through voluntary servitude. This servitude involves variable patterns of seriality and suspense, rhythms that are close to being (*eros*) and to non-being (*thanatos*). The detective case of *Killing Eve* performs what Deleuze is referring to, we argue, as not so much the incursion or return of an imaginary as a real arrhythmic response to a symbolic dead end. It calls, consistent with Deleuze, for a new foundation for being (like a foundation myth) that would follow the breakdown of law in our neo-feudal, globalized world.

This new foundation, as we will see below, is law negotiated via the construction of myth as a contract. *Killing Eve* stages Villanelle and Eve's *pas de deux* as a masochistic mythical case that shows the cruelty of the symbolic, for example, of non-being or not having a choice. This "*real* solution" to the collapse of law, we argue, is not reducible to the symbolic, nor is it a straight perverse provocation of the Other. Rather, it is an enactment or dance around the void of non-being. This void, or absolute negation as Deleuze explains, is "the no and the negation, and the death drive as absolute negation" (Deleuze 28). This dance around the void propels the whole detective investigation of *Killing Eve*. The case is never solved, or re-solved, but only staged repeatedly by Villanelle and Eve who stress the conversion of nothing into something, in arhythmical exchange.

This brings us closer to the unique existential problem that is Villanelle's predicament and why she is not a run of the mill *femme fatale*. *Killing Eve* is rife with bad mothers, and Villanelle is essentially a child still to deal with her mother (biological and symbolic). Cruel queens appear on every stage in every season. Carolyn Martens of MI5 is an indifferent and cold mother to her children. Dasha, Villanelle's trainer and mentor, is devoid of maternal feelings, and Villanelle's biological mother makes an appearance in Season III only to be killed. It is expected that as an assassin, Villanelle rebuffs orders and her resistance hinges on fast modes of aesthetic transformation. As fast as she moves from city to city quickly for a kill, all of Villanelle's costumes change as well. Her quick transformations of the image through various disguises and fixation on her own mirror image suggest that she sees no lack, stain, or recognition of the mirror.

Killing Eve, like the popular American Netflix show *Tiger King*, significantly suggests what viewers suspect: that making money in our late capital globalized world of inequality means being cruel, harm to others, and/

or harm to self. Luke Jennings, who wrote the novels behind the BBC TV series, based Villanelle on Idoia Lopez Riano, a Spanish hitwoman known as *La Tigresa*, who worked for a Basque terrorist group. Villanelle, like the Tiger Queen, was often seen admiring herself in the mirror. Her vanity, like Villanelle, is perhaps the only thing that interfered with her killing of 23 people (Hannan; Harrison). Yet vanity, an amazing salary and fetish objects only temporarily satisfy Villanelle. As a prolific killer, master of death and "dead" herself, Villanelle ultimately starts wanting to quit killing for The Twelve and is no longer interested in death—the challenge for her is eros.

Villanelle, as vehicle of *thanatos* and death, believes that Eve is a bridge to *eros*, which *Killing Eve* displays through a word play with the two main characters' names. Moreover, the name play is not an accident and built into the series as a playful art of staged sayings (*dire*) where meaning comes through phonemes or pulsions more than representation. In *L'etourdit* (1972), Lacan introduces the idea of an art of saying (*l'art dire*) that is an act of saying. This idea is later expanded in *Seminar XXIII*, where Lacan explains how Joyce managed to tie the knot of the sinthome through *l'art of dire*, which is *dieure (deus/dire)*, a word that is not with the paternal metaphor but God infused with negation. *Killing Eve* proliferates names and referents like Villanelle as a demonstration of its sinthomatic form, and refusal of paternal metaphors.

Both Villanelle and Eve contain two "E's" and one "V," which put together evoke the homonymic words "evil" or "villain." "Villanelle" is not simply a code name that the Russian Oxsana adopts but also a cherished fragrance brand that she uses to make her mark. It is the moniker she chooses to suggest being undetectable yet lethal, like a tigress after her kill who only leaves a scent or vapor. Jennings' book explains the origin: "Villanelle was the favourite scent of the Comtesse de Barry. The perfume house added the red ribbon after she was guillotined in 1793" (Jennings 27). Moreover, "Villanelle" is also a word that means both a pastoral dance song, and poetry—specifically a free form ballad poem with 19 lines and five tercets. Poetic villanelles were popularized in the 19th century but revived in the 1930s, as with Dylan Thomas "Do not go gentle into that good night."

The shows hinges around the song and dance of Villanelle who is both a ruthless killer and masochistic child looking for a real (and her symbolic) mother. Each series of *Killing Eve* constructs a pastiche of masochistic staging around Villanelle the child and Eve, as oral mother. This makes it necessary for us to reconsider the relationship between the child and the mother, the detective and the villain, to inflect it beyond the contractual agreement of two adults getting in (masochistic) play. Indeed, *Killing Eve* stages the formal characteristics of the Deleuzian masochism as if a template.

However, Deleuze does not consider two further points. First, when a "child" like Villanelle enters this contract, it may experience and exhibit omnipotence. Second, the temporal staging of *Killing Eve* involves repetitions as well as interruptions. Interruption is not the same as suspension, or what Deleuze calls masochist "suspense." These are points at which the subject "loses control" and appears to succumb to fate, destiny, or power beyond her reach. These interruptions signal the appearance of *ananké* or necessity (Lacan, *The Four Fundamental Concepts of Psychoanalysis*; Freud).

Ananké is this accident and interruption that is endemic to logocentric exposure. Freud discusses this at the end of "The Economic Principle of Masochism." She is mythological dis-figuration, the contrary corollary or negative capability of logos and *ananké*. As the asymbolic and arrhythmic necessity within logos, *ananké* does not reference anything in particular but is an interruption that intones the real beyond representing. The struggle of logos and a*nanké* foregrounds poetic invention through voluntary servitude. Villanelle and Eve circumnavigate the necessity that emerges from the marks, cut, or schisms in speaking being. Eve and Villanelle refuse captivity in "imago" representation and seize upon the interruptions of *ananké* as an opportunity to invent:

> The last figure in the series beginning with the parents is that dark supremacy of Fate, which only the fewest among us are able to conceive of impersonally. Little can be said against the Dutch writer, Multatuli, when he substitutes the divine pair *ananké* and *logos* [my trans. from the Greek] for the fates of the Greeks [Moiré]; but all those who transfer the guidance of the world to Providence, to God, or to God and Nature, rouse a suspicion that they still look upon these farthest and remotest powers as a parent couple—mythologically—and imagine themselves linked to them by libidinal bonds. In *Das Ich* and *das Es* I have made an attempt to derive the objective fear of death in mankind also from the same sort of parental conception of Fate. It seems to be very difficult to free oneself from it. (Freud 265)

Freud's essay on masochism shows how the libidinal reduction of *logos* is *ananké*. Fate appears at the end of speech as the "fear of death" or when facing the void. The dialogue in *Killing Eve* is weak, even unremarkable, and nonsensical, only punctuated by the interruptions of *ananké*, acts of killing or suspense that face *ananké*. Working through the body and not representational speech, Villanelle and Eve test fate to lay bare the intimate opposition of being and speaking, opportunity and necessity. *Ananké* is the negation lurking within the law and speaking being. She is a presence that appears only briefly through a violent, but creative mimetic struggle and arhythmic stage. *Killing Eve*, à la Deleuze's masochist aesthetic, stages such a battle. In the *condansation* of Eve and villanelle, *ananké* emerges as an interruption within logos. Moreover, artistic generation, in general, taps into the necessity or negation with symbolic representation.

Deleuze links masochistic suspense to a primary negation and non-being. It drives every sexual and symbolic act of *Killing Eve*. *Killing Eve* stages primary negation, not as foreclosure, but as not-being or what Deleuze describes as the "negative at work in destruction, [which] always manifests itself as the other face of construction" (Deleuze 30). From a Lacanian perspective, a sinthome is made possible, a viable arrangement which considers all the things (and all the relationships) that do not exist, including the sexual and symbolic. Lacan offers *Sinthomatic* invention as parallel to Deleuze's masochistic invention. Both involve invention out of nothing, creation *ex nihilo*, and voluntary servitude to construct a rhythmic mode of resisting the symbolic order.

The reading below does not seek to replicate Deleuze or Lacan. It borrows the formal characteristics of masochism and the demise of the Law to explore the particularities of rhythmic lived experience. As a performative show, *Killing Eve* demonstrates the movement of a masochist contact on three levels: encounters around a weak symbolic as relative to gender, the use of humor to reroute after the collapse of law, and generativity out of necessity and the interruptive oral mother. Each element of the contract plays out in *Killing Eve's* three seasons as a singular mythic performance with plural stages of *condansation*; the show revolves around Villanelle and Eve's digressions between desire and *thanatos*, logos and fate (*ananké*), being and nothing. These stages bear life after a paternal rule of death and sexuality. As riffing on masochist and hard-boiled forms, each season of *Killing Eve* exhibits a different dance floor of coldness through short and long trajectories of cruelty and play.

Season I: Heed My Desire

Eve is a bored low-level operative in MI5. She catches the attention of Carolyn Martens when she makes some clever observations about an elusive assassin, Villanelle. Eve has been following the case out of personal, amateur interest. Carolyn recruits Eve in her clandestine team of MI5 operatives and installs her at a secret London location, a working space with computers and surveillance equipment. Spread on a wall-mounted world map are all the known moves of the prolific assassin. "Wow" says Eve, "it is like walking into my own head."

The opening of the series is different from the usual detective dramas and merits our attention: unlike the ordinary hysteric who would normally ask "Why am I having this mandate, why have you chosen me?" Eve finds herself inside her own fantasy and is totally seduced by it. What she is about to discover is even wilder than her wild dreams. She finds out, for example, that her young assistant, Kenny, is Carolyn Martens' son. Carolyn always treats him with contempt. Eve also wakes up to the cozy arrangements between MI5 and the KGB and is quickly immersed in fast-pacing, dangerous work, traveling and risking life while leaving her caring yet jealous husband and his Thursday bridge club miles behind. Eve has just entered a world of utter lawlessness and precarious privilege, populated by people who share power and are not enemies, who can do what they like but are not immune to surveillance, loss of power, and death. In fact, they are just as expendable as the pawns they operate.

If Eve discovers a world she did not know existed, Villanelle lives in a world that does not know she exists. Villanelle is a contract assassin and talented linguist who can pass as English, Italian, or French. Her handler, Konstantin, visits her in her Paris apartment and hands her a postcard with a web link to instructions for her next job. Villanelle tries to buy Konstantin's affection with gifts and surprise parties for his birthday. Konstantin always rebuffs her, anxious to maintain a professional relationship. He is a cruel father: "Who do you love more, me or your kid?" asks Villanelle. Again, she is rebuffed. At the end of series one, Villanelle does not hesitate to try to kill Konstantin when instructed to do so. In the meantime, she treats herself to luxury clothes. She is seeing carrying expensive bags to her apartment and wearing whatever makes her conspicuous or visible. After one of her hits, she buys a designer bedspread seen in the bedroom of one of her victims.

Villanelle can be petty and childish. The opening scene of the very first episode defines her attitude: she is seated across a blue-eyed blond girl who is eating a huge ice cream in a café. Villanelle exchanges glances and makes funny faces at the little girl. Then as she leaves and walks past the child, she deftly pushes the ice cream bowl into the girl's lap.

In her apartment, Villanelle plays dead to shock Konstantin into response. He is not fooled. "Would you be sad if I died?" she asks. He does not respond. Nor does he lavish praise when she exclaims "I was sensational!" Konstantin is the reticent paternal figure by proxy, assigned to the role and not having chosen it. "Who worries about you, I do" she says on another occasion. Finally, she stages a birthday party for him, dresses up as him, and fills the room with balloons. He refuses to play along.

Eve is guarded and intuitive but by no means an accomplished detective. Eve's "incompetence" is a tactic used, like Stasi East German agents, to flush out information. Unlike Villanelle, she does eschew fetishistic objects (costumes, sex, confusion) to abject herself and everyone around her, including her husband. Her fascination with the elusive assassin shows its imaginary origins when they exchange glances for the first time through the mirror in the female lavatories of a hospital. Eve later realizes she has met Villanelle and describes her in sensual detail: full lips, smooth skin, delicate features.

Eve does not abandon her position as detective and does not know her desire but finds herself in the position of the victim, pursued by Villanelle with unwanted and terrifying attention. This lack of contact inaugurates alternating rhythms, for example, masochist suspension (Eve) and sadistic speed (Villanelle) to resist symbolic fixation. At first, Villanelle watches Eve. Unnoticed as always, she steals Eve's suitcase in Berlin. As if by magical thinking, she tries to possess the person as if they are their belongings. She stalks Eve while denouncing her to Konstantin, saying "I do not think about her." Back in London, Eve receives a new suitcase full of expensive clothes and a note: "Sorry baby." She is thrown into confusion and reverie. The game of seduction that started in the mirror enters a new phase: appearance and disappearance; seeing and not being seen; omnipotence and abandon; wooing and seduction trail-blazed by as many deaths as it takes to dislodge Eve from her immediate context, to make her "available."

Assault on all fronts: the world goes around in pushes and fragments, pursuits and chases reversed: Eve is supposed to be on the trail of Villanelle, but it is Villanelle who traces Eve, makes herself available to the gaze and calls the shots. The rhythm is that of the appearance and disappearance of one woman, two women. At the same time, this game seduces Villanelle into visibility. Seduction is a strategy of rhythms: making an appearance and retreating; demanding attention and repelling it; catching a glimpse of oneself in the mirror, the vanity that veils death, the reflection of beauty in the eyes of the other. This imaginary game of several instances of posturing and play-pretending is obviously sexual but bereft of *jouissance*. It is counterbalanced by the clinical efficiency of the killings and the *jouissance* Villanelle extracts in return: "Look me in the eye," she orders one of her male victims as the life is snuffed out of him. The impotence of the paternal order to uphold the gaze is phenomenal, as is the ease with which Villanelle kills in public. The Other looks but cannot see Villanelle, which is why she risks appearing to Eve as an aesthetic and oral mother, not as a symbolic desiring Other.

The encounters of Villanelle and Eve become real when the former breaks into the latter's house while Eve admires herself in the mirror wearing an expensive dress that Villanelle sent her. In this sense, Villanelle pretends to be the imaginary phallus but is the uncastrated child trying to make herself into a real phallus for the oral mother. Villanelle interrupts the reverie by her very real presence and tries to reassure Eve that she means no harm. But all the same, she must display her aggressive superiority and pins her to the fridge holding a knife to her throat. Villanelle tries to explain to a very scared Eve that all she wants is to have dinner with her. This mock-normality of the one dressed for dinner—prelude to sex in the classic couple parlance—goes awry with Eve's spirited resistance. She calls Villanelle a psychopath, revealing she knows her real name. Villanelle soon leaves but a relationship has been established between the two women. The visual economy of the scene sums up the affective tensions: face to face with a knife between them, body to body minus the erotic promise, the knife (tip of aggression) represents an aggressive de-eroticized phallus.

Eve and Villanelle will meet again in Moscow, where Villanelle returns to take care of an old associate in a state prison, and Eve will piece more of Villanelle/Oxsana's biography together, assisted by Kevin and making the most of Carolyn's mysterious friendship with the KGB agents. While her husband jealously snaps at her, "You are not saving the world," Eve will experience the ideological precarity of the post-Cold War world, which culminates when she finds out that Carolyn had visited Villanelle in prison.

If fantasy teaches us how to desire (Žižek 25), Eve will grasp the forcefulness of Villanelle's passion when she meets Anna, a former teacher and object of love of Villanelle (25). Villanelle had a fixation of Anna, who mentored her language learning at school and whom she made a widow and, consequently, available. Anna admits having had sex with her—"she seduced me" is said simultaneously with Villanelle. It seems that Villanelle uses a mixture of coercion and seduction as her method. We begin to realize that this is her working mode of operation, a repetition that makes Villanelle perfect, bored, and infallible. In this context, the *pas de deux* with Eve is presaged as an un-choreographed dance, where Villanelle, like a bullfighter, shadows her prey. Eve and Anna are mythic feminine beings who ignite Villanelle's "tigress" into a tussle of repetition-replication that iterates patterns from her past, for example, the exacerbation of ignorance, the repetition of advances and rebuffs, the ignorance (of the Other), and the secure knowledge qua repetition of the same. Moreover, even a monster's *pas de deux* involves a contractual rhythmic stage, like the matador's dance with a bull: *tercios, picadors, banderillos,* and a final lancing accompanied by graceful passes with a large red cape.

Eve begins to claw back at Villanelle's power when she starts copying her tactics: she steals the passport hidden in the clothes left at Anna's place, leaving her a note "Sorry baby." The next time they will meet alone will be in Paris where Eve breaks into Villanelle's home, in the season finale. Eve admits to Villanelle that she thinks about her all the time. They sit on the bed facing each other. Eve asks Villanelle what she wants, to which she replies that she wants a job, a flat, and someone to watch movies with. The two women's reflection is amplified by three mirrors as they lie back on the bed next to each other. Then, suddenly Eve stabs Villanelle in the abdomen. She panics and wants to help, but Villanelle vanishes.

The last scene of Season I completes the cycle of repetitions and mirrorings, conjoins eroticism with aggression, albeit clumsily, and establishes a rhythmic relationship between the two women. It is possible to argue that in attempting to kill Villanelle, Eve attempts to kill her double, Lilith, as a symbol of feminine *jouissance*. It is also plausible to argue that by stabbing her counterpart Eve introduces a symbolic cut in the frenzied unraveling of events. Restraining Villanelle is what had to happen to accomplish a suspense of desire, symbolic meaning, and law with (some) limits. In classic Lacanian terms, the scene also playfully confirms the proposition that "there is no such thing as a sexual relationship." Here, the non-rapport *sexuelle* is laid bare. Vanheule explains that the sexual relationship does not create a bond between subjects; only love does that (Vanheule 75).

In a loveless mechanized universe, there is no leeway for psychic investment. Thus, everyone always finds themselves close to the Real of sexual non-rapport, to all kinds of non-rapports in which subjects and objects are involved.

We would like to propose a more nuanced approach to the meaning of the scene. Season I is about woman as object a (Eve) and symptom of man. The season suspends all fantasies of the "classic" woman who exists as the fantasy object (a) and cause of phallic desire, as rubbish. Season I inaugurates the series as being about killing classic myths of femininity and creation. Eve Polastri is not the Eve who represents the first woman, Garden of Eden and the Not-all. She is also not the "not all woman" in a non-relation to Adam, for example, the hole in a phallic chain of being. Instead, Killing Eve shows how in late capitalism, "woman" makes its own double negative world of femininity that suspends the w-hole signifying chain. Villanelle and Eve perform and construct this double negative interruption, not via castration or symbolic limits, but in a dance over and around an inoperative paternal rule. Indeed, as all seasons of *Killing Eve* show, there is no "leaving" the garden for Villanelle and Eve since every territory and leader of this dystopian world is bought by The Twelve. *Killing Eve* is a cosmos: "It seems that our time can only think . . . wealth and money" (Agamben 29). This world has no consideration of personhood as unique, non-possessable, or appropriable.

In the past, sadism and masochism were deployed by women as ways of resisting patriarchy.[2] In the lesbian detective genre, the detective confronts the challenges of sexuality via her own detective work and the female victim of violence and murder, the dead body, solved all kinds of uneasy questions of femininity and vulnerability. Now, in their apparent sexual attraction, Villanelle and Eve are always heading toward a meeting or a clash, supercharged by the uncertainties of their symbolic positions. The uncertainties of their own libidinal investment unfold in post-Cold War/capitalist drama, underlined by a random and rapidly changing balance of alliances which are hard to predict and, worse, to rely on. Thus, when they finally catch up with one another, both exhausted by the chase and frustrated by the lack of resolution this meeting affords—what is the point of catching your killer if you cannot apprehend them? Eve has little else to do than to stab Villanelle.

In this moment, when traditionally the detective apprehends the killer, Eve refuses to enact the typical case. The cop lays down her claim to any symbolic identity and swaps places with the killer. The lack of control this act brings up upsets Eve into trying to kill Villanelle, in which she almost succeeds. As caught up in their *condansation*, Eve attempts to cut the villain out of Villanelle, not as a detective but to halt unrestrained desire. In the meantime, Villanelle has had plenty of opportunities to kill Eve and never did. This deferred encounter opens up space for more surprise encounters and performances, of making oneself visible or invisible as Villanelle does. The serial killer offers many opportunities and clues for pause or reflection upon her demands for Eve to validate being. Instead of erasing Eve,

Villanelle stresses her need to be seen by Eve and even lays her childish omnipotence down at her feet.

It is possible to argue that the unfinished scene echoes the passion of the master and the slave in modern times. Once, the master once was the one who enjoyed the surplus of labor but renounced *jouissance* (enjoyment of profit) to create more *jouissance*, or, demanded renunciation from all to create profit for some (Tomšič 217). Now, the function of the master signifier turns into an empty ritual (218) and nothing drives the relationship between the master and the slave (Deleuze and Sacher-Masoch 77). The ending of the first episode displays the hilarity of this endless gliding for anyone who assumes either position.

But there is more to the picture than meets the capitalist eye: these formal inflections allow for a pattern of appearing and disappearing, coming close and going away, non-being and not being nothing, establishing, we argue, a rhythmic regularity which re-moves Villanelle out of being invisible, dead, not represented or recognized. This is accomplished through the bond with Eve, whose masochistic interest stems from the boredom and a lack of *jouissance*—the pointlessness of a castrated existence. That relation is cherished by both in delay, in deferral, and in not taking place.

Villanelle views Eve as a bridge toward what in Deleuze approximates the impersonal ideal (Deleuze and Guattari 23), beyond the demands for love addressed to the cruel father and beyond wealth and conspicuous consumption. With Eve, Villanelle leaves a trace of "being there," a mark in the symbolic to be picked up by whom it may concern; a plea for a return gesture, for the reciprocation of rhythm; a plea for an object. Thus, Villanelle does not kill Eve so that they can only ever exchange places. She is abandoned in Eve—and that is terrifying and exhilarating. This exchange involves a perfect masochistic logic: the exchange of being the detective and killer, mother and child, lover and beloved. As such, the bond between Villanelle and Eve is a relation beyond symbolic validation. They validate one another on the level of being (and *jouissance*), as beings whose non-being is not nothing. With this bond, a contract is staged and a mythic scene is established: an assemblage or Gestalt, the two meeting in sexual desire with a knife between them.

The formal arrangement of the first series, the *mise an abyme* transforms no thing (lack of representation), to nothing, a game of eros and thanatos. The regularities of this exchange are rhythmic: deferral as futile chase and chance encounters, infallible evidence that the other does exist; mirroring: hunter–hunted, detective–killer; Villanelle and Eve always escaping death and capture as opposed to dying—being there by circumscribing thanatos. Their *condansations* affirm that there is something there, something that must be known and addressed, apprehended (in both senses of the word), captured (in both senses of the term), stopped (dead). In constructing a bond with Eve, Villanelle tries to invent herself out of thanatos, to purge her sense of boredom and non-being into the mythic idea of not being nothing.

Deleuze argues that masochistic transformation pertains to the Law (Deleuze and Guattari 44). We might say that transformation is achieved not only via distortion and exchanging places, but also via interruption, which involves an inability to control or effect the desired result. Necessity is interruption whose unpredictability and lack of control opens a space for invention, for example, fate as last vestiges of the Other, the not-whole, that establishes a sinthomatic letter beyond the Law.

However, the series contrasts the game of The Twelve to the real investigations of non-being and not-being-nothing of Villanelle and Eve. The two women stay alive via an archetypical contract: the inflections of the detective-killer relationship open to a contract between the masochist child and the generative mother. The formal logic of interruptive necessity in masochism installs a relation where there was none. Villanelle and Eve invent a passage from nothing to no-thing, disfigurement to performance, serial suspense to the confluence of eros and thanatos. They also inscribe themselves in a circuit of drives, which is both erotic and maternal, as in generative. The oral mother is not a child-bearer but the mother of art, necessity, and invention. Moreover, Villanelle and Eve's bond involves an element of surprise, as only just, which is formative for the masochist invention. This surprise comes through adjustment to *ananké*, or the interruption that is the advent of suspended desire in the scene. She is the way in which something begins beyond Logos, an invention that exceeds the control of the subject. The masochist stage involves a *tyche* or fate that arises out of suspended desire and only becoming visible when one exchanges places with the other.

This is a dimension we wish to foreground as significant in the theatrics of *Killing Eve*. Beyond the collapse of law, *Killing Eve* works through the particulars of the interpersonal situation. Through masochist invention, the show tries to establish proof of being as fragile and vital, in the literal sense of the term. Villanelle and Eve create a mythic and primal relation of being and non-being beyond the Name of the Father where there was none. Together, they invent a passage from nothing to no-thing, seriality to suspense, thanatos to eros.

The ideal, dramatic, and formal properties of the first episode relate to the mythical, dialectic, and imaginary—which underlines the difference between negative and negation and evokes a transcendental order (Deleuze 35), all being negotiated through the formal contract of the masochistic praxis. In the dialectic relation, masochism installs a scene that is being enacted like Lacan's "Father, Can't You See I'm Burning?" on several levels (Lacan, *The Four Fundamental Concepts of Psychoanalysis* 59). The primary level is monstrous, says Deleuze, while a secondary and minor invention is staged. The mythic masochist scene—here we harken back to Lacan's *en souffrance,* the *untertragen*, reality as *unterlegt* [underlying]—is staged once and then replayed and refined throughout the series.

Thus, through the typical masochist scenario recurring ad infinitum, *Killing Eve* makes a sinthomatic mythic investigation. This happens in serial stagings of suspended *reconnaissance* as *meconnaissance*, as interrupted by fate, leading to characters' surprising lack of control. Cruelty accompanies the unexpected, as an event beyond the regulation of characters, especially the savvy killer Villanelle, who thinks she has everything under control. In this context, invention occurs when they venture into encounters beyond their control that create an opening for eros. Indeed, the erotic attraction between Eve and Villanelle makes a frightfully feminine *condansation* that contrasts with the vagaries of the big Other, which remain contingent and incomplete but also tiresome, dull, and lawless. Of all the characters in *Killing Eve*, Adam and God are not exactly the main event in this show. Rather, Lilith and Eve come to the fore in a new creation, through a bond of non-being but not being nothing. Their *pas de deux* moves, in fact, beyond a game to the beat of mother *ananké*.

Season II: Reductio: Aggression/La Tigresa

Season II begins with the aftermath of the stabbing, and it meanders its way to finish with Villanelle and Eve's second meeting in the Roman ruins. If Season I established a relationship that could sustain being through precarious patterns and rhythmic repetitions, Season II could be considered as an elaborate prolonged preparation of a second meeting anticipated as a union but turning out to be a déjà vu in reverse. In the meantime, the in-between time, Villanelle and Eve will be sustained by imaginary similarities to one another, will be working on the same side, and will try to rescue one another before being separated, once again, by the intransigence of their own desire. In the meantime, symbolic womanhood is replaced by femininity as the interruptive power of *ananké*, the very force that brought the two women together at the end of Season I.

Season II suspends all ideas of woman as object a, or object of fantasy and a finite investigation. The case of catching Villanelle is superseded by the digressions of the detective job, which suspend all ordinary demands and freeze progress in terms of "solving" the case. This second season of *Killing Eve* is all about movement without aims, sufficient diversions, and digressions on and from the stabbing or cut in the body that started in the flux of events, for example, the wound inflicted by Eve's hand upon the cherished body of Villanelle, which has now become a mark of affection.

Season II contains a lot of movement with no direction. It opens at the *Gare du Nord* train station in Paris, where Eve drops the murder weapon (bloody knife) in a trash can before getting on a train back to England. After arriving in the UK, Eve is not sure where she is going or why she did what she did to Villanelle, so she goes to a pub and gets drunk. Flummoxed, mystified, and bewildered, Eve somehow staggers home, then cooks dinner for no one in particular. Music plays in background by Kim Wilde's "Kids in America" as a mock ridicule of Americans, like Eve, caught up in serfdom to a global cartel. Having lost all hope of career advancement, Eve accepts being treated like a kid by her boss Carolyn Martens, who ironically calls Eve multiple times, and is ignored by Eve who sits naked in the bath, crying.

Villanelle does not die. She vanishes at the point of death, re-emerging in the trauma ward of a Parisian hospital from which she escapes in stolen children's pyjamas, before crossing the Channel as a stowaway in a family car. Weak and unable to look after herself, Villanelle abandons herself to the hands of a Good Samaritan Julian, who lives in a big house with his senile mother. The house is full of porcelain dolls and locked doors so that mother does not escape. Once again, Villanelle endures imprisonment until the stab wound heals, kills Julian, and releases mother into the streets, in a scene that strongly suggests being liberated from a life of stillness, control, and coercive heterosexual conformity.

Love is not an option. Fascination is. Villanelle caresses her stub wound in the bath, while Eve claims that she knows her better than she knows herself, recognizes her propensity to play to the gallery when killing, and describes her as an omnivorous parasite, a hungry caterpillar. Villanelle mentally reciprocates to playing to the gallery by performing one of the most spectacular assassinations of her career, killing a man in the red-light district of Amsterdam, in full view of an unsuspecting audience who think they are witnessing a sadomasochistic sexual ritual. On several occasions, Villanelle and Eve are shown pensively in front of a mirror. After a tip off, Eve and her team come very close to apprehending Villanelle in a London hotel. Eve watches the scene from the spyhole of a hotel room—the voyeurism of the scene is obvious—but Villanelle escapes, assisted by Konstantin. The latter repeatedly tells Villanelle that Eve is no longer interested in her. She is after another female assassin known as the Ghost. At home one night, Eve finds a lipstick in her pocket and when she applies it a sharp blade hidden inside it cuts her lip. The jilted lover has made her mark. The object of love eludes her, but the new cut clearly evokes the old one and the desire to pause, to stop, to draw a line.

Appearing and disappearing, highly conspicuous in Amsterdam but always capable to vanish, Villanelle defies both surveillance and the gaze, because she knows that one can deceive both not by hiding but being too present, an excess in the field of vision. This happens in Episode 3 when Villanelle goes to the school of Eve's husband, Niko Polastri and leaves an apple on his desk (a private signal to Eve). The bullying campaign to remove Niko continues when Villanelle calls up the school pretending to be a student with multiple complaints against him.

Since love is not allowed, seductive mirrorings spill over into the public arena when Eve convinces Carolyn Martin to hire Villanelle to extract information from the Ghost. To lure Villanelle, Eve offers herself as bait.

For the second time, Villanelle will visit Eve at home, inflicting a test of trust upon her by challenging Eve to swallow poison pills to prove her integrity. Eve does that and Villanelle breaks down in mock panic, before starting to laugh manically at her clever trick. From then on, a contract of trust defines their real interaction in an underworld where enemies can once again find themselves on the same side.

The lesson that can be gleaned from both scenes is the following: when stagnation threatens, one must move things forward by offering oneself up as victim to the cause, fodder to the cannons, or food to the hungry caterpillar. This epithet is used by Konstantin to refer to Villanelle as "a parasite . . . the hungry caterpillar . . . you think she loves you then she makes her hate you." Eve's substantial offer to be a lure mocks the pound of flesh typically rendered in the castration complex. It is an all or nothing sacrifice of surrendering, of being given to the desire of the other. It looks masochistic. The omnivorous other, however, does not wish to devour and ingest but to regurgitate and, as in the case of the pills, to (cause one to) spit out, to preserve (the beloved) at the point of death: limit conditions replayed.

Having successfully dealt with the Ghost, Villanelle is hired by Carolyn to assist in the investigation of billionaire Aaron Peel. She befriends his sister Amber in an A.A. meeting pretending to be a rich American girl. At the meeting, Villanelle speaks true words in jest, confessing she is bored and feels nothing. Boredom is the symptom of an impotent symbolic. Villanelle exclaims "BORING" for the first time in Season II, Episode 4. She yells and draws the words out, shouting out loud at the Rijksmuseum and there is an echo.

This echo and her repeated exclaiming of the word "BORING" appears again in Episode 6, where Villanelle is used as an enticement to lure the software company Faraday (an analogue to Facebook) founder, Aaron Peel. At an A.A. Villanelle gets real in a terrifying confession of her life as BORING, which, on the one hand, might be reducible to the psychotic's cry; as in there is no Other, no symbolic connection, only the psychotic in their delusion, which is dangerous for anyone to penetrate. On the other hand, as Walter Benjamin and artists like Cézanne note, deep boredom or idleness allows for creative contemplation and visualization of the inconspicuous or fleeting. Confessing her boredom at A.A. may be the beginning of the end of Villanelle's acting. It is an actual moment where she can provide a real expression of the pain she feels at having no inner life and intimacy.

Previously, Villanelle eases the blankness and boredom by acting out never feeling. She is blank inside but now less barbarian after confessing her boredom with killing and awareness of being empty. Here again, Villanelle exceeds the genre hard-boiled *femme fatale*, in admitting to boring semi-human and unsure even of how to be satisfied. Moreover, she does not entirely conform as psychotic since, as she eschews treating the symbolic as a mere semblance, as in the way the psychotic uses it to construct a regularity of existence out of copied routines of daily life (Vanheule 10–11).

The other side of the boring is ideo-political. In *Malign Velocities*, Benjamin Noys gives an account of the relationship between the libidinal machine that is capitalism and how subjects are emplaced in it due to a transfer of libido (Noys 40). Noys comments on the boredom of everyday life: "The experience of most work is of profound boredom and pointless-ness . . . work is the eternal hell of the same, as Baudrillard would put it, repetitive and often ridiculous tasks to no good or even useful end. Accom-panying this experience is the erotic reverie, an experience of endless var-iation and exploration of erotic possibility both at and beyond work in a libidinal acceleration" (46).

As not simply Villanelle's cry, boredom is also a problem for Eve. Her new job chasing Villanelle is a lot more interesting now that Eve is completely immersed in the *jouissance* of digression that accompanies Villanelle. Of course, the more one indulges in the fantasy of an altered life, the more one finds oneself closer to the collapse of the Real at the heart of it, since "the fantasy of integration is the fantasy of abolishing fantasy" (Noys 47). Ideas of closure indulge fantasy and are stripped in Season II, which contains a lot of boring digressions or movements without direction. Boredom is not prized in a culture of hyperattention and scattered awareness like the *Killing Eve* cosmos. This

> low tolerance for boredom, does not admit the profound idleness that benefits the creative process . . . someone [like Eve and /or Villanelle] with a greater tolerance for boredom will recognize, after a while, that walking as such is what bores him. . . . Only human beings can dance. It may be that boredom seized him while walking, so that after—and through—this "attack" he would make the step from walking to danc-ing. Compared with linear walking straight ahead, the convoluted movement of dancing represents a luxury; it escapes the achievement-principle entirely. (Han 13–14)

When Eve and Villanelle admits their boredom, the object, end, and aim of their action dissolve and shift entirely into enjoyment of the process itself.

We could, therefore, argue that two major forces prevail in Season II. On the one hand, the ineluctable trajectory toward the Real, the catastrophic second meeting, on the other, the attempt to uphold the Other through continued contractual relations with The Twelve. Both Villanelle and Eve seem to offer themselves to the Other, affirm the arbitrariness of the bigger game, and become cogs and wheels in an immoral and chaotic universe. On the other hand, symbolic relations may account for life but are not satis-fying, whereas libidinal investments do (Vanheule). Libidinal attachments and love are a reminder to Villanelle and Eve of another trail, a bridge to interruptive necessity and fate. The rest is dry symbolism. Achievement cul-ture is and remains an empty symbolic universe. *Pas de deux-ing* in and out of surveillance, in and out of private and public domains is a step toward satisfying but without love is simply the erotics of a masochistic game. Season II is a game of seduction and dissimulation. When Eve visits Villanelle in her London flat unannounced, she finds her in bed with a man and a woman. "Don't be jealous," Villanelle says.

Still, Eve has learned something of Villanelle's elusive ways: how to enjoy in full view and despite the symbolic eye. As the season ends, action moves to Rome, where Villanelle is invited by Aaron Peel and the MI5 crew follows. Once again, Villanelle is practically a hostage in Aaron's luxurious villa and Eve's team is assigned to rescue her if in danger. There is an open channel of communication between the two women and when Eve makes love to fellow MI5 employee, Hugo, we are led to believe that Villanelle is actively listening. The following day, a series of threats, assassination attempts, and bloodshed result in both women saving each other's life and escaping together from their assassins. And this is how they reach the ruins of the Roman villa that host the denouement of the second season.

"Why did I come here (to Rome)?" Eve wonders aloud. "To save me," replies Villanelle. Let us suspend the interpretation of the final scene until we go over Season II, again, one more time. Season II suspends symbolic womanhood and shows its *Reductio* through interruptive encounters that tap into transformations of the drives; everything is relativized, and there is an exchange without meaning. In this sense, *Killing Eve* mocks investigative detective efficiency and genre formulaic pursuits of truth in lieu of episodic acts without direction. While it appears that this monstrous *pas de deux* is going nowhere, that is exactly how the show shifts into performative gear, through stagings of fight or dance that are repeated, in content and form; eternally returning, inverting the same thing, and uncannily doubling as key to the show/case itself.

The main characteristic of Eve and Villanelle's relationship is delay/deferral. Theirs is not a relation based on connection but upon interruptions because of their encounters. If there is no such thing as sexual relationship, then the present series illuminates this impossibility, further problematizing castration and gender. We could propose this phrasing: "*this* is not a sexual relationship." We could say that the significant semantic difference between "this is not" and "there is not" constitutes the territory in which femininity can(not) possibly be in the capitalist discourse.

A woman less, a woman more but no woman in the end? Villanelle is not the opposite of Eve but possibly another instantiation of Carolyn Martens, the sexualized woman who does not fall for weakness or subordination and exposes the fantasy of the common good and the decent order. And while in the classic noir-female detective genre perversion normally lies hidden, here it constitutes the ambient environment in which no woman falls in love, and no one loses control. Yet unlike Carolyn, Villanelle wants to (and still believes she can) be loved.

At the same time, masochism no longer holds a relation to the superego, to guilt. Villanelle spends like there is no tomorrow; kills and spends with equal pleasure; the relation to money is pivotal here; the lack of normative guilt parallels the lack of normative sexuality and allows us to establish clear links between capitalism and the libidinal order. As already argued, Villanelle's addiction to objects is not just capitalist consumption, but a metonymy of the self. Villanelle has a relationship with the world in her own image. Ultimately therefore, and to come back to the point of seduction, the big game is not sexuality, it is surviving, being, a pulsioning repetition of the psychotic and the bored.

The fact that they are all skating on thin symbolic ice becomes apparent in the final scene of the second season, when Villanelle and Eve enter the world of Roman ruins. Riffing on the symbolic power of Rome and the decadence of Roman rule, the last episode is set in these crumbled ruins. It ironically seizes upon this site for their underground meeting, as a space for Eve and Villanelle, the subversive dissidents to discuss the true rot and ruin to which they are subject, for example, the rogue entity controlling society as the ruinous rule of The Twelve. Eve and Villanelle are now truly on their own, in a world which does not exist, or exists beyond all previous symbolic realms. This world is an inoperative location full of underground tunnels and cloisters, a belowground space for discussing a failing and lawless state. The ruins appear a seemingly suspended city to show the existence of their non-existent non-rapport. Yet, Villanelle is expert at negotiating wreckage and ruins, adept at trashing places and destroys pristine structures (aggression). Indeed, at this point, challenge is to rise up from the ruins around and on top of them, to find an egress from being serfs of The Twelve, and their corporate labyrinth with no exit but death.

The labyrinthine ruins and setting directly link the characters' psychic interiority and exteriority. Lacan is the opposite of Piranesi (Holms). The latter uses the ruins to reveal lost worlds, whereas the former is picking up stones to restore an illusion of meaning. Indeed, Lacan finds meaning in the ruins (past). Yet, we argue that the labyrinth exhibits the logic of interiority and exteriority, not simply what is behind the stones. The Lacanian ruins are the site of active negotiation and movement. To put it differently, they do not constitute a site of Heideggerian dwelling but a point of passage characterized by repetition, traversal, and interpretation. Lacan argues that in the psychoanalytic clinic, desire, always marked by alienation in the field of the Other, is found again (*retrouver*) in fragments, as something forgotten: "*Le méconnaître est condamner la découverte à l'oubli, l'expérience à la ruine* [To ignore it is to condemn the discovery to oblivion, the experience to ruin]" (Lacan, *The Language of the Self* 38).

Eve and Villanelle are driven into this setting with their *pas de deux* past a failing paternal metaphor, into a dance with the minotaur that is both without and within. To make turn from the Name of the Father, they circle like Ariandne and Theseus in the labyrinth of ruins, and they *pas de deux* by following a string in the dark. Yet, Eve is overtaken by anxiety and attempts to flee, indicating that it will take a longer time to find their own passageway.

What is ruined and ruinous at this moment, the repetition of the first stab in the dark? Eve resists Villanelle's offer of unconditional love and elopement. Her repeated "no" infuriates Villanelle, who complains: "You are ruining the moment!" Eve hesitates, and is not sure if she is ready yet to dance without any symbolic rules. Yet all is not ruined. The last episode leaves a thread for the two women to reunite (*après-coup*) in a *pas de deux* after the ruins. Season II ends without us knowing whether Eve dies from Villanelle's gunshot, and whether Villanelle defeats the monsters of boredom and commandments to "obey." It ends without closure in a reiteration of the case's impossibility, their relational stalemate as a recurrence, and as a hard-boiled riff on the sublime to the ridiculous. On top of that, it becomes apparent that the ruins of the past can never be recomposed into a full landscape. Villanelle shoots Eve in the ruins of the Roman Villa Adriana in Tivoli. Once again there is no closure. Only suspense.

When Villanelle shoots Eve, Season II entirely expels symbolic womanhood, as the object of male fantasy, and simultaneously ushers Eve and Villanelle into this feminine cosmos and passageway to quiescent ruins. Villanelle is Ariadne, leading Eve through the labyrinth into a chthonic creation, a world where sacrifice, woman, and instinct rule. Digressing from Athenian law (the rule of law per se in the *polis*), Villanelle helps Eve pass through the opaque labyrinthine ruins with panache, beauty, and grace. Season II ends with a flipping of nature and culture where law and The Twelve are shown to be more beastly and cruel and impassable than nature, the irrational, or animal instinct.

Yet, Villanelle exhibits no swagger when Eve threatens to walk away, as stuttering and shrinking before finally shooting Eve. The fact that Villanelle shoots Eve from a distance when she tries to leave is not an accident, and the gunshot is not fatal. It is a graze, a stroke, a skimming strike like that of a bullfighter who does not wish to kill his minotaur. This ending is another mutation of their suspended serial and staged interactions. At the same time, Season II ends in a more performative and gladiatorial manner than ever, playing to an invisible gallery, with Roman decay as an emblematic backdrop. In this remainder space, Eve and Villanelle wander away from servitude to a decadent inoperative rule, but at the last minute Eve gets cold feet about going on the run with Villanelle, an assassin, to Alaska, so Villanelle pulls the gun. After Eve's collapse, the camera pans out from the Roman ruins while threading back (enriched) to indicate that this will be a disaster that is survived. It is in these underground ruins that a mythic passage and unofficial contract between Eve and Villanelle is rehearsed, tested, and maintained.

Season III: The Bridge: Killing Eve's Dialectic without Synthesis

While Season II displays the death of symbolic womanhood, Season III of *Killing Eve* stages a multiplicity of mother figures, monsters, and mentors that push Eve and Villanelle into a dance with *ananké*. The mother is central to Season III of *Killing Eve*, not only as support for law, or what is left of it, but also as a force for arrhythmic invention. In *Coldness and Cruelty*, as well as *Killing Eve*, there is a turn toward the oral mother who relates to fate *(ananké)* that Deleuze describe as "The mother herself . . . the third of the Fates alone . . . the specific element of masochism is the oral mother, the ideal of coldness, solicitude, and death, between the uterine mother and the Oedipal mother" (Deleuze 55). Season III permits us to extend Deleuze's idea of the oral mother and explore *ananké* as the mother and motor of Eve and Villanelle's *condansations*.

Season III of *Killing Eve* is less about solving the case of "who killed Kenny," which is a lost cause typical of the show. Rather, it is about the total collapse of the law and the emergence of bad mothers who lead Eve and Villanelle into a turn on the bridge from *thanatos* to *eros*, a turn from The Twelve. All the action in *Killing Eve* Season III revolves around maternal feminine *jouissance* and contractual *ad hoc* arrangements besides the law. The turn to *ananké* follows a parade of bad mothers who attempt to replace the father and make the child into the phallus. For Deleuze, the oral mother is not the Oedipal one who colludes with the father, nor is it the Uterine mother who is the cloacal and swampy mother, partner of the primal horde father. As the mother of masochist invention, the oral mother does not dominate or overpower with *jouissance* but engages necessity to invent, play, and desire differently. Eve and Villanelle go through a lot of cruel mothers before turning on the bridge toward fate.

Season III opens with Eve, not dead, but done being employed in any official position with intelligence. Separated from her husband, separated from everything to do with intel, Eve is turned around after barely surviving Villanelle's gunshot. She is off the grid and going through the motions while working as a dishwasher at a Korean restaurant. This is interrupted when Carolyn unofficially seeks out Eve's services to help find Kenny. At first, Eve rebuffs Carolyn's offer of employment but ends up following the case. Ironically, Eve's objections, "I don't work for you anymore, not after what you did in Rome," ignite a search that consumes the entire season. Moreover, there is no pretense of respect between Eve and Carolyn, who finally fall out for good in this season.

Investigations in *Killing Eve* have moved out of the realm of law entirely into a contractual search. The death of Kenny demonstrates how phallic mothers like Carolyn look and try to be strong men, yet depart from law, overworking themselves, and killing everyone around them. Admittedly, in

Episode 6 of Season III, Carolyn confesses that she "doesn't have the mother gene" to Geraldine, her daughter. Geraldine shows up in Season III to grieve her brother Kenny, nauseating Carolyn with kindness. Her daughter is a painful reminder to Carolyn of how she herself hired Kenny into intelligence and kept him close to the killer The Twelve cartel since Season I. Given The Twelve are liable for Kenny's death from the beginning, Carolyn's search for the cause of Kenny's death is entirely disingenuous. Moreover, even while Carolyn mourns her son's death, that does not stop her from going into work the very next day where she is told to "go home" by Paul—a rival work mate and more "pious" disciple of The Twelve—Carolyn's nemesis.

Season III stages a myriad of mothers, many of whom are bosses—Carolyn, Dasha, and Hélène—all attempting to humiliate, but being humiliated, by both their biological and work children. Carolyn's assistant Mo literally works on the Kenny case until he is also rubbed out by a member of The Twelve. This is after Mo tells Carolyn, "I found the thing linking to the "thingy," you know Paul to the Twelve." This dialogue, like so much of the discourse in *Killing Eve*, does not straightforwardly reference but uses word play to suggest, since no one who directly speaks survives. The symbolic lines between family, work, boss, lover, and parent are more crooked and unclear than ever among The Twelve and particularly between Carolyn and Konstantin.

Carolyn and Konstantin are deviant boss parents, who, like The Twelve, use their authority to spawn death, spread destruction, and set off dissension to consume, capture, and devour their progeny. Konstantin's daughter, Irina feels continually replaced by Villanelle. In Episode 2, Konstantin avoids going home and stays in England after accidentally killing Kenny to siphon money from The Twelve and then frame it on their accountant, Charles Kruger. He hires Villanelle to kill Kruger, which she does while he sits in a car next to Carolyn. Villanelle shows that while she kills for The Twelve, she can and will kill the mother. Konstantin's plan (which he tells no one) is to take the money and abandon, not only The Twelve and Carolyn, but also Villanelle and possibly his own daughter Irina. By the end of Season III, it is revealed that Konstantin slept with Carolyn and their son is Kenny. He also sleeps with Carolyn's daughter Geraldine after abandoning his own daughter Irina, who is incarcerated in a detention center for evaluation after running over her stepfather.

The serial TV version of *Killing Eve* is different from the mystery series by Luke Jennings, because it keeps Konstantin as a continually unreliable presence for all three seasons. In preserving Konstantin, the TV show hangs onto a remainder of law, or Oedipal fantasy regarding the father as a constant presence. Yet, even in Season III, Konstantin provides no fatherly loyalty, protection, or trustworthiness to his daughter Irina, his biological son Kenny, his ex-lover Carolyn, Dasha, or even Villanelle, whom he appears to like more than Irina. In all three seasons, the only constant about Konstantin is his existence itself. He somehow manages to hold on to life in Season III after Carolyn shoots him for killing Kenny; he embezzles money from The Twelve, and collapses in the subways, almost dying of a heart attack.

In book one, *Killing Eve, Codename Villanelle*, Konstantin dies quickly and is killed by Villanelle, his own apprentice. The book version kills the father early on to lionize Villanelle who repeats his own advice to her, while delivering the final blow: "Trust no one, she says, and placing the barrel of the Glock against his ribs, squeezes the trigger" (Jennings 201). The book series is perhaps more uncompromising about retaliation in a world of lawless and useless paternal figures. Yet, the TV series uses humor between Konstantin and female characters, especially Villanelle, as comic relief to show his fatherly feebleness. As if to indulge and show Oedipal relations as a ridiculous fantasy, *Killing Eve* mocks Konstantin's "support" of women, mentees, and children, showing his abandonment of former lovers (Carolyn, Geraldine), negligence of his own son and daughter, desertion of Villanelle, and his part in the death of the accountant, Dasha, and the accountant's wife. Interactions with the cruel mothers, especially Villanelle's biological and work mothers, are not only humorous but also heart-breaking.

Season III begins when an old school Russian retired KGB agent, Dasha, a gold medal gymnast who still wears the award around her neck—turned hitwoman for The Twelve—shows up at Villanelle's wedding and crashes the party. As her original work mother, Dasha mocks the attempted marriage and makes it clear to Villanelle that she has no life outside The Twelve. Conversations between Dasha and Villanelle usually end up in fights, or death threats. They relate via *thanatos,* which is like the relay between Konstantin and Villanelle, Carolyn and Eve. Bosses of The Twelve are primal horde parents who accidently kill their own children. Neither Villanelle nor Eve wants to get back to work for Dasha—the uterine, swampy mother and partner to the primal horde who unmoors them both back into the sadistic boss boat.

Eve meets Dasha in Season III and questions her about corrupting Villanelle in a bowling alley. Here, Dasha appears old, but bold, unrepentant, and monstrous, bragging about mentoring Villanelle to Eve: "I broke her back, I gave her wings and made her perfect killing machine." Eve underestimates what Dasha will do to drive a wedge between her and Villanelle. In Episode 4, Dasha follows Eve's husband Niko where he has fled to Poland, then pitchforks him through the neck, pretending it was Villanelle. Still, Dasha's power is provisional, since she reports to The Twelve who control her and Villanelle. Dasha, Carolyn, and Konstantin are aggressive, sadistic, and omnipotent—reverse apostles—who feel empowered by encouraging servitude from their acolytes.

Moreover, all members report to Hélène, mother of The Twelve, whom Villanelle finally meets in Episode 7, Season III. This episode opens at Helene's house, which is an *unheimlich* display of medieval armor, knives, rough wooden chairs, and tables. She embraces her like a mother after asking Villanelle about her wound and says: "Do you know why I love you?

Because you are an agent of chaos. . . . It's monstrous but it's beautiful. You are a beautiful monster, Villanelle. You wouldn't be able to kill me before I kill you. You are a child; you have no idea what you are dealing with."

Hélène directly embraces her as both a serial killer and a child. Subsequently, the uncanniness of the excessively close mother, and encounters like these, hasten Villanelle's longing to leave The Twelve. They sabotage her attempts at omnipotence, and all being by reducing her to a maternal phallus. After getting sick of Dasha's orders and Hélène's delay in making her a keeper, Villanelle visits mother Russia with information that she receives from Konstantin about her biological mother. She makes this trip, because Villanelle knows what Hélène said is no doubt correct: Villanelle is still a mental baby, caught in the maternal realm, brewing in primordial love/hate.

Just as Villanelle challenges God to appear and validate her being there, in Season III she challenges the mother to revolt against *thanatos* and help her get a life. She does not. Like Dasha driving home how Villanelle will never get married, Carolyn shuts Villanelle down when in the Royal London theater, she begs for a real job not as hitwoman for The Twelve. Carolyn cruelly demeans and refuses to help Villanelle, as another cruel mother who refuses to acknowledge her existence (being/*eros*) except as tool of *thanatos*/death: "you exist to kill and if you stop killing you are useless." Using her creative powers for domination, the bad mother's message is: Since I made you, I can kill you. Her mentors mock Villanelle's demands throughout Season III such that she ricochets between Hélène, Konstantin, Dasha, and Carolyn until she visits her own biological mother in an entire episode that begins and ends with a long journey.

Correlatively, Season III contains a lot of trains, buses, and vehicles that symbolize turning, movement, and a crossing from one mental and physical space to another. The train is a repeated motif when Konstantin has a heart attack on the subway train platform, and when Villanelle sends Eve a double decker red birthday bus cake in Episode 4, which she promptly throws out. Eve later in Episode 7 attempts to retrieve the cake box by jumping into a garbage dump to locate Villanelle, who is, of course, in transit. These trains and other assorted vehicles perform a bridging function as semipublic (not spaces controlled by The Twelve) means of transportation: "they are ambiguously connoted transitional spaces and times—womb-like cocoons protecting us from the external world while at the same time exposing us to mortal dangers. [They are] Iconic containers -on-wheels of fears and desires" (Sabbadini 131). Trains, bridges, and buses symbolize a moving link function in *Killing Eve* and spark a change in direction for Villanelle, which happens after a trip home.

When Villanelle arrives at her birth home in a rural Russian village, the family are all there, but only Pyotr, her brother, recognizes Oxsana (Villanelle's birth name). She meets her mother's youngest son Bor'ka, who says he needs 50,000 rubles to see Elton John. Oxsana's mother (Tatiana) comes in sobbing, pretending to be happy to see her. At one point, the family are spread around the table all singing Elton John's "Crocodile Rock," in a scene of absurdist surrealism. Attempting to find out what happened to her father whom she tells her brother "taught me how to fight," Villanelle asks, "Where's Dad?" No one answers and the absurdism escalates when at the local fair, Villanelle wins the dung throwing contest. The youngest, Bor'ka loses a cooking contest and Villanelle tries to console him after seeing their mother tell him he is stupid and embarrassing.

Tatiana sees Villanelle soothing Bor'ka, and angrily tells Villanelle: "You are not welcome anymore. You are not a part of this family. Get out of my house." This harkens back to the song and conforms with what Lacan says about the mother's desire as like an all-consuming crocodile: "The mother's desire is not something that is bearable just like that, that you are indifferent to. It will always wreak havoc. A huge crocodile in whose jaws you are— that's the mother. One never knows what might suddenly come over her and make her shut her trap" (Lacan, *The Other Side of Psychoanalysis* 112). Being rocked by a crocodile involves a dangerous grip like when Tatiana shuts her trap on Oxsana twice by kicking her out after she travels a long way to visit and by formerly abandoning her when she was a baby at an orphanage for being "annoying." Villanelle has not yet freed herself of the mother/mentor's desire, so Tatiana's rejection accelerates her spiral into destructive *jouissance*.

In response, Villanelle actually speaks her pain while shedding crocodile tears and reminds Tatiana of the past before killing her, "You can carry an innocent little girl out of the house, but it will be harder to get an adult to go along." This season uniquely displays Villanelle approaching self-awareness, having emotions, and even attempting to connect or heal. Still after her biological mother's rejection, she reverts to acting out, stabs her mother, and then torches the whole house, but not without saving and leaving money for Bor'ka and Pyotr who sleep in a separate barn. This episode ends with Villanelle returning to the UK, back on a train, cocoon-like looking out a window and singing Elton John. This trip home eventually allows her to see the futility of making demands upon the mother.

In Series 3, Villanelle executes many maternal figures, including a Spanish mother in Andalusia (nod to Buñuel's *Un Chien Andalou*) with a poison dart whose baby she steals and later deposits in a trash can. Yet, after killing her biological mother, the Spanish mother, and her work mother Dasha, Villanelle does not feel liberated, her mood plummets, and the sadness returns as killing fails to cheer her up. These killings are stabs at the past, too many ineffective cuts. Villanelle's killing is acting out, an attempt to make a limit (on the mother) that no longer works. What we see here is the capitalist confusion of psychic elements annihilates the subject who sees itself as "nothing," the non-object of the other's desire, replaceable, not unique, a commodity. However, this uncastrated state of not-being-the-other's object also protected Villanelle in the past with the reassurance: when I am nothing, nothing escapes me as surplus or loss. Still, after the visit home, Villanelle beings to shift strategies and engage Eve to make transition and suspense the new cut. They give up trying to kill each other and revolve together in *condansations* to leave a mark on one another.

Departing from fixture in sexual and detective positions, the two characters inch closer to a transitional space and passage of escape. Villanelle slowly shifts away from narcissistic investments in her own body, into a play with fate via Eve. Her child-like mind fixates on Eve as an aesthetic ideal and oral mother exactly because she has no symbolic value in a highly aggressive phallic and sexualized universe. More importantly, by the end of this season, we see how Villanelle provisionally relies on Eve as an oral mother in order to embrace *eros* and be released from the feeling of being erased (*thanatos*) by bad mothers and their crocodile rock. Likewise, when Eve stops reporting to Carolyn and simply follows necessity on the Kenny case, she is released from the Oedipal mother who pays lip service to the failed MI5 father.

This release allows Villanelle and Eve to shift into obeying *ananké* in a play on the Oral mother. One might view Eve and Villanelle's performance as akin to those of Leopold von Sacher-Masoch and Wanda, who were political resistors. Their performative actions display how citizens then and now in globalized late capital are existentially controlled and caught up in a political system of tyranny that believes itself to be above the law.

The Twelve as Fifth column highly global and professional white-collar bosses are the truly politically powerful and felonious criminals. As John C. Coates of Harvard Law School predicted in "The Problem of Twelve,"

> Three ongoing meta-trends are reshaping corporate governance: indexing, private equity, and globalization. These trends threaten to permanently entangle business with the state and create organizations controlled by a small number of individuals with unsurpassed power. (Coates 1)

Together, they stage a dance of voluntary servitude that departs from the serfdom and non-existence of answering demands from The Twelve. Instead of suffering to avoid facing the real, Eve and Villanelle stage a voluntary play submitting to *ananké*.

After circling the drain of unregulated law and combatant mothers, a scene near the end of Season III literally puts Eve and Villanelle on the dance floor. In a meeting at a ballroom, they watch dancers until an usher tells them: "we encourage all to the dance floor, rhythm or no rhythm." At this point, Eve steps on Villanelle's feet as if to demonstrate their arrhythmic *pas de deux* and Villanelle says, "Are you leading or am I.?" Hélène's replacement for Villanelle enters and rudely interrupts Eve and Villanelle's dance discussion of a kill-free future. Her replacement Rian is a Scottish serial killer, and Villanelle's obvious double. Also, the name "Rian" is a nod to the last name of Idoia Lòpaz Riaño, the real-life *La Tigresa*, and person upon whom Villanelle's character is based ("Killing Eve"). Riano was a Spanish ETA hit woman and serial killer for Basque terrorist groups that *Killing Eve* makes into Rian and Villanelle's uncanny double.

As soon as Villanelle spots Rian, she knows it means a threat to her existence and status as a serial killer. Villanelle gives Eve the money she took from Konstantin (a gesture that confirms they are together) and follows Rian, who leads her to the subway. In a last-ditch humorous attempt to avoid eliminating Rian, Villanelle shouts, "Jump! Jump!" to indicate that they are in the same boat as serial killer serfs for The Twelve. Stalwartly, Rhian says, "Autonomy is overrated, sheep are better than wolves." They fight, then Villanelle ends up killing her by throwing her onto the subway tracks before an oncoming train. To separate from Hélène—the mother of bad mothers and The Twelve—Villanelle must kill her double Rian, and thus sever ties with *la Tigressa*, her serial killer self. This is a further step in the *pas de deux*, which allows Villanelle to veer away from The Twelve.

Following the dance floor interruption, there is an *ad hoc* meeting of The Twelve where Carolyn shoots Paul instead of Konstantin for killing Kenny and The Twelve all disperse. Eve and Villanelle depart from that explosion into the show's last scene where they are standing, turned toward each other, on a bridge. It is no accident that the season ending occurs on a bridge, which is suspended over water since the water is connected to the mother as movement, flow, and wellspring of life. As Gaston Bachelard notes, water is "the spring of being, motherhood. Water flows its constant movement responding to the environment and to possibility" (Bachelard ix). The bridge is a suspended conduit and contractual overpass that provides them passage over dark maternal forces that threaten to rise, surge, and flood. It is an ungrounded link that allows Villanelle and Eve to imagine an alternate existence. The Season III ending shows the two women finally connecting instead of attempting to kill one another on a bridge that is like their relation—a variable, contractual, and suspended link.

Their conversation is short and begins by establishing that they both killed Dasha, uniting over killing the primal mother. Given Dasha almost killed Eve's husband Niko and tried to kill Villanelle early on, she remarks how this mother's death "is romantic." This humorous word play is a literal bonding of *eros* over *thanatos*.

Yet, they acknowledge that the mother monster is not entirely dead and exists within them: Eve: "I think that all of us have monsters in us, but most people keep them hidden." Villanelle: "I think your monster encourages my monster." Eve: "Help me." The bridge permits the two women to engage in a suspension of symbolic structures to indulge the possibilities of fate like Coleridge's suspension of disbelief (Sabbadini 130). Villanelle and Eve's meeting on the bridge is a performative play not fixed by any concrete ground, representation, or institutional power. As an in-between space, the bridge allows them to imagine crossing over and above the "mother monsters" that reside not only beneath and beside them, but also within.

On the bridge, Eve and Villanelle find a freedom of imagination and suspense of understanding like what Deleuze describes in *Coldness and Cruelty* as: "In masochism we find a progression from disavowal to suspense, from disavowal as a process of liberation from the pressures of the superego to suspense as incarnation of the ideal. . . . Suspense points to the new status of the ego and to the ideal of rebirth through the agency of the maternal phallus. . . ." (Deleuze 127). Their re- and de-territorializing of detective and sexual forms flips the power structure and satirizes traditional detective forms, like the James Bond series.

Villanelle and Eve meet on the bridge as transitional space for engaging temporal intervals between two events or time periods. While there is not much representational dialogue between the women, the bridge allows them to turn from past identities toward a cartel-free future. This movement, like the bridge, connects them across disparate and binary categories of enemy and friend, past and future, policewoman and assassin. A bridge is what Donald W. Winnicott calls a "transitional space" that is a playground for individuals to engage in play or "the perpetual human task of keeping inner and outer reality separate yet interrelated" (Winnicott 230). In this way, Eve and Villanelle's play obeys fate to harness an *inner* driven movement that is manifest in *external* interruptions and repetitions. In a play that accepts *ananké*, as a figure of the oral mother and fate, necessity becomes Eve and Villanelle's final dance partner on the bridge.

After a discussion of their prospects and hopes, Villanelle vows to stop killing and go AWOL from The Twelve. By the end of Season III, Eve also vows to stop working for British MI5. These realizations crystalize on the bridge suspended above water that allows for a transitory play (*parlêtre*) with speaking being. On the bridge they invent how they might connect disparate aspects of self (psyche) and society (*soma*) over time. It allows dwelling not in fixture or representation but through speaking being as characterized by repetition and a temporal life passage. Heidegger first noted how, "the bridge does not first come to a location to stand in it; rather a location comes into existence only by virtue of the bridge" (Heidegger 154). Standing apart but together on the bridge, Villanelle and Eve make it a location through a movement that eschews fixed ground. They play-act to find (*retrouver*) a future out of fragments, or something forgotten that might revive their lives from ruin.

Conclusion

Killing Eve constantly reminds us of the failure of the symbolic to verify meaning in being or to access to the real truth of the reality. In fact, when characters fully access the truth, they often die. Intelligence, the law, and the truth are all cloaked and suspended. Hence, the show's play on words and the dance of simulated metaphors between Villanelle and Eve where fake names, serial interactions, humor, and word play are the closest we get to an unveiling of the truth. The human ability to accept reality as a play of illusion is a fundamental necessity for active existence. Full participation in the play of the cosmos requires giving up the illusion that language completely represents.

The end scene displays the two women accepting how even The Twelve as so-called keepers of the truth are unable to control the facts. Villanelle and Eve cross over the water for rebirth around *ananké*, to become participants in the play that drives speaking being (*parlêtre*). This play is not simply a child's play, but the play of the cosmos where our lives are driven by fate and necessity. Villanelle and Eve's embrace of *ananké* correlates to *amor fati* and Nietzsche's idea of necessity controlling being through the rhythm of eternal. Embracing *ananké* involves the acceptance or love of what is to come, *amor fati* as the fact that all beings are subjects bound by becoming. Necessity is pre-symbolic and mythic, a driven force that never fully appears and takes a multiplicity of veiled forms: the oral mother, ananké, and, as we will see, Eurydice. Scholars reexamining Heidegger's reading of Nietzsche posit "a non-metaphysical originality in Nietzsche's cosmological philosophy of play" (I. A. Moore 70). Instead of overcoming, Nietzsche's idea of the eternal return is the incessant, all-embracing, all-providing, and all-eliminating rhythmic play of beings as becoming in the world. This dimension of "play" in Nietzsche's philosophy involves a non-dialectic engagement of chance, like the play of a child or an artist.

It would be tempting to view *Killing Eve's* three seasons as a dialectic, with teleology culminating in synthesis. However, each season suspends closure and resolution at the end to intensify the unsolved and stage the accidental. The show's refusal of movement toward synthesis accords with Deleuze and Blanchot's eschewal of the dialectic and positive ontology in lieu of movement of thought, and movement of becoming (Kaufman 153). While there is a lot of movement and travel in *Killing Eve,* this movement does not end in any resolution or smoothing out of conflict.

Season I ends with Eve stabbing Villanelle in bed, Season II ends with Villanelle shooting Eve in the Roman ruins. Season III ends with Eve and Villanelle in a simulated shoot-out scene, backs to one another, slowly walking further apart as if in a hard-boiled gun draw until Eve turns back to match Villanelle's gaze. This play comes after Eve's cry for "help" when Villanelle tells her to "Stand up Straight and look at me. Now turn around and face the other way (back-to-back). Now we walk and never look back. Don't turn or look back." The rest of this episode lacks dialogue as they both turn back and the music plays, "Tell me I'm your baby, that you'll kiss me forever." This turning back (*Kehre*) is not only a play with the hard-boiled genre in a fake draw but also a play with femininity through fate that allows them to turn back toward one other, rather than toward the power of a gun.

The end scene "turn" (*Kehre*) is related to what Maurice Blanchot says about the myth of Orpheus in *The Space of Literature*. Here, he engages the myth as central to the book—the real center of symbolic representation that displaces itself. The myth of Orpheus points out how any and all attempts at saying are a betrayal, as illustrated when Orpheus turns back to look at Eurydice: his seeing is a betrayal of his saying and singing (Blanchot 172). This myth explains how the inevitable acquisition of language is an oscillating movement between the real and representation, where to speak is to kill. This oscillating movement occurs when Orpheus sees Eurydice, when in Lacanian terms symbolic representation substitutes for the real. As a non-signifying muse and negative capability Eurydice, like *ananké*, is the partner of *logos* whose death sparks *eros*, music, and life. Music, arrhythmically speaking, does not yet signify; it is the oscillating movement of turning when Orpheus sees Eurydice, "the real acceding to symbolic."

Orpheus' turning is not sublimation, but a praxis of creative movement out of negation, or the very holes in signifying chain itself. Blanchot describes this type of inventing as "a gift whereby he refuses, whereby he sacrifices the work, bearing himself toward the origin according to desire's measureless movement—and whereby unknowingly he still moves toward the work toward the origin of the work" (Blanchot 174). It is a performance that shows its own oscillation between appearing and disappearing. This type of creative praxis is akin to what Lacan says about Joyce's writing as turning around "the fourth term, it happens, is the sinthome. It is just as surely the Father, in as much as perversion means nothing other than *"turning* to the father" [*version vers le pére*] and that, in short, the Father is a symptom, or if you prefer, a *sinthome*" (Lacan, *The Sinthome* 6). As in perversion, sinthomatic creating involves a turn from paternal metaphors around discourse. However, unlike the pervert who wishes to eradicate the symbolic and deconstruct the Other, sinthomatic praxis engages the real to articulate differently.

Eve and Villanelle's play on the bridge stages this movement between signifying registers. It is a praxis like Joyce's writing of the enigma to engage the body in an art "that is dance. This would allow me to write the term *condansation* a little differently" (Lacan, *The Sinthome* 62). The end scene where they turn is a *pas de deux* not infused with any image or word but a praxis of performatively engaging negation. Trailing necessity compels Eve to betray Villanelle at the Season I ending, and then what compels Villanelle to betray Eve in the Season II. However, by the end of Season III, the two women stop betraying each other and turn together to betray The Twelve. This turn away from The Twelve is *Killing Eve's* resistance play with symbolic traditions of detection, like James Bond, and myths like Orpheus. The show articulates differently through multiple dance stages that mark out *ananké* as mother of invention. Subsequently, the show makes its own supplemental myth, which our article uses to play with Gilles Deleuze's mythic and masochistic oral mother and Maurice Blanchot's myth of Orpheus.

The end bridge scene is simulation of a shoot-out where both women walk away from one other then turn but not to kill. Rather, theirs is an orphic turn back to each other as performers on the bridge. Through the myth of *ananké* as mother of invention, *Killing Eve* makes its own serial art of detection and dance. Instead of returning to a "toxic, lawless, workplace," Season III shows how Eve and Villanelle stop acting out for an oedipal and uterine mother to face *ananké*. The two women turn in a movement that is a performative act not meant to create synthesis but to engage. The simulated shoot-out on the bridge at the end of Season III is a turn from symbolic servitude into voluntary bodily invention. In saying little or nothing, their turn (*Kehre*) allows Villanelle and Eve to depart from detective cliché and stage their own *condansations*. Season III ends on the bridge in a play that turns from detective investigation into a real case. *Killing Eve* does not resolve or amalgamate the other seasons, but it bridges them to invent a serial televised artform of invariable detection and dance.

Notes

1 As a twist on the hard-boiled *femme fatale*, Villanelle is more like what *The Big Book of Female Detectives* (Penzler) calls "Bad Girls" who are less intentionally bad than caught up in an inescapable system of criminality. Literary corollaries include "The Winged Assassin" by L. T Meade and Robert Eustace and "Extenuating Circumstances" by Joyce Carol Oates.

2 Linda Williams writes an introduction to the edited volume *Viewing Positions* that refers to both John Berger's 1972 *Ways of Seeing* and Laura Mulvey's 1975 "Visual Pleasure and Narrative Cinema." Williams like Mulvey and Berger is foundational for connecting gender to active or passive looking and critiquing the "male gaze" in Western art and "classical" Hollywood cinema (1). Williams relates the tradition of gendered active or passive looking to both Christian Metz and Jean-Louis Baudry, who extend the idea of the disembodied spectator in their work (Williams, *Viewing Positions* 2).

Works Cited

Agamben, Giorgio. *Creation and Anarchy: The Work of Art and the Religion of Capitalism*. Stanford University Press, 2019.

Bachelard, Gaston. *Water and Dreams: An Essay on the Imagination of Matter*. Translated by Edith R. Farrell, Fourth printing 2006, Dallas Institute of Humanities and Culture, 2006.

Blanchot, Maurice. *The Space of Literature*. Translated by Ann Smock, University of Nebraska Press, 1982.

Coates, I. V. *The Future of Corporate Governance Part I: The Problem of Twelve.* SSRN Scholarly Paper, ID 3247337, Social Science Research Network, 20 Sep. 2018. *papers.ssrn.com*, https://doi.org/10.2139/ssrn.3247337.

Declercq, Frédéric. "Lacan on the Capitalist Discourse: Its Consequences for Libidinal Enjoyment and Social Bonds." *Psychoanalysis, Culture & Society*, vol. 11, no. 1, Apr. 2006, pp. 74–83, https://doi.org/10.1057/palgrave.pcs.2100068.

Deleuze, Gilles. *Masochism: Coldness and Cruelty.* Zone Books, 1991.

Deleuze, Gilles, and Félix Guattari. *A Thousand Plateaus: Capitalism and Schizophrenia.* Continuum, 2008.

Deleuze, Gilles, and Leopold Sacher-Masoch, editors. *Masochism.* Zone Books ; Distributed by the MIT Press, 1989.

Desutter, Laurent. "Reciprocal Portrait of Jacques Lacan as Gilles Deleuze." *Deleuze and Lacan: A Disjunctive Synthesis*, edited by Boštjan Nedoh and Andreja Zevnik, Edinburgh University Press, 2016, pp. 32–43.

Freud, Sigmund. "The Economic Problem of Masochism." *Collected Papers*, edited by James Strachey, vol. 5, The Hogarth Press, 1950, pp. 255–68.

Gompertz, Will. "Killing Eve: Will Reviews Season Two of the Award-Winning Drama." *BBC News*, 7 June 2019. *www.bbc.com*, https://www.bbc.com/news/entertainment-arts-48547153.

Han, Byung-Chul. *The Burnout Society.* Translated by Erik Butler, Stanford Briefs, an imprint of Stanford University Press, 2015.

Hannan, Martin. "The Real Villanelle ... and How She Killed Her Victims." *The National*, 20 May 2020, https://www.thenational.scot/news/18450783.real-villanelle-killed-victims/.

Harrison, Ellie. "Killing Eve: The Real-Life 'Psychopath' Who Murdered 23 People and Inspired Villanelle Character." *The Independent*, 14 May 2020, https://www.independent.co.uk/arts-entertainment/tv/news/killing-eve-villanelle-real-inspiration-jodie-comer-idoia-lopez-riano-la-tigresa-luke-jennings-a9513881.html.

Heidegger, Martin. *Poetry, Language, Thought.* Harper & Row, 1971.

Jennings, Luke. *Codename Villanelle.* Mulholland Books, 2018.

Kaufman, Eleanor. *Deleuze, the Dark Precursor: Dialectic, Structure, Being.* Johns Hopkins University Press, 2012.

"Killing Eve: How My Psycho Killer Was Brought to Life." *The Guardian*, 5 Aug. 2018, http://www.theguardian.com/tv-and-radio/2018/aug/05/killing-eve-how-my-psycho-killer-was-brought-to-life-luke-jennings.

Lacan, Jacques. "On Psychoanalytic Discourse." *La Salmandra*, translated by Jack Stone, 1978, pp. 32–55, https://web.archive.org/web/20140729192754/http://web.missouri.edu/~stonej/t67894312xxxv.html.

——. *The Four Fundamental Concepts of Psychoanalysis.* Translated by Jacques-Alain Miller, WW Norton, 1998.

——. *The Language of the Self: The Function of Language in Psychoanalysis.* Translated by Anthony Wilden, Johns Hopkins paperbacks ed, Johns Hopkins University Press, 1981.

——. *The Other Side of Psychoanalysis.* W. W. Norton, 2007.

——. *The Sinthôme: The Seminar of Jacques Lacan, Book XXIII.* Translated by A. R Price, 1st edition, Polity, 2016.

Leader, Darian. *Why Can't We Sleep?* Penguin, 2019.

Moore, Alison. *Sexual Myths of Modernity: Sadism, Masochism, and Historical Teleology.* Lexington Books, 2016.

Moore, Ian Alexander. "Fink's (Heideggerean) Nietzsche, or The Possibility of a 'Verwindung' of Metaphysics." *Purlieu,* vol. 1, no. 1, 2010, pp. 54–76.

Noys, Benjamin. *Malign Velocities: Accelerationism & Capitalism.* Zero Books, 2014.

Penzler, Otto, editor. *The Big Book of Female Detectives.* Vintage Crime/Black Lizard, 2018.

Sabbadini, Andrea. *Boundaries and Bridges: Perspectives on Time and Space in Psychoanalysis.* Karnac, 2014.

Tomšič, Samo. *The Capitalist Unconscious: Marx and Lacan.* Verso Books, 2015, p. 256.

Vanheule, Stijn. "Capitalist Discourse, Subjectivity and Lacanian Psychoanalysis." *Frontiers in Psychology,* vol. 7, 2016. *Frontiers,* https://doi.org/10.3389/fpsyg.2016.01948.

Williams, Linda Ruth. *Critical Desire: Psychoanalysis and the Literary Subject.* E. Arnold ; Distributed exclusively in the USA by St. Martin's Press, 1995.

——. *Viewing Positions: Ways of Seeing Film.* Rutgers University Press, 1998.

Winnicott, D. W. *Playing and Reality.* Tavistock, 1971.

Žižek, Slavoj. *The Ticklish Subject: An Essay in Political Ontology.* Verso, 1999.

Chapter 2

Repetition to Revolution

Jordan Peele's *Us*

Jennifer Friedlander

Us centers on the Wilson family, Adelaide and Gabe (parents) and Zora and Jason (their daughter and son) as they arrive at their Southern Californian summer house, which used to be Adelaide's childhood home. When Gabe announces that he has planned for them to meet the Tyler family (Gabe's friend, Josh, his wife, Kitty, and twin teenage daughters) at Santa Cruz Beach, Adelaide expresses uneasiness. The audience knows what Gabe does not yet know: that she had an eerily disturbing encounter there as a child. The film begins with a flashback, before the opening credits, to young Adelaide in 1986 on the day that will come to haunt her and the narrative of the film. It opens with a TV, presumably being watched at home by young Adelaide, airing a commercial for "Hands Across America." Adelaide is then shown with her family at an adventure park on the Santa Cruz Beach boardwalk when she wanders off into a desolate exhibit called "Vision Quest," with the tagline, "Find Yourself." Inside she wanders through a creepy hall of mirrors and when the power suddenly goes out, things take an uncanny turn: her mirror reflection becomes out of sync with her movements. She sees not her face but the back of her own head—the impossible position of seeing oneself as an object to be seen by others. When the girl turns around, it quickly becomes apparent that rather than facing her mirror image, Adelaide is confronted by an embodied doppelgänger.

As the present-day Adelaide tells Gabe about her misgivings regarding the impending beach excursion, the film intersperses another flashback, one that we are to understand reflects what Adelaide is thinking. This brief scene shows a young Adelaide in the waiting room while her parents speak with a therapist about the aftermath of Adelaide's childhood ordeal. We learn that Adelaide did not speak after returning from the house of mirrors, a condition that the therapist diagnoses as PTSD. The therapist suggests that her parents encourage Adelaide to "tell her story" in other creative forms like art and dance. Her father responds somewhat incredulously to the therapist's diagnosis, retorting, "She wasn't in Nam; she got lost." Her distraught mother is more accepting of the therapist's words, pleading, "I just want

DOI: 10.4324/9781003194033-4

my little girl back." Her father, by questioning the connection between her speechlessness and her disappearance, and her mother, by recognizing (even metaphorically) that this is not her "little girl," both unknowingly stumble upon two interrelated dimensions of the truth of Adelaide's disappearance. In retrospect, these comments can be read as subtly foreshadowing the major twist of the film: that (as her Mother alludes) the Adelaide who went into the Vision Quest is not the same little girl who emerged from it, and that (as her father senses) trauma is not responsible for her lack of speech. We discover in the shocking final moments of the film that Adelaide's doppelgänger attacks the "real" Adelaide and takes her place. The reason why the "Adelaide" who escapes from the hall of mirrors cannot speak is not because she has survived an unimaginable horror, but rather because she is a shadow figure who had never learned how.

This discovery comes as a shock for viewers, who are led throughout the film to root for this substitute Adelaide in her life and death struggle to protect her family from the doppelgängers (the "tethered") who have emerged to launch a coordinated and comprehensive attack on their counterparts. We learn that everyone has a "tethered" shadow figure who is condemned to live underground in brutal conditions. As described in the film by Red, who is Adelaide's presumed doppelgänger-turned-original-Adelaide:

> . . . whatever happened to the girl happened to the shadow. . . . When the girl ate, her food was given to her, warm and tasty, but when the shadow was hungry, she had to eat rabbits, raw and bloody. On Christmas the girl received wonderful toys, soft and cushy, but the shadow's toys were so sharp and cold they'd slice through her fingers when she played with them.

Red has been long planning an intricate revolt that she calls "The Untethering," in which the tethered surface from their underground confines in red jumpsuits and armed with giant scissors, with the goal of killing their counterparts and taking their places in the above-ground world.

Before considering how this twist operates for viewers of the film, I focus on the ways in which this discovery (that "Adelaide" is herself originally the tethered counterpart who abducts the little girl and lives in her place) is widely interpreted by viewers to be a revelation for "Adelaide" herself. Viewers and critics alike tend to agree that the film indicates that Adelaide has repressed knowledge of the switch due to the traumatic nature of the circumstances and that it only comes to surface in her memory as a result of the tethered revolt. But, I argue, in order to take up this position in relation to the film, the spectator would have to make the foundational mistake upon which the narrative depends: namely, that repression is a secondary phenomenon of trauma (and returns in the distorted form of the symptom).

The film, I contend, highlights that this understanding of repression is the condition of possibility for the error that enables Adelaide's double to slot seamlessly into her life. In particular, I argue, the film demonstrates that the commonly held view of trauma as creating repressed memories which later come to be accessed with clarity (after catharsis or "working through") should be complicated by the Lacanian-Zizekian claim that it is the rhythm of repetition that is primary and constitutive. As Slavoj Žižek neatly puts it, "repetition precedes repression" (*In Defense of Lost Causes* 320).

Based on this insight, rather than frame the central twist of the film around the question of Adelaide's "remembering," I suggest that we complicate it by rethinking what is meant by "remembering" and "forgetting" in terms of Freud's 1914 paper, "Remembering, Repeating, and Working Through." As Freud explains, if trauma involves the symbolically unintegratable, then it could never be "remembered," since it "could never have been 'forgotten' because in a sense it was never consciously experienced" ("Remembering, Repeating and Working-Through" 149). Rather than "remembering," the person "repeats" it as an "action," "without, of course," Freud notes, "knowing that he is repeating it" ("Remembering, Repeating and Working-Through" 150). As Lawrence Friedman highlights, not only does Freud's account challenge our usual understanding of what is involved in "remembering," but it also complicates how we think about memories themselves. Whereas conventional approaches to memories take an epistemological track in asking whether they are known to the person who experienced the events, Freud introduces a radically ontological approach to thinking of memories. He questions the very existence of memories as "retrievable episodes," suggesting that past events do not appear to us organized in the form we come to call "memories,"—they only come retrospectively to be considered as such. As Friedman puts it, that "memories are often not anecdotal, not naturally segregated . . . often not thoughts (just connections), frequently not incidents (but habits and character), sometimes not even actual (but just virtual)" (Lacan 54). We repeat what cannot be remembered not because the memory has been repressed, but rather because it never held nor could ever hold a place within the symbolic.

Within this context, I advocate against reading the final twist in *Us* as an act of "remembrance," and instead suggest that the film demonstrates the role of repetition of the Real (the failure of symbolic integration) over that of return of the repressed. Such an interpretation, I suggest, also helps to frame the film's political orientation. To be specific, I argue that the film highlights how repetition carries transformative political potential. As Žižek describes, the "failure to integrate some 'impossible' kernel of the Real can activate the "impossible," which the symbolic has foreclosed (*Enjoy Your Symptom! Jacques Lacan in Hollywood and Out* 91). Repetition, in this sense, is not only of the impossible, but can also bring about the impossible by unleashing its barred potential.

Repetition/Return: Tuché and Automaton

Catherine Malabou highlights the foundational role that temporality plays in understanding both psychic and social reality: "according to Aristotle, everything that comes to pass is due to one of . . . two modes of temporality" (Malabou 118). The two modes of temporality referred to here, which Lacan innovatively develops, are *tuché* and "automaton." Lacan draws upon these concepts in order to forge a distinction between two registers of phenomenon that undergird psychic processes: return versus repetition. He refers to the movement of signifiers within the symbolic order as "automaton" and their interruption by "the encounter with the real" as *tuché* (Lacan 53). Automaton functions via "return," in the sense that, as Bruce Fink describes, "it involves the Return, coming back, or insistence of signs" (Fink 225). But in *tuché*, a surprising encounter with the Real, the signifier has no place to which to return, so in Lacan's Freudian terms, this "chance" encounter can only be "repeated" as opposed to "returning" (Lacan 54).

This Lacanian point has ramifications for understanding trauma. Repetition is often taken to be an effect of trauma: since trauma cannot be reproduced by/returned within the symbolic system, we are fated to repeat it. Lacan, however, emphasizes that, rather than a result of trauma, repetition functions as a condition for trauma to emerge. The repressed trauma is installed retrospectively through the act of repetition itself. "What is repeated," Lacan emphasizes, "is always something that occurs . . . *as if by* chance." Repetition, thus, can be seen as inaugurating trauma via an encounter with a coincidence that might otherwise appear insignificant. Roberto Harari offers the example of encountering numbers on one's train ticket that match the date of one's birthday. As he puts it, "as innocent as it seems, the repetition of the same ending digit in the ticket numbers precipitates a traumatic situation because it may be construed as something inassimilable" (Harari 104)). Such a coincidence moves from being insignificant in the sense of lacking importance, to becoming insignificant in the more disruptive sense of being unable to be made significant or meaningful— unable to be returned within the symbolic system. As Žižek describes, " . . . the unconscious trauma repeats itself by means of some small, contingent bit of reality. . . . " (Žižek, *Enjoy Your Symptom! Jacques Lacan in Hollywood and Out* 14). Lacan asserts that "there is no question of confusing with repetition either the return of the signs, or reproduction, or the modulation by the act of a sort of acted-out remembering"—"in Freud's texts," he tells us, "repetition is not reproduction. There is never any ambiguity on this point: *Wiederholen* is not *Reproduzieren*" (Lacan 54).

In the film, Adelaide attests to the disruptive potential of repetition/tuché when she confides to Gabe more details about what happened at Santa Cruz beach and implores that they should go back home. She recounts (as if from the position of the original Adelaide) that as a young girl, she wandered off from her parents on the pier and entered the house of mirrors and encountered her double. She tells him that a number of "coincidences" have occurred since their arrival to Santa Cruz, which, for her, function as a "sign" that the "girl is getting closer." As in Harari's account, none of these coincidences in themselves carry ominous portent (clock numbers lining up to 11:11, a frisbee landing perfectly within a circle of the same dimensions on their beach blanket, etc.). The examples of coincidences to which Adelaide refers operate as repetition/tuché in terms of either content or form (or a combination of both). The number sequence 11:11, for example, not only contains its own immanent repetition but also shares a direct connection at the level of content to Adelaide's childhood experience the day of the switch. Adelaide witnesses the numbers 11:11 on a sign held by a man at the beach that day, reading: "Jeremiah 11:11." But it was the original Adelaide who saw this, not the one who takes her place. Thus, in retrospect, this repetition highlights the constitutive absence at the heart of the psychic structure of repetition: the palpable emergence of what is lacking. The coincidence of the frisbee landing on its shadow image creates a coincidence at a more formal level. Rather than "reproducing" or "returning" symbolic content attached to the distressing event, the frisbee coincidence emerges as a fragment bearing the impossible formal logic of the real. It repeats the uncanny encounter at the house of mirrors, through the symbolic impossibility of doubling.

Lacan distinguishes reproduction/return as obeying the laws of similarity and difference held by the symbolic register, whereas repetition flouts these rules by carrying a connection to the real. Reproduction, Lacan tells us, belongs "to the optimistic days of catharsis," when it was thought that "the primal scene" could be reproduced in the same way that a painting of "the great masters" can be reproduced "for 9 francs 50" (50). Freud quickly moved away from this position in favor of repetition, which, by contrast, latches on not to the success, but rather to the failure, of the symbolic to confer identity and meaning. In this way, repetition, unlike reproduction/return, is not limited to what already exists, but rather carries with it the potential to introduce what could have existed if not foreclosed by symbolic operations. In this sense, Lacan insists that repetition always "demands the new," an insight that, I suggest, bears significantly on both the psychic and political possibilities offered by the film. As Harari stresses, rather than consist as a "reproduction of stable traits," repetition occurs "as if by chance," and involves "surprising, disconcerting, uncannyfying . . . circumstances" (61).

Repetition/Language/Difference

In furthering the argument that doubling in the film should be interpreted in terms of the rhythms of repetition rather than reproduction, I turn to how the film illuminates the way in which "minimal difference," as Alenka Zupančič emphasizes, is central to repetition. This kind of difference points not to the difference between one entity and another, but rather to an entity's difference from itself. The relationship of the tethered to those above ground, I suggest, works to highlight the internal split of the subject. As Erick Neher, in his account of the film, nicely puts it, "Nyong'o [who plays Adelaide and Red] manages . . . to embody the film's theme of mirrored duality, but also to disrupt that duality, to find the normalcy within the monster and the monstrous within the normal" (Neher 111). The artifice of the double, thus, should be interpreted in terms of Žižek's claim that "the foreign body, the intruder, which disturbs the harmonious circuit . . . run by the 'pleasure principle' is not something external to it, but strictly *inherent* to it" (Žižek, *Enjoy Your Symptom! Jacques Lacan in Hollywood and Out* 55).

The notion of "minimal difference" brings together two functions of the signifier: the creation of difference from sameness and the creation of sameness from difference. The sitcom *Seinfeld* provides an example of this first function of how excessive similarity can create difference.[1] Jerry's best friend, George, often calls him for help when he gets into predicaments so uniquely ridiculous that they could only happen to George. As soon as Jerry answers the phone, George, without any introduction, immediately blurts out his problem. Jerry invariably responds by pulling the phone away from his ear with exaggerated mock-surprise, asking: "Who is this?" This gesture carries comic effect by playing with how a too-close resemblance can indicate difference: when it could ONLY ever be George, then of course it can't be George. The joke works by highlighting that when resemblance fails to include lack—is too complete—it brings with it a destabilizing excess.

Michael Frayn's 1999 novel, *Headlong,* by contrast, demonstrates the inverse function of the signifier, conferring sameness through difference. Here, the protagonist desperately wants to believe that a painting he has come across is a lost masterpiece by Bruegel. When his research leads to ever-mounting anomalies between his painting and Bruegel's known works, rather than be discouraged by these inconsistencies, he reads them as support for his belief that he must, indeed, have a genuine Bruegel. How could it not be a Bruegel, he reasons, when it goes to such lengths to distinguish itself from a Bruegel? In this case, only difference can confirm its identity (Frayn).

Both of these operations disturb the sense of coherence within a given entity rather than between one entity and another. Minimal difference, which appears as "the gap that separates a thing from itself, the gap of repetition," can be thought of in terms of the Lacanian Real (Žižek, *In Defense of Lost Causes* 321). The relationship between the characters and their tethered counterparts, I argue, should be read within this context, even though the above account depends upon the crucial dimension of human existence above ground that is not mirrored by the tethered: the use of language. Red's ability to speak, thus, offers a clue that she might have once lived in the world. The signifier is responsible for introducing the cutoff difference/

meaning by introducing the "minimal difference" that marks the subject's relationship to itself—its inability to perfectly match an element in the signifying system with the place it occupies. This logic is mirrored in the very possibility of the switch between Adelaide and Red, even though the other tethered figures do not have language: in a system structured by the signifier, positive identity can never be secured; meaning is only every provisionally secured by differential relationships.

Giuseppe Civitarese explores this concept of "minimal difference" prior to the cut of the signifier that differentiates the subject from the object. He locates this "constitutive *non*-coinciding of the subject with itself" directly within the "rhythm of unpleasure-pleasure" characteristic of masochism (Civitarese 907, italics in original). In the context of the "'pre-history' of the subject," traumas encountered at the level of the object, he contends, are "experienced in the body" (889, 896). He argues for the centrality of rhythm (specifically, of unpleasure-pleasure in masochism) to the process of the "transindividual constitution of the subject" (896). In *Us*, this "rhythm of unpleasure and pleasure" appears to operate as the most palpable way of clearly dividing subjects from their tethered counterparts. As we learned from Red, every enjoyable act above ground (from eating, to celebrating holidays, to falling in love) is inverted into a horrific ordeal for those underground. These divergent experiences of Adelaide and Red appear to result solely from the structural position each figure occupies rather than according to any innate qualities.

But the film also presents us with a key exception to this logic, one that is intricately tied to rhythm: dancing. Acting on the advice of the therapist who advises Adelaide's parents to encourage her to dance as a creative outlet for her to express her presumed trauma, the tethered child, whom they mistake for Adelaide, becomes a passionate and accomplished dancer. When the replacement Adelaide enjoys dancing above ground, rather than suffer below, the original Adelaide (Red) also enjoys. Red's pleasure from and talent in dancing marks her as an exception among her tethered peers, for whom, Red tells us, it was only after she danced, that "the Tethered saw that I was different, that I would deliver them from this misery." Although Red's ability to speak acts as a clue for viewers for distinguishing her as the original Adelaide, it is her dancing (and the pleasure it brings her) that, for the tethered, differentiates her from them. Dancing, in the film, originates with the tethered girl who is now living the life of Adelaide. While reflecting upon the conditions that prompted the tethered revolt, Red marvels: "and to think, if it weren't for you, I never would've danced at all." In short, rhythm, specifically dancing, marks the site of shared pleasure between the original Adelaide (Red) and the replacement Adelaide, as well as constituting the only activity that disobeys the oppositional logic, established within the film, for governing the tethered to their counterparts. Thus, rather than function as a way to mark the difference between subject and other, rhythm operates here as the locus of the subject's minimal difference from itself—a minimal difference that, in turn, becomes the vehicle for the transformational rhythm of repetition.

Repetition and Jouissance

Žižek, following Lacan, highlights how repetition of symbolic failure produces jouissance—a painful enjoyment that lies "beyond the pleasure principle." Return/automaton, by contrast, follows and depends upon the symbolic logic of the pleasure principle. In other words, repetition opens us up to an encounter in which jouissance overwhelms attempts at symbolic containment. Indeed, jouissance itself functions as a form of repetition, both in terms of the repetition compulsion that pushes us beyond the pleasure principle, and in terms of the drive, which generates surplus pleasure from its repeated failure to reach its goal. Repetition, thus, works to unleash unrealized transformative "potential" that the symbolic attempts to suppress, a potential that may take on a political dimension. *Us* offers a demonstration of such a political possibility. The political potential, I argue, involves a temporality that follows the logic of the drive, rather than desire, however. As Žižek emphasizes, "in the shift from desire to drive, we pass from the lost object to loss itself as an object." In drive, we do not seek "impossible fullness" but rather "we directly enjoy lack itself" ("The Liberal Utopia: Against the Politics of Jouissance"). Whereas desire ostensibly pursues impossible satisfaction that leads us to suffering, drive pushes us to repeat suffering that leads us to satisfaction (in the form of surplus jouissance).

Although race is barely discussed in *Us*, I agree with Harry Olafsen, against Richard Brody's claim that "the Wilson's [the protagonist family] are black, a fact that, as depicted, has little overt effect on their lives" (Olafsen 21). Olafsen points out that "this is simply not the case," a position he supports not only by the diegetic circumstances of Gabe's failure to reach the same level of socio-economic privilege as Josh, despite the men having the same occupation, but also the extra-diegetic knowledge of Jordan Peele's sustained commitment to critiquing manifestations of racial inequality in the contemporary U.S. (the U.S./*Us* connection has been widely commented upon).

In the film, what are ostensibly depicted as markers of the failure of Gabe (Adelaide's husband) to reach the excessive level of socio-economic success enjoyed by Josh turn out to be highly effective in the struggle against the tethered. For example, as Olafsen describes, "Gabe purchases a rundown boat to compete with Josh's luxury yacht" (21). Gabe's disappointment is palpable when, after excitedly relaying the details of his boat purchase to Josh, it is revealed that he failed to get the "flare gun" which Josh has. But, as Todd McGowan and Ryan Engle point out,[2] not only is the flare gun utterly useless when Gabe tries to attack one of the tethered with it, but also the faulty engine of Gabe's own boat is used to considerable advantage in helping him to throw his tethered double off the boat. Also, a defective door in their summer house, responsible for Jason getting locked in a closet during the previous summer, comes in handy in his escape from his tethered counterpart. The strategic use of these flaws, I suggest, complicates the aspirational logic of capitalist accumulation and points to the importance that the film accords to lack. By showing lack as advantageous to survival and accumulation as an obstacle to survival, the film is consonant with McGowan's critique of consumer culture. McGowan emphasizes that rather than see lack as an impediment to our satisfaction, we need to accept that our satisfaction depends upon loss. In particular, he argues that our recognition of our satisfaction in the present can derail the future-oriented, promise-driven logic of capitalist accumulation. As he tells us, "capitalism depends on a psychic investment in the promise of the future and that a sense of one's [present] satisfaction is incompatible with the continued survival of capitalism" (McGowan, *Capitalism and Desire* 244). The critique of consumption in *Us* complements McGowan's project by challenging the capitalist structure of desire, in which lack appears as contingent and therefore potentially able to be filled by the right objects. By contrast, in structure of the drive, lack plays a constitutive role, through which subjective loss is repeated (generating jouissance) rather than provisionally concealed, and it is in the mode of the drive (and specifically in repetition) that the film's political potential manifests.

The drive does not simply bind us to suffering; it also transforms our suffering into (the painful pleasure of) enjoyment/jouissance. This type of suffering not only makes us miserable but also gives us reason to live. As Adrian Johnston, building on Žižek's insights, describes, drive, as "repetition without teleology," changes the nature of our suffering and unmoors it from symbolic anchoring (Johnson 186). Desire, on the other hand, as a "teleology without repetition," locks us to our suffering, by "refunctioning" it (as Mari Ruti puts it) into something that will pay off down the road (Johnson 186; Ruti 11). The purposelessness of jouissance carries with it the potential to introduce what cannot be made sensible within the established symbolic coordinates. The production of unintegratable excess, thus, highlights the incompleteness of symbolic order—its constitutive lack—and opens the door for the emergence of the "impossible," or in Calvin Warren's terms, of the "world-destroying."

Warren argues, from within an Afro-pessimist framework, that "[b]ecause anti-blackness infuses itself into every fabric of social existence, it is impossible to emancipate blacks without literally destroying the world" (Warren 239). He locates this world-destroying turn within the tradition of "black nihilism," which seeks not the eradication of hope, but rather "*hopes* for the end of political hope" (244, italics original). Future-oriented notions of "political hope," he contend, "perpetuate black suffering by placing relief in an unattainable future, a future that offers nothing more than an exploitative reproduction of its own means of existence" (233). Warren invokes the "death-drive" (as "being-toward-death") as the "essence of black suffering, since no escape from the Political is possible without "ending blackness" (224–25). But where Warren seeks to "break this 'drive'—to stop it in its tracks—as a way 'to end the cycle of insanity that political hope perpetuates,' Žižek and related scholars highlight the radical political potential of death drive in bringing forth 'world-destroying' conditions" (243). In Žižek's reading, the death drive strives not to "annihilate" the organism, "but rather the symbolic order, the order of the symbolic pact which regulates social exchange"—the very sphere of the Other to which desire addresses itself and operates to consolidate (Žižek, *From Desire to Drive*). Death drive, in this sense, operates as a repetition of failure that produces jouissance.

Us, I suggest, illustrates this point by highlighting the necessary role of repetition in launching a radical, revolutionary act. The repetition of the 1986 sanitized demonstration of superficial solidarity into a world-destroying revolt unleashes the politically destabilizing dimension of jouissance, which was foreclosed by the symbolic framework of the original event. Repetition acts as a motor for unleashing the disruptive political excess that the symbolic works to contain. A form of political hope, perhaps then, becomes possible if we locate both its origin and its aim in the suppressed potential of the past, and not in the illusory promises of the future. In the next section, I pursue the critique of a politics of hope through the work of Lauren Berlant.

Present Time of Crisis

After the tethered doubles of the Wilson family invade their home, each doppelgänger breaks off in direct pursuit of their counterpart. Adelaide, left in the house and handcuffed to a table, asks Red: "What do you want?" Red's answer is unexpected: "We want to take our time." Why does Red reply with this temporal request rather than the spatial demand of, "we want to take your place?" In attempting to address this question, I briefly return to consideration of the unique role that rhythm plays in the link between Red and Adelaide. In particular, I suggest that Lauren Berlant's focus on slowness and the present offers a valuable lens for interpreting Red's declaration, but that Berlant's framework, in turn, benefits from a deeper engagement with repetition and jouissance.

I have argued that rhythm, expressed in the film through dance, marks an interruption into the logic governing the oppositional relationship between Red and Adelaide. Red's dancing carries with it a trace of her humanity—garnering her a special, indeed revolutionary, status among the tethered. A concern for rhythm's connection to humanity is expressed in an inverse way in Adelaide's unease about her son's (Jason's) difficulty in snapping to the beat of a song played on the car radio. This challenge emblematizes

Jason's slightly "off" behavior throughout the film. Viewers widely speculate that Jason (the son of a "tethered") betrays his status through odd behavior. Adelaide, intent on getting him to feel the proper beat, snaps instructively to the music as she tells him, "Jason, Get it in rhythm." That the "Untethering" would be framed in terms of time/rhythm is significant: it highlights the transformative role rhythm plays in both constituting and bringing forth an exception to the symbolic—an impossible act.

Berlant sheds further light on Red's invocation of a rhythmic goal. She shares with Warren the aim of disrupting future-oriented logic which casts our current suffering as the necessary price for the (empty) promise of future happiness. In particular, she attends to how, under increasingly brutal socio-economic conditions, fantasies of "the good life" become both less tenable and increasingly intractable (Berlant 2). She argues for more finely attuned attention to the present, due largely to what she sees as its affective potential: we encounter the present "affectively" "before it becomes anything else" (4) The present, for Berlant, is thus "profoundly political," fluttering with the potential of what it will have come to be (4). This affective potential is also an indicator that the present is beset by "crisis," in both the structural sense that its meanings are not yet determined and in the contingent sense that it presents a sphere of increasing precarity. As a corrective to what she calls "trauma discourse," which configures crisis as an exceptional intrusion into the everyday, Berlant coins the term "crisis ordinariness" to refer to the present as a state of perpetual crisis. By emphasizing "scene[s] of exception" that appear to "shatter . . . some ongoing, uneventful ordinary life," "trauma discourse" works to reinforce the present as a fixed, neutral sphere, rather than as a political space within which meanings have not yet become cemented (10).

Berlant's insights regarding the ways in which the framing of trauma as an exception can naturalize present conditions are complicated by Žižek's rethinking of modes of ideological operations. In addition to understanding ideology as a naturalizing force, through which contingent phenomenon are made to appear inevitable or obvious, Žižek highlights how ideology also operates in the inverse mode by dismissing structural inevitabilities as mere contingent exceptions. Like the proverbial "few bad apples" onto whom systemic violence is deflected, trauma discourse, for Berlant, obscures the way everyday existence "force[s] people to adapt to unfolding change" (10).

Berlant focuses on the present not only as a space of precarity and crisis, however, but also as a space for moments of reliable, albeit fleeting, relief from hopelessness. Eating beyond satiation, for example, figures prominently for Berlant due to a combination of its betrayal of normative values of self-sovereignty, its dependable satisfaction among pervasive disappointment and uncertainty, and its detachment from the future-oriented, neoliberal logic of goal-oriented productivity (17). Eating here functions as an activity through which subjects negotiate agency amid the unmeetable demands and daily struggles for survival. Such pleasures function in her account as "small vacations from the will:" "interrupt[ions to] the liberal and capitalist subject called to consciousness, intentionality, and effective will" (116).

But framing these relief-seeking practices as a form of "interruptive agency" seems at odds with Žižek's position that ideology requires precisely such breaks—moments in which we feel we are able to evade its expectations (99). Rather than designate these pleasures as acts of interruption from the unrelenting pressures of neoliberal productivity culture, we might see them as providing the necessary breathing room for enduring its continuation. Berlant, thus, risks falling into the same trap that she seeks to avoid: Namely, by designating these pleasures as interruptions to or breaks from ideology, she overlooks the ways in which they constitute ideology itself.

Although Berlant's work strenuously critiques the discourse of future fulfillment, she frames loss and obstacles as contingent impediments to our satisfaction, rather than as constitutive to our satisfactions, subjectivity, and the social. Berlant, thus, overlooks the ways in which the impediment not only sustains us in desire but also fuels the fantasy that our dissatisfaction is contingent rather than the result of constitutive lack.

The difficulties in Berlant's view of the impediment as contingent become clearer when considering her view on optimism:

> all attachment is optimistic, if we describe optimism as the force that moves you out of yourself and into the world . . . [O]ptimistic relation[s] are not inherently cruel. They become cruel only when the object that draws your attachment actively impedes the aim that brought you to it initially. (1)

This view of optimism resonates with a different Freudian insight, that our survival "must be attributed to the external disturbing and diverting influences . . . [which] oblige [us] to diverge ever more widely from [the] original course of life to make ever more complicated detours before reaching the aim of death" (Freud, *Beyond the Pleasure Principle* 45–46). Berlant's notion of optimistic attachments, thus, may be seen in terms of the human tendency, noted by Freud, toward "lengthening the road to death" (*Beyond the Pleasure Principle* 48). But, I argue, whereas Freud comes to locate this impetus "beyond the pleasure principle," Berlant seeks to locate our survival within the parameters of the pleasure principle. For her, optimism involves an

> orientation toward the pleasure that is bound up in world-making, which may be hooked on futures, or not. . . . Even when it turns out to involve a cruel relation, it would be wrong to see optimism's negativity as a symptom of an error, a perversion, damage, or dark truth: optimism is, instead, a scene of negotiated sustenance that makes life bearable as it presents itself ambivalently, unevenly, incoherently. (Berlant 14)

But, I argue, despite Berlant's aim to strip away from optimism any residue of constitutive negativity, repetition, and jouissance, that, within Freudian-Lacanian psychoanalytic accounts, is foundational to subjectification, her examples suggest, to the contrary, that unacknowledged negativity/repetition/jouissance accompanies the impetus for life. Optimism, she contends, can orient us to "ordinary pleasures [that] induce conventionality" (what I take to be within the realm of the pleasure principle), or, she adds, to pleasures that defy "rational calculation" (which I take to indicate that they lie beyond the pleasure principle). The pleasure of eating falls into this latter category in constituting a surplus jouissance, which, rather than serve our biological needs (life of the organism), comes to overhaul them (thus serving the life of the subject). Here, Berlant captures how jouissance is both life-preserving and organism-destructing when she tells us that, "Paradoxically . . . there is less of a future when one eats without an orientation toward it" (Berlant 117). Thus, against the thrust of her own argument, Berlant illuminates the contradictory tension of the pleasure principle's orientation toward stability (and sustenance of organic life) and jouissance's push toward excess (as both a threat to organic life and as that which makes livable).

Berlant ventures most closely into this psychoanalytic terrain when she raises the provocative question of "whether cruel optimism is better than none at all?" (16). Within a Lacanian framework, the answer can be nothing but a resounding "yes." All attachments that make life worth living introduce a threat—or at least an indifference—to the flourishing of organic life. Jouissance names these cruel attachments beyond pleasure principle; it leads us to compulsively chase "traumatic enjoyment," with no concern for how these pursuits might affect organism-sustaining needs (McGowan, *Psychoanalytic Film Theory and The Rules of the Game* 55). As McGowan stresses, jouissance does not only leads us to suffering and self-sabotage, it is also the "sine qua non of our vitality . . . the meaning of life:" jouissance "gives the subject a reason to keep going" (*Psychoanalytic Film Theory and The Rules of the Game* 54–55). Aaron Schuster perhaps answers Berlant's question by asserting that "the measured pleasure [of the pleasure principle] is not enough to sustain life" (Schuster 118). This claim brings into stark relief the life-preserving role of jouissance. Our jouissance causes us great suffering, but without it, life would not be worth living.

Repetition to Revolution

The revolutionary act undertaken by the tethered appropriates the form of the failed 1986 "Hands Across America" fund-raising event, aimed at tackling poverty. The concluding scene of *Us* depicts the tethered standing hand-in-hand in an unbroken line as far as the eye/camera can see (in the original historic event, the line was beset by large and frequent gaps). Rather than dismiss the repetition of "Hands Across America" as another kitschy reference to 1980s' popular culture (of which there are several scattered throughout the film), I suggest that it plays a significant political role. Against most critical opinion, I agree with Todd McGowan and Ryan Engley regarding the importance of this action (McGowan and Engley). They emphasize that the film transforms a gesture of imaginary unity into a cut of the Real. I argue that this possibility is realized through repetition in which the symbolic's internal negativity enters into the symbolic itself, destabilizing its coordinates of possibility. In this case, the symbolically excluded (the tethered) insert themselves into a place within the symbolic universe built around their very exclusion (the excluded upon whom "Hands Across America" depends). It makes way for the emergence of otherwise impossible transformations within the political realm and unlocks a potential space of freedom for the subject as well, not as Berlant would argue, on the basis of the pleasure principle, but rather through the rhythmic work of repetition and its production of jouissance.

Notes

1 I draw upon these examples for slightly different purposes in my book *Real Deceptions: The Contemporary Reinvention of Realism*. New York: Oxford University Press, 2017 (Friedlander).
2 Here, I reference Todd McGowan's and Ryan Engley's brilliant "Why Theory?" podcast episode on *Us (McGowan and Engley)*.

Works Cited

Berlant, Lauren Gail. *Cruel Optimism*. Duke University Press, 2012.
Civitarese, Giuseppe. "Masochism and Its Rhythm." *Journal of the American Psychoanalytic Association*, vol. 64, no. 5, Oct. 2016, pp. 885–916, https://doi.org/10.1177/0003065116674442.
Fink, Bruce. "The Real Cause of Repetition." *Reading Seminar XI: Lacan's Four Fundamental Concepts of Psychoanalysis: Including the First English Translation of "Position of the Unconscious" by Jacques Lacan*, edited by Richard Feldstein and Maire Jaanus, State University of New York Press, 1995, pp. 223–32.
Frayn, Michael. *Headlong*. 1st American ed, Metropolitan Books, 1999.
Freud, Sigmund. *Beyond the Pleasure Principle*. Translated by James Strachey, Norton, 1989.
——. "Remembering, Repeating and Working-Through." *Collected Papers.*, translated by Joan Riviere et al., Hogarth Press and the Institute of Psycho-analysis, 1950, pp. 147–56.
Friedlander, Jennifer. *Real Deceptions: The Contemporary Reinvention of Realism*. Oxford University Press, 2017.
Harari, Roberto. *Lacan's Four Fundamental Concepts of Psychoanalysis: An Introduction*. Other Press, 2004.
Johnson, Adrian. "Repetition and Difference: Žižek, Deleuze and Lacanian Drives." *Lacan and Deleuze: A Disjunctive Synthesis*, edited by Boštjan Nedoh and Andreja Zevnik, Edinburgh University Press, 2017, pp. 180–202.

Lacan, Jacques. *The Four Fundamental Concepts of Psychoanalysis.* Translated by Jacques-Alain Miller and Alan Sheridan, W.W. Norton & Company, 1998.

Malabou, Catherine. "'Father, Don't You See I'm Burning?' Žižek, Psychoanalysis, and the Apocalypse." *Repeating Žižek*, edited by Agon Hamza, Duke University Press, 2015, pp. 113–26, https://doi.org/10.1215/9780822375470-008.

McGowan, Todd. *Capitalism and Desire: The Psychic Cost of Free Markets.* Columbia University Press, 2016.

——. *Psychoanalytic Film Theory and the Rules of the Game.* Bloomsbury Academic, 2015.

McGowan, Todd, and Ryan Engley: *Why Theory.* https://soundcloud.com/whytheory. Accessed 21 Dec. 2021.

Neher, Erick. "Interpreting Horror: Jordan Peele's Us." *Hudson Review*, vol. 72, no. 1, Spring 2019, pp. 111–14.

Olafsen, Harry. "'It's Us:' Mimicry in Jordan Peele's Us." *Iowa Journal of Cultural Studies*, vol. 20, June 2020, pp. 20–32, https://doi.org/10.17077/2168-569X.1546.

Peele, Jordan, et al. *Us.* Monkeypaw Productions, Blumhouse Productions, Dentsu, 2019.

Ruti, Mari. *Penis Envy and Other Bad Feelings: The Emotional Costs of Everyday Life.* Columbia University Press, 2018.

Schuster, Aaron. *The Trouble with Pleasure: Deleuze and Psychoanalysis.* The MIT Press, 2016.

Warren, Calvin. "Black Nihilism and the Politics of Hope." *CR: The New Centennial Review*, vol. 15, no. 1, 2015, p. 215, https://doi.org/10.14321/crnewcentrevi.15.1.0215.

Žižek, Slavoj. *Enjoy Your Symptom! Jacques Lacan in Hollywood and Out.* Routledge classics ed, Routledge, 2008.

——. *From Desire to Drive: Why Lacan Is Not Lacaniano.* https://zizek.livejournal.com/2266.html. Accessed 20 Dec. 2021.

——. *In Defense of Lost Causes.* Verso Books, 2017.

——. "The Liberal Utopia: Against the Politics of Jouissance." *Lacan.Com*, https://www.lacan.com/zizliberal.htm. Accessed 20 Dec. 2021.

Chapter 3

Radical Temporalities of Trauma, Melancholia, and Disaster

Lacan, Blanchot, Sebald's *Austerlitz*, von Trier's *Melancholia*

Eve Watson

Unconscious Effects in Disaster, Mourning, and Melancholia

There is a certain eventfulness to accidents of destiny such as trauma, disaster, and mourning that make these states impactful and significant. Psychoanalytically, each of these states is understood to run a different course to teleological time as chronological sequencing is perverted by the impacts of these respective states on the subject. These impacts are determined by the subject's psychic organization, which, in turn, is determined by a subject's own structure, with structure referring to unconscious choices, forgettings, repressions, and a singular history which determines how a subject will respond to a catastrophe or disaster and organize a process of mourning. Laying someone or something to rest has a palliative and restorative function and an unmourned loss has consequential and, as we shall see in the case of Jacques Austerlitz, the protagonist of W.G. Sebald's novel, *Austerlitz*, catastrophic effects. For Justine, the principal character in the film *Melancholia* (Trier), the impending disaster offers her a way out of her melancholic impasse by liberating her from psychic imprisonment and ultimately offering her repose.

Let us begin with a consideration of the unconscious in terms of a series of temporal moments. Lacan describes the unconscious not in terms of locale or place but as "a temporal pulsation" and something that closes up as soon as it opens (Lacan, *The Four Fundamental Concepts of Psychoanalysis* 143). This is due to a particular mode of repetition that repeats because it misses the mark, and the moment of this missed encounter is the opening and almost instantaneous closing of the unconscious. The moment of opening is the gap which beckons speech and remembering, as the unconscious is structured like a language, while the moment of closing is the capture in the gap of the impossible lost object which causes desire, the *object a* (Lacan, *The Four Fundamental Concepts of Psychoanalysis* 144–45). The *object a* causes desire and satisfaction to circulate around it and is a point of orientation. It is timeless and genderless, but it is not wayward as it responds

DOI: 10.4324/9781003194033-5

to certain attributes of the Other. It is in play when desire draws us close to someone or something or when the drive is implicated.

The subject is coincident with the temporal opening and closing of the unconscious. Lacan clarifies this when he says, "if I have spoken to you of the unconscious as something that opens and closes, it is because its essence is to mark that time by which, from the fact of being born with the signifier, the subject is born divided" (Lacan, *The Four Fundamental Concepts of Psychoanalysis* 199). The subject, as such, is born via signifiers, which are traces or marks that cleave the subject's division from the *object a* and subsequently from its "beingness." In this sense, language operates as a cause for the subject who is separated from their own being (Lacan, "The Position of the Unconscious" 708). This is what is meant by the idea that the letter not only bars the subject but also kills being ("The Position of the Unconscious" 719). This castrating function of language causes the real of being and the overwhelming proximity of experience to be excluded from the field of the symbolic. This process of symbolic castration is precluded for the psychotic subject, with the consequence that full access to the symbolic register is rendered impossible (Lacan, *The Seminar of Jacques Lacan: The Psychoses: Seminar III* 13).

In the event of a traumatic experience, the subject can be subdued and crushed by the Other and the psyche overwhelmed by the catastrophe. The disaster or trauma fills the division that is constitutive for the subject. This causes a stoppage in the signifying chain which the subject returns to in a kind of traumatic closed repetition. This is a point of fixation and as we shall see in the case of Austerlitz, it insists in a coded and hidden way and to which melancholia is superimposed . In melancholia, the proximity of the object disturbs the subject and sutures the necessary distance from the object that typically supports desire. This occurs when the subject is unable to separate from the object and this produces another form of subduing and crushing, in this case, of the libido and the life-drive.

In mourning, Freud poses that loss is worked through by a process of relinquishing the lost object as well as the subject's identifications with it. Our memories and hopes linked to the person or thing we've lost are run through, and each one is met with the judgment that the loved one is no longer there (Freud 245). This process of surveying and re-assessing images and thoughts of the lost person eventually exhausts itself, freeing up the ego to be uninhibited again and the mourner will choose life over death (245). As a result of mourning, imaginary identificatory connections are remade with symbolic coordinates, which both re-establish the object and organize a necessary distance to it. Darian Leader offers an example of this process in his book on mourning and melancholia, *The New Black*. After her mother's death, a woman dreamt of speaking about her mother's death to a faceless third party. The dream marked the introduction of a basic triangulation and instead of dreaming of speaking directly to the dead and departed, it "showed that the loss was being registered, transformed into a message to be transmitted to someone else and accepted, at some level, by herself" (Leader 59). This is a symbolic re-imagining and inscribing of the real hole left by the departed.

Freud recognized that the main barrier to the work of mourning was the mixture of love and hate. The problem of separating from the lost object is added to by a powerful ambivalence comprising loving and hateful impulses toward the departed (Freud 250–51). The more our loving feelings for the dead person are swamped by feelings of hate, the harder it is to separate ourselves from them (Leader 168). Rage against those who left can be devastating in both mourning and melancholia because it confronts the subject with their fundamental ambivalence toward the lost one in addition to their abandonment by them. How, as Dylan Thomas put it, to express "rage, rage against the dying of the light"? (Thomas 148). Freud observed that in "the crushed state of melancholia" the unconscious hatred of the one who is lost turns back on and engulfs the subject who rages against their own self as they once raged against the one who is lost (Freud 248). In this, the subject unconsciously identifies with the lost object and becomes what they cannot bear to give up, and the hatred toward the other is introjected. Moreover, the melancholic subject doesn't realize they've lost something precious, unlike the bereaved who knows what they've lost (245). This has the combined effect of exhausting and crushing the subject. Ultimately, the subject has the choice of killing the dead or dying with them. The melancholic choice is to die with the dead.

The circumstances of Justine and Austerlitz's lives suggest not only the existence of ambivalence but also significantly good reasons for it. Justine's mother's consuming hate for her father, matched only by her father's feckless narcissism, offers no room for acknowledging their daughter's significance to them. Her sister's accomplishments in education, career, and marriage highlight her lack of phallic value in the parental constellation, adding to her insignificance. Justine's languid posture and melancholic exhaustion point inexorably to an inaccessible loss revealed by the extraordinary effect on her of the impending disaster of the arrival of the planet Melancholia. The beckoning disaster effectively re-starts her clock and offers an escape from drowning in a timeless and deadening ennui.

For Austerlitz, this psychical clock momentarily stopped on arriving as a young boy at Liverpool Street train station on the *Kindertransport* from Germany to England. His life up to then was forgotten and under a veil of repression this forgotten memory became a point of fixation, a nucleus of symptomatic formation. Without knowing why, he became obsessed with train stations and cultivated an extraordinary knowledge of their history and architecture. One day, he wandered into Liverpool Street train station and without warning recognized the about-to-be-demolished platform and remembered it as the scene of his arrival as a boy. Shaken to the core, the sudden and traumatic instantiation of this hidden archive led to a prolonged period of melancholia that lasted until Austerlitz re-emerged driven by a quest to rediscover his parental family of origin. This quest is the centrifugal force of the latter part of the novel. It represents Austerlitz's psychical work to symbolically mediate the catastrophic and unbearable weight of the traumatic loss of his parents and his childhood with them. The novel traces how this, in fact, entailed bearing more loss as traumatic repetition worked itself out and as the quest become whether Austerlitz's desire for life would prove stronger than his melancholic identification with the lost and the dead.

Austerlitz: From Timeless Melancholia to a New Time of Quest

> For the history of every individual, of every social order, indeed of the whole world, does not describe an ever-widening, more and more wonderful arc, but rather follows a course which, once the meridian is reached, leads without fail down into the dark. . . . (Sebald 24)

W.G. Sebald's extraordinary palimpsestic novel, *Austerlitz*, is a triumph of over-determination and an account of subjective experience that goes far beyond narrativization. It is filled with sadness, trauma, secrets, lies, tragedy, and survival that are discernible not so much in major episodes or events but in simple moments dynamically articulated by the co-protagonists, Austerlitz and the novel's narrator. In this, Sebald brilliantly captures in his writing the curious fact that when we enunciate ourselves, we convey several things at once. Freud discerned from his patients our habit of embedding the important things in simple, quiet, and practically indiscernible banalities and rhetorical wanderings that only the astute listener or the patient reader will pick up. Austerlitz takes this up when he says, "we take almost all of the decisive steps in our lives as a result of slight inner adjustments of which we are barely conscious" (189). These are the "decisive steps" or, as Lacan puts it, the "trails" left, which constitute the subject (Lacan, "The Position of the Unconscious" 703).

For the reader, the novel is a travelogue of Austerlitz's journey into the labyrinthine corridors of his past and a terrible confrontation with his traumatic and forgotten childhood that began with wandering into Liverpool Street train station. There, he suddenly recalled sitting in that station where he was met and then adopted by a childless Welsh couple, the morose minister Elias and his wife. The inescapable, terrible, and epiphanic nature of that experience is captured in Austerlitz's own words of the devastating effect of the return of this memory:

> All I do know is that when I saw the boy sitting on the bench. I became aware, through my dull bemusement, of the destructive effect on me of my desolation through all those past years, and a terrible weariness overcame me at the idea that I had never really been alive, or was only now being born, almost on the eve of my death. (Sebald 194)

He realized that the accumulation of his extraordinary and substantial knowledge over the decades—he was brilliant at architecture, history, engineering, and many other subjects—had served him as a substitute or compensatory memory (198). Thus, the remembering of his first arrival at the train station is not only a recovered memory but also an epiphany that both stops and starts time. It was ruinous to his sense of linear time and the basis, as Austerlitz describes it, of "a silence of unfathomable profundity" (232).

For our beguiling protagonist, his experience that " . . . certain moments had no beginning or end, while on the other hand his whole life had sometimes seemed to him a blank point without duration" (165) came to be located within a different time which can be broadly described as an agonizing breakdown in which a melancholic silence outside of time reverberated to another rhythm and beat of being outside of documentable history and measurement. An enforced period without work, industry, and scheduling propelled a wandering into remote, indistinct, and heretofore hidden aspects of himself. It transpired that Austerlitz's disaster was not his traumatic journey to England, nor indeed his forgetting of it, but its re-emergence as an overwhelming force of "unfathomable profundity" which would take him to the depths of despair and back. It was then he realized that he had in fact long been a witness to what he could not recollect.

The utter failure of language to capture his state of mind reached a crisis as he tried to write a book which can be understood as the creation of a legacy. How does one make a legacy without some point of origin, some fundamental question which in his meetings and dialogues with the novel's co-protagonist made apparent were missing? Austerlitz muses on this, using an architecture of the cityscape, saying:

> If language may be regarded as an old city full of streets and squares, nooks and crannies, with some quarters dating from far back in time while others have been torn down, cleaned up and rebuilt, and with suburbs reaching further and further into the surrounding country, then I was like a man who had been abroad a long time and cannot find his way through this urban sprawl any more, no longer knows what a bus stop is for, or what a back yard is, or a street junction, an avenue or a bridge. The entire structure of language, the syntactical arrangement of parts of speech, punctuation, conjunctions, and finally even the notions denoting ordinary objects were all enveloped in impenetrable fog. By his own admission, Austerlitz realised that in spite of his efforts to convey himself through intelligent enterprise, often brilliantly, and through his efforts at sociability and courtesy, what he had in fact been successful in doing was isolating himself from his lifelong unrelieved despair. (Sebald 178)

Coming to terms with the architecture of his life as a construction of fictions, lies, and his own traumatic forgetting is a shattering experience for Austerlitz that forces him to consider his fate. This time the choice of life or death will be his choice.

The rejection of his false filiation and the fictions of his life story correspond to what Lacan designates as an "instant of the glance," a moment of subjective realization in which a logical movement is possible; it paves the way for the crystallization of a hypothesis that aims at the real of the problem (Lacan, "Logical Time and the Assertation of Anticipated Certainty" 168). This temporal moment is one of instantaneity as it interrupts and is coincident with a moment of opening and closing of the unconscious circuit. Such an "instance" of the unconscious is co-efficient to the retroaction of the signifier, and this is followed by a "time for understanding" which builds on the hypothesis formed in the preceding temporal movement. It introduces meaning and cause and involves the making of a judgment, as the moment that introduced it, the "instant of the glance" vacillates ("Logical Time and the Assertation of Anticipated Certainty" 168). Austerlitz, after a period of severe and deep melancholic despair, in which the object is so close that he is unable to move, embarks on a new temporal movement, a "time for understanding."

His long quest to re-find and reclaim his origins and, in particular, his mother took Austerlitz to Prague's infamous Theresienstadt ghetto and was a sign of respair, to re-claim a term that has fallen woefully out of use. The reader enters the quest's rhythm and profundity and is obliged to endure its obligatory and compelling nature in lengthy descriptions of townscapes, the beautiful rendering of the Eastern music that so moved Austerlitz, and in the story of Dan Jacobson's search for his grandfather, and another wandering Jew, the rabbi Heshel. The obsessive but ultimately fruitless effort to discover his mother in the infamous Nazi propaganda film made of the ghetto ushers in a "moment to conclude." This can be inferred in how Austerlitz listened to the melodies of the Parisian music players, which evoked his Eastern, Germanic, and Welsh origins. He describes the sounds as an inexplicable mystery that touched him as he watched a snow-white goose "standing motionless and steadfast among the musicians as long as they played" (Sebald 384). This goose is an "idiot," to give it another idiomatic meaning, and undoubtedly refers to Austerlitz himself. He movingly describes the scene as that in which he "listened there in the tent beneath that shimmering firmament of painted stars until the last notes had died away, as if it knew its own future and the fate of its present companions" (384). This goose-like "idiocy" is a recognition, a moment that concludes what has come before. He has reached the end of the road and what was previously understood is integrated by Austerlitz and his quest concludes. He has arrived at a place where he can rest.

Melancholia versus Disaster

Lars Von Trier's *Melancholia* (2011) cinematically conveys a crushing state of melancholia and its notably different psychic time. The film begins with Justine arriving hours late for her own wedding reception, which she repeatedly absents herself from. This other chronology that Justine follows is the result of something irrevocably lost and unmoored and the narrative suggests that this object is centered within the network of her parental and sibling relationships, and in particular her parents' irreconcilable relationship. In being unmoored, the object is retained and the introjection of the lost object causes the ego to be diminished by the unrelenting punishment of its critical agency to such an extent that the subject is exhausted. The is excellently rendered in the film in Justine's inability to move, bathe, and even eat.

Justine's recovery in the face of the planetary disaster suggests a release from the overwhelming power of an introjected non-relinquished loss and savage self-punishment. The time of the melancholia and the "time" of symptoms is interrupted by the impending disaster which signals the end of the world. Her vitality returns with the appearance of the planet Melancholia. This is an important confirmation that the disaster, in fact, is yet to come and has not already happened. Her sense of self is restored, she is disinhibited and no longer exhausted. Justine, thus, embraces a recognition that places her in a cut caused by the impending disaster. This is a real intrusion into the signifying articulation of time, aesthetics, logic, and in the seeming efficiency of discourse. This different time is no longer the dead time of the melancholia but is a time that opens up at the very point that it closes for those around her who are overwhelmed with anxiety and find themselves in a time without knowledge, routine, or joy.

Justine's subjective re-emergence is the reclamation of an alienation that is familiar and significant; everyone like her is alienated and no less than her are the consequences of the representational movement of one signifier to another. The implicates the Other, making our very subjectivity alienating. In other words, my own subjectivity is not my own, even my cause is not my own, and the stakes are limited to a choice: "your money or your life," or "liberty or death" (Lacan, "The Position of the Unconscious" 713). Either choice involves a loss and disappointment: one involves living with certain symbolic advantages, and the other is a petrified life without symbolic support. The kicker is that in the end this is a false dialectic as money of course doesn't circumvent death. It seems that for Justine this dialectic is suspended by the death-bearing planet and offers a momentary relinquishing of this forced choice. A new horizon of truth and being has opened that she cannot close herself to. She accepts this and there is little to do but build a tepee against it and wait for the big bang.

It turns out that we are poorly prepared for disaster. We may dream of it and we may even fantasize it but when it happens, our response is determined by our psychical structuration and any defenses we can muster. This means some of us fare better than others: some may be less overwhelmed by an onslaught of the real or suffer from anxiety induced by the failure of words and the disappearance of narrative-framing which organizes time and events teleologically by historicizing, supplying meaning and promises of the future. A subject ravaged by the real can induce madness. Justine's lack of despair and anxiety in the face of the looming disaster stands in stark contrast to the terrifying and despairing anxiety of those around her. Such anxiety is the position of the praying mantis facing the Other, proposed by Lacan as analogous to the anguished subject bereft of its indices of recognition and knowledge (Session 14 Nov 1963 Lacan, *Anxiety. Book X. The Seminar of Jacques Lacan.* 3). A disaster is a logical time that reveals the subject's organization of anxiety: how trauma is refracted through particular signifiers, how certain conditions of enjoyment operate, and the importance of history, stories, and constructions in providing a mythology and temporality for the subject. Justine whose rhythm is out of time with the world of linear time and meaningful order is open to the time of the disaster. This is why, unlike those around her, she does not descend into madness.

It turns out that life carries a disastrous heaviness which is a consequence of refusing to accept that death and limit are its companions. We conceal death from ourselves in different ways: in the empty ways we talk about it, in delimiting it to something that happens to others, and in thinking of it as something indefinite, what Heidegger calls the "tranquilized everydayness" that we cling to in order to cover it up and console ourselves (297). A registration of death is its acceptance as an unfillable void, the integration of the Other as an unbridgeable alterity within. For Heidegger, an existential conception of death overturns the factical and ontical tendency of beings to avoid it, and an ethical stance toward death is an "authentic acceptance" of the certainty of one's own (302). This is, as only Heidegger could put it, its "ownmost possibility" (304) or what Lacan describes as "the subjective realization of being-towards-death" (Lacan, "The Function and Field of Speech and Language in Psychoanalysis" 231). Justine is someone who opens out to being incorporated into the Other. Her knowledge of death is honest and ethical. The planet Melancholia liberates Justine, because it is a privileged externalization of her own subjective subsumption to the Other and even as it kills her, it promises her liberation from the object.

Blanchot's Horizons of Death and Disaster

In his aptly titled essay, "The Human Race," Maurice Blanchot considers the transformational stakes of disaster. Pondering the connection between "destructible" and "destroyed" in light of Robert Antelme whose writing is based on his experience of the concentration camp, he proposes that in perceiving himself as indestructible, there is no limit to man's destruction

(Blanchot, "The Human Race" 68). He states that "man is the indestructible who can be destroyed. This resounds as a truth and yet we cannot know it as we know some preconceived truth" ("The Human Race" 61). The attacks of one person against another are not only the elimination of their personhood and the decline of the collective tie but it places them outside of the world, rendering them "a being without horizon" ("The Human Race" 62). This is a problem of truth which is exacerbated by our tendency to anthropomorphism, which is a version of self as power and its expression is "understood as the ultimate echo of the truth, where everything ceases to be true" ("The Human Race" 63). Blanchot uses this to consider affliction as a state which causes us to disappear into the horizon of the affliction with which we merge. This loss of identity is a loss of self, it is a state of powerlessness even for the torturer who can never eliminate the presence of the Other ("The Human Race" 64). In dispossession of oneself, in radical need and abject deprivation, what is asserted is the strangeness of the other, their absolute otherness, which in spite of its horror and stupor brings lucidity ("The Human Race" 64). Blanchot notes that for Antelme what is at issue in his writing is not historical report, autobiography, or storytelling but "*speaking*" (italics in original, 66). There is the necessity of speech through which the Other "was alone able to be received and brought within human hearing" ("The Human Race" 66). The effect of the camps and of being released from them, he says, was a delirium of speech whose authority came from "therefore," the very necessity of its saying ("The Human Race" 67). But as necessary as it is, it is also impossible to bridge because two people talking together so often talk to forget ("The Human Race" 68). The importance of a "necessity of saying" is explained by Blanchot:

> Memories are necessary that they may be forgotten: in order that in this forgetfulness—in the silence of a profound metamorphosis—there might at last be born a word, the first word of a poem. (Blanchot, *The Space of Literature* 87)

This is remarkably apperceptive of the importance of "saying" and the possibility it conditions for the construction of something entirely new (a poetic word) that will capture and punctuate the experience of the disaster. This takes the "eventfulness" out of it in a new construction that will singularly capture its traumatic and catastrophic affect.

Blanchot also explores the significance of passivity and destitution for the suffering of the subject in times of disaster. In *The Writing of the Disaster*, he proposes that passivity is measureless, it is the disaster defined not as a past event but as the "immemorial past" which can return in ghostly form (Blanchot, *The Writing of the Disaster* 17). There are two types of passivity: the passivity of quietude and the passivity of non-quietude (*The Writing of the Disaster* 5) that the general discourse overwrites with the activities of unity, coherence, and order. Blanchot traces an important etymology in passivity: it is a semantic movement that includes passion, past, and *pas* (*The Writing of the Disaster* 16). This is a passivity bereft of self that is an alterity, a non-dialectical place where being lacks but does not give way to non-being. He refers to the patience of passivity, a time of time's absence, the time of dying which has no support other than language that is at best fragmentary but gives voice to the ambivalences of being that are paradoxical such as passivity/activity, inertia/dynamism, voluntary and involuntary (*The Writing of the Disaster* 20). Speaking, he poses, is "responsible passivity" and it "gives the response, answering to the impossible and for the impossible" (*The Writing of the Disaster* 20).

To conclude, we do well to think deeply about the double salvo of patience and speaking as well as passionate passivity in broaching disaster as a horizon of life and death, being and non-being. Justine's embrace of death is a passionate passivity that is truthful, but it does not give voice to the deepest ambivalences of being that Blanchot proposes are necessary to go to the very horizon of human possibility and propel the creative, our very "mot-tility." The problem for Justine is that she enters and becomes the void rather than deploying her passivity before the void as a renewed impetus for life. She embraces a real death in order to come to rest. Austerlitz comes to inhabit two contradictory worlds at once and is lost in an abyss with the past and the present worlds on either side. This was ultimately pierced by the moment of traumatic glance on the train platform, the time of understanding of his origin-quest, and its conclusion. The effect of this was the supplanting of his helplessness and anxiety with knowledge, passion, and repose.

Works Cited

Blanchot, Maurice. "The Human Race." *On Robert Antelme's The Human Race: Essays and Commentary*, by Robert Antelme, translated by Jeffrey Haight, Marlboro Press/Northwestern, 2003, pp. 61–68.

———. *The Space of Literature*. Translated by Ann Smock, University of Nebraska Press, 1982.

———. *The Writing of the Disaster*. Translated by Ann Smock, University of Nebraska Press, 1995.

Freud, Sigmund. "Mourning and Melancholia." *The Standard Edition of the Complete Psychological Works of Sigmund Freud*, edited by Josef Breuer et al., vol. 14, Vintage, 2001, pp. 239–60.

Heidegger, Martin. *Being and Time*. Oxford Blackwell Publishing, 1962.

Lacan, Jacques. *Anxiety. Book X. The Seminar of Jacques Lacan*. Translated by Cormac Gallagher, Unpublished, 1962. http://www.lacaninireland.com/web/wp-content/uploads/2010/06/Seminar-X-Revised-by-Mary-Cherou-Lagreze.pdf.

———. "Logical Time and the Assertation of Anticipated Certainty." *Écrits: the first complete edition in English*, translated by Bruce Fink, W.W. Norton, 2007, pp. 161–75.

——. *The Four Fundamental Concepts of Psychoanalysis*. Translated by Alan Sheridan, Karnac, 2004.

——. "The Function and Field of Speech and Language in Psychoanalysis." *Écrits: The First Complete Edition in English*, translated by Bruce Fink, W.W. Norton, 2007, pp. 197–268.

——. "The Position of the Unconscious." *Écrits: The First Complete Edition in English*, translated by Bruce Fink, W.W. Norton, 2007, pp. 703–21.

——. *The Seminar of Jacques Lacan: The Psychoses: Seminar III*. Translated by Jacques-Alain Miller and Russell Grigg, Routledge, 2000.

Leader, Darian. *The New Black: Mourning, Melancholia and Depression*. Penguin Books, 2009.

Sebald, W. G. *Austerlitz*. Translated by Anthea Bell, Penguin, 2002.

Thomas, Dylan. "Do Not Go Gentle Into That Good Night." *Collected Poems: 1934–1953*, edited by Walford Davies and Ralph Maud, Phoenix, 2003.

Trier, Lars von. *Melancholia*. Zentropa Entertainments, Memfis Film, Zentropa International Sweden, 2011.

Part II

Speed

Chapter 4

Uncut Gems

Dashing between the Red and the Black

Jessica Datema and Manya Steinkoler

The film *Uncut Gems* depicts the frenetic pace of late capitalism via the hustle in motion of a middle-aged Jewish jewelry district merchant, the desperate Howard Ratner (Adam Sandler). Ratner is drowning in gambling debts, flailing his arms against the unrelenting current to stay financially afloat. Ratner believes in, strives for and chases after the ever-hoped-for monetary return through gambling and gem sales. After Ratner arranges for the rare black opal to be smuggled out of Ethiopia and shipped to his jewelry shop in NYC, it finally arrives. This gem is the *piece de resistance* that is supposed to get Ratner out of the red and into the black but only plummets him further into debt.

Howard Ratner's unyielding devotion to the gem exemplifies a loyalty toward late capitalism akin to what Giorgio Agamben calls "*pistis.*" *Pistis* means "faith," and Agamben points out how this word was transformed from a sign on the front of an ancient Greek bank, to the language of the early church, into the credo of late capitalism (Agamben 69). In *Uncut Gems*, it is Ratner's constant faith in turning over a deal that propels all the film's real/reel motion as it rolls toward the disastrous end.

Ratner is the exhausted subject of late capitalism whose non-stop movement is prolonged by *pistis* itself, the hope and faith that the Uncut gem will solve all his problems. In the end, *Uncut Gems* leaves him (and us—the audience) anxious, oscillating between exhilaration and despair, perched on the edge of our seats. Running on empty, Howard Ratner has too many balls in the air in pursuit of the black opal until—both to his and to our surprise—he's shot point blank in the chest. No more movement. No more movie. No more Howie.

Uncut Gems shows how faith in the church of late capitalism is reducible to the pursuit of profit. Howie Ratner dies a true believer. His world is our world where the protocols of citizenry are abdicated to get back in the black. Subsequently, human value is reduced entirely to the fiscal, and not moral or social debt. Citizens are reduced to their monetary assets, shedding the antiquated burden of the name of the father and the sacrifice it entails.

DOI: 10.4324/9781003194033-7

The film exposes how instead of being re-territorialized subjects situated in desire or history, citizens pursue the dangling carat of *pistis* until it demolishes all anchors. As Maurizio Lazzarato notes in his recent critique of global capitalism, "Debt has reconfigured sovereign disciplinary and biopolitical power. . . . It constitutes the most deterritorialized and most general power relation" (Lazzarato 89–90). Citizens have become slaves to the market, subjects reduced to the money drive. Whereas we used to make sacrifices under a religious order, now the only sacrifice demanded is the *pistis* of late capitalism.

The Pistis Principal: Running on the Rat Wheel of Late Capitalism

The entire film unwinds as Ratner's movement toward the yield he imagines will be obtained by the black opal. The jewelry store owner is exemplary of what Agamben discusses as a compelled subject under "capitalism [who] lives in a continual indebtedness, which neither can nor should be paid off" (Agamben 71). We call this "the Pistis Principal" since it is a compulsion that runs on nothing but faith in the financial system. Devotion to the *pistis* principle accelerated in America after the crash of 2008 when life without debt became impossible.

Ratner's labors in *Uncut Gems* exemplify ordinary citizens whose exertions circularly amount to the hunt for more credit to pay off increasing debt. Stijn Vanhuele aptly describes this subject position as circulating "like go-carts on a racetrack . . . as if it were on wheels" (Vanheule 7). We see how in the discourse of the late capitalism, rotation and spinning wheels replace metaphoric anchoring or quilting via symbolic bonds. The lack that is constitutive of subjectivity becomes Uncut in service to the *pistis* principle of profit. Ratner is a post-modern Tantalus, condemned to the rat wheel of consumption eternally running after the black to get out of the red.

Howard's last name reveals how this circular rotation unravels all symbolic anchors. The Jewish surname "Ratner" stems from the German *"Rat,"* which means council, or *Rathouse*, that is, a city hall or a courthouse where law is enacted. Notably, an inflatable rat is used as a mascot of union strikes since "rats" aim to replace workers in the interest of profit; people are reduced to rodents, forced to survive by running on the wheel of paycheck to paycheck. This is the world we live in today.

As *pistis* replaces law, Ratner personifies this *acephalic* (headless) circulation, which undercuts and replaces both law and community. The name "Ratner" alludes to Howard's Ashkenazic Jewish ancestry, a history of community, family, and fatherhood which he abandons in pursuit of profit. Ratner's faith in the black opal becomes deadly, making him a martyr for money who erases all naming, memory, family, and community to run on the rat wheel of speculative fortune.

In the new faith of capitalism, symbolic law is never instituted via the cut. Rather, the *pistis* principal keeps Ratner on the move, enslaved to the hoped-for profit, without lack, interruption, or a pause. Here, we see the importance of the adjective "uncut" in the film's title. What Freud called the anchoring metamorphic rock of castration is replaced by the *jouissance* of the ever-errant black opal. *Uncut Gems* refers not only to the black opal, a stone which remains unfinished and never set, but also to the psychoanalytic notion of castration as what is forsaken by the *pistis* principle.

Uncut Gems shows how nowadays everyone is "getting their rocks off" rather than having to make do with lack. Freud's "rock of castration" is the locus of loss and impossibility, the origin of social and moral debt (Freud 356–57). *Uncut Gems* depicts Ratner's refusal of lack as a pursuit of profit without pause—where no gem is ever enough—as what compels subjects of the *pistis* principle, reducing them to rats on wheels. Moreover, Freud warns that even psychoanalysis will succumb to the demand to "accelerate the tempo of analytic therapy to suit the rush of American life" (317). The black opal sutures the cut of Freud's rock metaphor, bypassing analysis, and the cut of the symbolic; it is a *gem fatale* that remains Uncut, a rock that is "real."

Had the Freudian rock been in place, castration would be the "cut" that would have permitted Ratner to limit *jouissance*. Castration is the way a subject detaches from the mother, allowing for identification. Identification comes from what Jacques Lacan calls the big Other, that is, the social symbolic order of speech which permits communication and co-existence. In the film, as in late capitalism, the big Other's demand to "keep it going" brooks no pause. Ratner's world is one without rest or sleep. It portrays the *24/7* infinity that Jonathan Crary describes as what drives the insomnia and restlessness of our neoliberal society (Crary).[1] This infinite movement is, in fact, the film's subject matter as shown in the endless plotless plot with no real development. *Uncut Gems* centers around Ratner's "quest" for the black opal that goes nowhere. Trailing the gem's rotation on the rat wheel, he moves from his jewelry store to his various residences, Sotheby's, his mistress' apartment, the basketball court, the casino, and finally, to a black metal bullet shot point blank into his chest.

Uncut Germs: When It Smells Fishy, It Is Fishy

When Howard Ratner's black opal initially arrives, it is packed in ice, smuggled through international customs in the body of a large fish. This delivery underscores the motif of fishiness that we see throughout the film. This fishiness is further indicated in the color scheme of the film itself. *Uncut Gems* is shot in vaporous, murky, luminous, almost radioactive tints as though underwater. The black opal is similarly tinted in spangled darkness, an opaque but radiant rock. Its murky luminosity is reminiscent of Ratner's shady and nefarious black eyes, goatee, and black tracksuit.

Howard Ratner appears a *kitsch* Mephistophelian figure of our era of *biothanatopolitics*, where the drive is the partner of our undying *pistis* to profit. This dark era is epitomized by a "precariousness of existence as well as the growing vacillation of institutions, of democracy, of the remnants of freedom [and]of the respect for the fantasy of the other" (Braunstein 3). As a shady spokesperson, Ratner blindly rushes after the gem until he accidentally plunges into an outdoor fountain. He loses his glasses like a fish out of water; yet there is no miracle of the fish to nourish, only further submerging to suffocate.

Uncut Gems gives us an eyeful of Manhattan's jewelry district as a SeaWorld of underwater treasures where Ratner's jewelry store is a microcosm of the deep-sea realm. The entire glass shop is a fish tank whose double glass doors constantly get stuck, literalizing the no way in or out of aquatic life, for example, swimming in the drives. The counters display Ratner's fishy merchandise; his legitimate acquisitions are always in question. At one point, the showroom also holds a pet goldfish. After an employee learns that Ratner sold him fake Rolexes, enraged, the man shatters the fishbowl. The film shows how everyone is drowning in the pursuit of profit, from the small business owner to his employees and his clients.

As slaves of late capitalism, the Amazoning of the world, Ratner and his motley rat pack swim out of sync. The jewelry store is the aquarium where they will all be ultimately engulfed in the frenzy of consumption. Here there is a parallel made with the Passover Seder in the film commemorating the exodus from slavery in Egypt, and epitomizing struggling citizens soaked in the red. We, all of us, have only been liberated to sink again as slaves to late capitalism, as the bottom feeders who fight over leftovers or the excess of one percenters who buy, squander, and discard. *Uncut Gems* shows how only the fortunate avoid drowning in the red (sea) and everyone else is left treading water.

The value of the gem, like the subject under late capitalism, is not part of a labor-based economy. Rather, its exchange value is based on the vagaries of asymmetrical financial institutions of power and black markets. Value has become equivalent to enjoyment of the transaction. In this sense, Ratner is a "multitasker" who gets caught up in the helter-skelter frenzy of flexible trades. Social critic Byung-Chul Han describes such "multitasking" as "not representative of civilizational progress. Rather such an aptitude amounts to regression and is commonplace among wild animals" (Han 12). Ratner runs on the roller coaster of instinct to juggle multiple deals, making him more akin to a wild animal in a state nature than a small business owner.

The film aptly shows our current socio-cultural and political reality of the sales transaction as at the highest enjoyment. It underlines how there is no cut or limit to the demand occasioned by the money drive. As subject to this *pistis* principle, human beings are not separated or castrated, but compelled objects themselves. In that sense, the characters are moving all the time in a circular rhythm of sameness without the possibility of creating meaning. Human value is no longer tied to labor, collective meaning, personhood, or community.

Uncut Gems reveals the situation of income inequality where the middle class swims alongside bottom feeders while the 1% remain above water. Our fishy contemporary world was presciently depicted in early capitalist Holland by Dutch Master Pieter van der Heyden's (1557) celebrated *Big Fish Eat Little Fish* (Heyden et al.). This 16th-century painting prefigures our modern capitalist moment of interminable consumption. In the marine world of capital, the only logic is to consume or be consumed, a logic that has made it to the White House. Ratner's jewelry showroom is his Opal Office where small business executives flounder in the sea of consumption. His showroom is an exaggerated microcosm of our uncanny market, motored by surplus value and devotion to fishy financial transactions.

As the global economy moves away from labor and exchange value to the imposition of institutional powers prescribing and imposing asymmetrical modes of exploitation, domination, and subjection, citizens are subjected to the charges of an autocratic and unpredictable economy. *Uncut Gems* shows how "Beyond the state it is money that rules, money that communicates, and what we need these days definitely isn't any critique of Marxism, but a modern theory of money as good as Marx's that proceeds from where he left off" (Deleuze 152). The film critiques our de-territorialized culture of hypercapitalism where mobilizing money trumps recognition, identification, and differentiation. Ratner is exemplary of a middle-class citizen, working non-stop who is unable to amass savings, pay off debt, or obtain a secure job with fixed income and health insurance, and who doesn't want to.

Stone-Blind

Ratner's store is screened in by glass not for transparency or easy access but to lock down and hide his assets. As a pervert, he uses "sight" and his jeweler's loupe not to see others but to control them as well as to surveil the circulation of his merchandise. This mercantile voyeurism is exhibited in an early scene in which Ratner watches his girlfriend masturbate, his merchandise, while he texts her from a hidden closet. In this scene, he enjoys precisely how she does not see him, a position which gives him mastery.

Uncut Gems includes scenes like these that emphasize the enjoyment of the very gaze that is at stake with the gem, one that is blinded by seeing. For example, the glass walls of Ratner's jewelry store exemplify his need to control others with the gaze. They permit him foreknowledge of when and how clients enter or exit his sparkling repository. It is worth noting that the lock on the door to his showroom frequently breaks and is eventually replaced by a wedge that allows him to scope out what customers are looking for before they enter. The point is that there is no gap in seeing that will occur to interrupt Ratner's span of sales or the *pistis* principle; he can use all errors, blindness, or mishaps to perpetuate profit.

The glass walls, cameras, and faulty lock display how Ratner deploys the gaze but remains blind to the others, including his own family. This is exemplified at his daughter's recital when his brother-in-law pulls Ratner out of the concert hall with some goons and punishes him for an unpaid debt. They strip him naked and lock him in the trunk of his own family car. Trapped in the trunk, Ratner is reduced to a body entirely in the dark. Blind and humiliated, he has no choice but to phone his wife who is forced to leave the theater and open the trunk. She is clearly so inured to her husband's shenanigans that she doesn't even ask what happened when he emerges from the car naked. Ratner's reckless blindness and disavowal of others directly foreshadows his death.

Most of the violence in the film is enacted by Ratner's own family who systematically assault and destroy neighborly kinship ties. With the black opal, Ratner becomes increasingly encircled by his own debt to other family members. These diminishing circles wield the very real threat of death and a more violent end than any creditor's retribution. At work under the surface is *pistis*, an untethered faith in money. This faith is not visible in any form except as a blind excess that usurps all relationships.[2]

Human subjectivity and ultimately life are reduced or distilled, as incremental value has been reduced to excremental value. Hoping that the opal will help him get back into the black, Ratner finds value only in running after *pistis*. Making this fact stunningly apparent, the camera literally runs through Ratner's colon in the film's opening shot. This opening shows the invisible path of the anal drive as the real/reel work of Ratner's entire life. The black opal is the anal object which promises to move Ratner out of the red and heal all familial and financial ills.

The theme of sight and blindness is suggested by the choice of gem. In ancient culture, the opal was thought to cure eye diseases and was believed to have the power to render its owner invisible. In ancient Rome, the opal was called the "Patron of Thieves." It is a jewel whose slippery and sliding scale value is used by thieves or those who profit from what cannot be measured; its value is tied to the movement of the drive. In gemology, the color of a gem is the color on the spectrum that does not absorb light. The opal, as opaque, depends purely on the market: it cannot, like other gems, be objectivity assessed. The fluidity of the opal's value is further underlined by way of its errancy in the film, driving Ratner's shady deals. Ratner's sales of the opal shift from basketball player to pawn shop, to girlfriend, to casino. He gets the opal into the black only to lose and swim after it into the red again and again.

Uncut Gems shows not only Ratner's lack of subjective division but also an absence of any filmic genre specificity in both content and form. *Uncut Gems* is a mixture of fiction and documentary, not reducible to either. Many of the actors were inducted from the diamond district to act in their first film, including the goons that follow Ratner around and eventually murder him. Untrained actors are convincing precisely because they are real, further collapsing the field of representation. While the film shows that no one is acting in late capitalism, at the same time it underlines that reality is an act all by itself.

The uncut aspect concerns the trajectory of the drive. The opening scene cross cuts between a mine in Ethiopia and a miner's wound and a camera running through Ratner's colon underlining the black opal as a drive object. *Uncut Gems* contrasts the miner with his maimed leg that is opened and bloody being carried off site with real footage of Ratner's colon. These visual links indicate not only the driven reel that constitutes the duration and form of the film, but also its content, which is a circulation around the black opal. Language is made possible by this rift into the real, which is why the movie begins with the mining of the hole. Mining the colon for the anal object is the story of the film, the begin and the begat of the consuming voraciousness of late capitalism and the *pistis* principle. The body is the final grab of contemporary neoliberal biopolitics—of late capitalism's literal "colonizing" of the body's space and spaces.

In the striking opening scene, there is a semantic equivalence made between the anal object, the opal, and colon cancer, that is, the object of a colonoscopy, as what we go digging for. The day laborer has found the black opal, the earth's precious turd, a find, and a kind of *pharmakon*, evoking the object as cure and poison, life and death.[3] The black opal offers Ratner an unfixed object to barter in a world where both life and value itself have become forms of waste. The black opal is the anal object that takes on value via circulation itself, a beyond of life and death. Ratner's infinite attempt to obtain the excretory object that does not satisfy exemplifies the "non-stop movement of global exchange" (Crary 5). The wit of the film illustrates that the constant circulation of late capitalism is reducible to the peristalsis of bodies *sans* castration. As a driven body running after the anal object, Ratner is reduced to the peristalsis itself; he has become his colon.

In this manner, Ratner exemplifies the passage in Genesis describing the time of a man's life span as dust to dust. Under late capitalism's *pistis* principle, the film suggests that humanity is both a colon and a colon. Howard rides the money drive until he dies on the floor of his showroom and all financial deals are put on ice. This is exactly what happens to his fish after the employee smashes its tank. His desperate attempts to save the fish momentarily by putting it into a drinking glass ironically symbolize Howard's entire life. Howard has become the dead fish.

Howard Ratner likes selling and buying things. He sports a rimless pair of Cartier glasses, a Salvatore Ferragamo logo belt; he stashes Rolex watches in his store, and most unusually, he displays a bizarre, bedazzled diamond Furby with darting little brown eyes to privileged clients. This necklace that looks like a gremlin is the hook Ratner uses to further land a sale. The *Baal* worship jewelry is a symbol of the modern monstrousness of buying. Ratner's faith (*pistis*) is in buying as a lure or getting people to buy into his sales.

The Furby was created for the market, a curio object between human and animal, culture and nature. It represents the perverse entropy of what Jaques Lacan calls an uncanny object that symbolizes the porous borders of profit, *pistis*, and price. The jeweled version of the Furby we see in the film was invented by the directors as an uncanny thing. It functions as what Nestor Braunstein calls "an unusual form of the object *a*, a segment of the real lacking a specular image that carries with it the *unheimliche*" (Braunstein). In an interview, the directors of *Uncut Gems* actually liken the pervie Ratner to the Furby as "the saddest dumbest *thing* that existed in the nineties" (Woodhead). The Talisman objects, like the black opal, are gems meant to stave off poverty and bring good luck. All that these treasures indicate is that the person donning them has become tragically hooked in pursuit of the deal.

Another way the film defies genre is shown in the role of Kevin Garnett. Garnett is an American former pro-basketball player who competed for 21 seasons in the NBA with the Minnesota Timberwolves, the Boston Celtics, and the Brooklyn Nets. In real life, he is known for his amazing dunks, athleticism, intensity, and defensive skills. In his debut film, acting as himself, Garnett plays a buyer. Ironically, the basketball player's last name, Garnett, is his real name but also fits with the idea of the black celebrity athlete as a gem. Garnett is introduced by a contact to Ratner as one who is interested in buying watches and jewelry. After Ratner pulls out the diamond Furby for effect, he whips out the precious black opal. The famous NBA player engages in a heated negotiation, asking how much Ratner originally paid. Ratner remains evasive, claims the opal is not for sale, that it has magical properties, was mined by African Jews, and tells his hooked customer that the gem is priceless.

Ratner conducts business like basketball players' practice; he keeps negotiations open by dribbling and shifting. He treats his gems like a basketball, as an extension of himself. Each sale is a play, and the black opal is the latest equipment in Ratner's acquisitive game. Excellence in the sport depends on dribbling the gems—in this case a black opal—which interests Garnett for its Jewish African value and resonance with black lives. We see how the object is being weighed with supplemental meaning. After much negotiation, Ratner gives Garnett the gem temporarily to wear so that Garnett will win, and he can bet on the game.

The basketball player promises to return it to Ratner with a victory, yet Garnet, like Howard, is never done with playing. They follow the money drive, and these moving unbounded negotiations are the only story of the film. In the basketball court of late capitalism, there is no conclusion, only more or less acceleration or stalling. The miserly aim with the anal object is to mine the gem/ball into the hole, the basketball hoop, the girlfriend, or bank, or back to its African or biblical origin, underground dust, where it will be safe and undetected forever. The basketball, like the black opal and the Furby talisman, cannot be taken out of circulation. Indeed, the hole—the basketball hoop, the colon, the ground that is mined—does not provide a limit but invites more movement. The ball in the hoop harkens back to Ratner's colon polyp. All this movement around the uncanny object underlines its unattainability. Instead of owning or maintaining their merchandise, Ratner, like Garnet, opts for playing around the hole to deflect, side-track, or pivot other players on the court. In the showroom of late capitalism, there are only infinite adjustments to the game, never conclusions.

Uncut Gems shows what happens to culture when the *pistis* principle becomes the new religion. Our global neoliberal world is one without pause, lack, castration, grace, reconciliation, or forgiveness of loans. There is only debt and interest-bearing anxiety. Daily life does not avoid death and the black market; it is our economy; we are in the bowels of the earth where cash is buried; we are the excretory object. The rule of capitalism's *pistis* principle has rendered life on earth a watery underworld where Ratner infinitely circulates like the polyp in his colon around the black opal he pursues. With no aim except profit, his movement has "no telos; it is essentially infinite yet precisely for this reason incessantly in prey to a crisis" (Agamben 74). The jeweler no longer aims to create or sell anything tied to labor or fixed value but is thrown between shifting positions of the red and the black.

Uncut Gems makes audiences feel Ratner's viral plunging, submerging, and saturation in the money drive. The black opal is the sliding scale viral object, or *pharmakon* whose *jouissance* forces Ratner into an underwater darkness where all revenue streams lead to debt. Ratner's life is jeopardized the closer he gets to experiencing the cut of castration and being in the red. In this manner, he exemplifies the citizen of late capitalism who "tends with all its might not towards redemption but toward guilt, not toward hope, but toward desperation; capitalism as religion does not aim at the transformation of the world, but at its [own]destruction" (Agamben 68). Howard ends up like the dead fish on the floor of his jewelry showroom; a casualty of the *pistis* principle where there is no division between life and debt.

Uncut Gems exposes how the American Dream has been reduced to the nightmare of the drive, as the pursuit of wealth has gone viral. The film shows how society has become sick from worship, not of the object itself, but from the *jouissance* of buying and selling. Since buying is no longer bound by political, religious, or legal limits, nothing curbs this *jouissance*. The gems have effectively become germs, and the virus has infected us all. Instead of buying as believing, or betting on the opal, might we learn from Howard Ratner's death and invent more reflective and binding rituals for democratic participation? Or do such binding rituals presuppose that we were already cut out in the first place? We are not sure. We only know that to cut the shit, we must embrace insolvency, idleness, and convalesce and mask up to protect ourselves from uncut germs.

Notes

1 "The injuring of sleep is inseparable from the ongoing dismantling of social protections in other spheres. . . . (Crary 18). Insomnia corresponds to the necessity or vigilance to a refusal to overlook the horror and injustice that pervades the world" (19). "Sleep can stand for the durability of the social, and that sleep might be analogous to other thresholds at which society could defend or protect itself" (25). A number of fundamental assumptions about the cohesion of social relations come together around the issue of sleep—in the reciprocity between vulnerability and trust, between exposure and care. "Crucial is the dependence on the safekeeping of others for the revivifying carelessness of sleep, for a periodic interval of being free of fear and for a temporary 'forgetfulness of evil'" (28).

2 "Uncut Gems" is a kind of post-modern accelerated updated version of Moliere's *The Miser*, where the social relation is reduced to money. In Moliere, the main character cannot afford to part with his money and is named "Harpagon," which means a five-pronged hook. This grappling iron hook is used for dragging or grasping, which is akin to the angling, spinning, and casting that Ratner does in the film (Moliére).

3 We might contrast this kind of gem with, say, Max Ophuls' "Earrings of Madame de . . . " (Ophüls et al.). Here, the earrings take on value via metaphor and circulation; they are invested with meaning and achieve their greatest value when they can be sacrificed. In *Uncut Gems*, "value" is reduced solely to circulation. There is no separation that would allow for subjectivity and meaning.

Works Cited

Agamben, Giorgio. *Creation and Anarchy: The Work of Art and the Religion of Capitalism*. Stanford University Press, 2019.

Braunstein, Nestor A. "Psychoanalysis, Too, Will Never Be the Same." *European Journal of Psychoanalysis*, May 2020, https://www.journal-psychoanalysis.eu/psychoanalysis-too-will-never-be-the-same/.

Crary, Jonathan. *24/7: Late Capitalism and the Ends of Sleep*. Verso, 2013.

Deleuze, Gilles. *Negotiations: 1972–1990*. Translated by Martin Joughin, Columbia University Press, 1995.

Freud, Sigmund. "Analysis Terminable and Interminable." *Collected Papers V*, edited by James Strachey, Hogarth Press, 1950, pp. 316–58.

Han, Byung-Chul. *The Burnout Society*. Translated by Erik Butler, Stanford Briefs, an imprint of Stanford University Press, 2015.

Heyden, Pieter van der, et al. *The Big Fish Eat the Little Fish*. engraving, published 1557. *National Gallery of Art*, https://www.nga.gov/collection/art-object-page.57872.html.

Lazzarato, M. (Maurizio). *The Making of the Indebted Man: An Essay on the Neoliberal Condition*. Translated by Joshua David Jordan, Semiotext(e), 2012.

Moliére. *The Would-Be Gentleman; That Scoundrel Scapin; The Miser; Love's the Best Doctor; Don Juan/Translated with an Introd. by John Wood*. Translated by John Wood, Penguin.

Ophüls, Max, et al. *Madame De...* Franco London Films, Indusfilms, Rizzoli Film, 1954.

Vanheule, Stijn. "Capitalist Discourse, Subjectivity and Lacanian Psychoanalysis." *Frontiers in Psychology*, vol. 7, 2016. *Frontiers*, https://doi.org/10.3389/fpsyg.2016.01948.

Woodhead, Hannah. "'There Was Sadness in the Eyes': The Story Behind Uncut Gems' Bedazzled Furby." *Vulture*, 9 Dec. 2019, https://www.vulture.com/2019/12/uncut-gems-bedazzled-furby-a-history.html.

Chapter 5

Running with Thieves

Baby Driver and The Beat My Heart Skipped

Angie Voela

In Western culture, rhythm inhabits, among other things, the fast pace of modern life; the incessant flow of information and data; the madness of capitalism; the desire to slow down, relax, and take time off; the working patterns of different professions; the profusion of musical genres; and, of course, the continuous circulation of commodities that fuels consumer capitalism. Rhythms and movement are also embedded in the personal trajectories of individuals as they navigate complex networks of socio-cultural values, communications, desires, and prevalent epochal (symptomatic) formations. The discussion of rhythm in relation to psyche and culture invites us to consider rhythm as an important, permanent yet variable presence in various relational fields, in which psychic interiority and material exteriority—which we only separate from heuristic reasons—compose, de-compose, and re-compose in recognizable patterns with duration. Rhythm engages directly with the ontological question of being and plays no lesser role in the experience of change than language, especially when change implies "crossing the line to a new and improbable identity" (Rajchman 13). To this decisive crossing rhythm contributes ground and passage in a systematic and measured manner.

A good way to grasp rhythm is by juxtaposing it to arrhythmia, cacophony, and chaos. For some psychoanalysts, the basic rhythm of psychic death and resurrection (Eigen) is the de facto basis of all psychic capabilities. For Deleuze and Guattari, rhythm mediates between chaos, be that internal or social, and ordered environments. Deleuze and Guattari write that from chaos, milieus and rhythms are born. A milieu is a coded environment, and a code is established by periodic repetition. Milieus are open to chaos, and rhythm is both the milieu's answer to chaos and the in-between with the latter: "In this in-between, chaos becomes rhythm, not inexorably but has the chance to" (345). Rhythm may also link milieus to one another: "There is rhythm when there is a transcoded passage from one milieu to another, a communication of milieus, coordination between heterogeneous space-times" (345). This dual conceptualization makes rhythm a very suitable tool for tracing changings states of being, especially in culture

DOI: 10.4324/9781003194033-8

where working through and interpretation are harder to follow than in the consulting rooms.

In contemporary culture, the themes of harnessing the forces of chaos and surviving catastrophe are often enmeshed with anxieties around the disappearance of salient points of reference, or the derailment of the capitalist machine into literal and metaphorical exploitation and thievery. European cinema and Hollywood echo these anxieties. In Audiard's 2005 film, *The Beat That My Heart Skipped* (*De battre mon cœur s'est arrêté*), a young man, Thomas Seyr, works in real estate, but, in reality, he is a thug who terrorizes tenants out of their flats and evicts refugees from squatted properties (Audiard et al.). Thomas is the son of a businessman involved in shady deals and a gifted concert pianist who is now dead. In *Baby Driver* (Wright et al.), Baby is a talented getaway driver who can only drive to the beat of his favorite music. The high-speed car chase and the music connect Baby to his dead mother, and it is this repetition, rather than the accumulation of wealth, that keeps him in the business. Baby is a loner. The only person close to him is Doc, mastermind of the robberies and paternal figure of sorts.

Baby is running with thieves and Thomas with thugs, but both are fundamentally indifferent to the structure, outsider-insiders to the profession that makes a mockery of honest labor in capitalism. Both have a visceral relationship with music and rhythm, yet it is speed that keeps chaos at bay. The dissonance in their lives is marked by the juxtaposition of classical or melodic music to the drumbeat of electronica and the noise of the car chase or the bar brawl. Baby and Thomas are not saints. They are complicit to thuggery, and endure rather than suffer, living an infinite duration of stretched, repetitive, unchanging time. Baby speeds and tears through geographical territories without much concern about the law—both the symbolic paternal law and the traditional separation of right from wrong. Thomas has forgotten how to play the piano. His life has its own regularities: alternating scenes of semi-legal activities in daylight and a nightlife of debauched entertainment, all punctuated by a steady drumbeat through the headphones, used by Thomas to draw a line under stressful events.

Bachelard argues that rhythm is integral to habit, with the latter being a formation of superseded temporalities, memories, and repetitions which creates a sense of duration (Bachelard, *Intuition of the Instant* 43). From his perspective, change as knowing oneself "means finding ourselves again in scattered personal events" (*Intuition of the Instant* 42), a rhythmic pursuit seen as a unifying process, eventually culminating in harmony. Bachelard does not see harmony as an ideal state of happiness, but as less fragmentation, fewer lacunae, less anguish, and less death. In this pursuit, rhythm appears on the side of life and keeps death at bay. Lacoue-Labarthe concurs on the proximity of rhythm to life and its fundamental opposition to death, as do Deleuze and Guattari for whom the refrain as rhythmic phrase ushers in the new and the improbable (*natality*). In the films we are discussing below, rhythm as part of life and change is an answer to death, to psychic stagnation and the difficulty of being born anew. Stagnation is best summed up by the infantile status of the two young protagonists and their dependence on the abusive father and the dead mother. Rhythm underlines the Oedipal relationship but exceeds and transforms it. In their rhythmic journey, Baby and Thomas are on a trajectory from helplessness to openness—to future possibility, music, and harmony. Rhythm serves both.

Rhythm mobilizes powers of chance. Falling in love can have a new rhythm which mobilizes psychic forces after prolonged periods of disengagement and mourning. Both films employ falling in love as a new rhythm. Here, love is not about the enchantment of the ego by the ideal image in the other but a way of establishing new habits, new realms, and new territories of being. Deleuze and Guattari consider falling in love, courtship, and the refrain of the lovers as rhythmic patterns opening to new assemblages (Deleuze and Guattari 360), deterritorializations enacting movement and change. They are, as we will argue below, rhythmic ways of undoing restrictive maternal and paternal ties, as well as responding to the aporia of death, the cesura of being, as Lacoue-Labarthe would call it, which posits the terrible question: *Am I dead or alive?*

So far, I have deliberately avoided giving rhythm a definition, highlighting, instead, some of its instantiations in contemporary philosophy. Deleuze and Guattari's opening lines in the chapter *1837: Of the refrain* raises rhythm to a wonderful aesthetic gesture of fragility and mastery:

> A child in the dark, griped with fear, comforts himself by singing under his breath. He walks and halts to his song. Lost, he takes shelter, or orients himself with the little song as best he can. The song is like a rough sketch of a calming and stabilizing, calm and stable, center in the heart of chaos. (Deleuze and Guattari 343)

The image of the child in the dark invites us to listen—listening being the privileged mode of relating between the analysand and the analyst. Listening to rhythm is not antagonistic to listening to the signifier or to seeing or, indeed, to the game of another child who endeavors to represent the absence of the mother with the rhythmic recitation of an antithetical pair of vowels (o-a), a reel and a piece of string. Granting rhythm due importance in psychoanalysis, and anteriority to the *fort/da* game, argues Civitarese, allows for a new aesthetic which enriches psychoanalytic theory and practice (Civitarese).

The aim of this chapter is to explore the uses of rhythm between psychoanalysis and to certain strands of continental philosophy. The emphasis, as indicated above, is on movement and transformation, with equal attention to psychic interiority and the systematic examination of external events which locate the individual in intersubjective and epochal relations. Deleuze and Guattari, Bachelard, and Lacoue-Labarthe offer a range of concepts which allow us to elaborate a rhythm-based language for such a systematic examination. In *A Thousand Plateaus*, Deleuze and Guattari develop the refrain as a key concept for conceptualizing how individuals and environments compose into territories or assemblages. The refrain traces movement between assemblages, passage from one to the other, change over time, and de-composition and re-composition through movement and rhythm. The concept will be used to establish a rhythmic appreciation of the exterior and forces, of the outside.

The apparent Bergsonism of Deleuze and Guattari, who claim that we do not have systems, only lines and movements (Deleuze and Guattari 386), does not always sit well with psychoanalysis. In the present chapter, it is "moderated" by drawing on Bachelard, who, in *The Dialectic of Duration*, proposes a way of thinking rhythm and duration beyond rather than against Bergson. Bachelard acknowledges the vital importance of the Bergsonian rhythm but argues that we cannot accept the endless flow of time without postulating certain lacunae when we examine psychic temporally (Bachelard, *The Dialectic of Duration* 81), or a void "between the successive states characterizing the psyche's development, even if this void may be simply a synonym of the difference between states that are differentiated" (*The Dialectic of Duration* 81). It further allows us to begin in media res, when chaos returns and things fall apart, and one is called to either *run through* or *work through* the predicaments of modern life.

Below, rhythm in *The Beat That My Heart Skipped* and *Baby Driver* are discussed in three moves. The first, titled *Arrhythmia of care*, focuses on the patterns of living in the sphere of an uncaring and exploitative father, the forces of habit surrounding this relationship, and how the young protagonists regulate paternal desire in a setting that seems impenetrable to change. The second section, *Movement, stasis, nothing*, focuses on the prolonged mourning for the dead mother and a memory carefully preserved in recordings of the maternal voice. Both sections deal with rhythm as an endeavor to fix a fragile point as center in the middle of chaos (Deleuze and Guattari 344). Rhythm sustains the subject in its loneliness in the middle of the frenetic pace of modern life. Drawing on Lacoue-Labarthe's concept of *desistance*, I argue that, between the dead mother and the indifferent father, one has little to hold on to apart from their own rhythmic dis-semblance from death. Lacoue-Labarthe's philosophical inquiry into subjectivity is suffused with psychoanalysis, allowing us to further establish rhythm as a primary component of psychic life and an antidote to the cesura of death.

The advent of new rhythms is discussed in section three, entitled *Passing through the imperceptible*. Drawing on Deleuze and Guattari, I show how new rhythms achieve regularity by organizing new assemblages and making incursions into the (parental) domain of established habits. The possibility of the new starts by chance and blossoms with abandoning oneself to the other, characteristic of falling in love and the Deleuzian *becoming-child*, by which Baby and Thomas allow rhythm and music to re-infuse their body. Recurrent passage and movement to and from new assemblages effects psychic transformation in and with the external milieu. In that section, I endeavor to do two things: establish a clear connection between psychic interiority and changes occurring in the external environment and show how the Deleuzian conceptualization of rhythm-refrain as spatiotemporal transformation chimes with psychoanalytic processes like *working through* and *moving toward* psychic progress. I also draw on Knoblauch's important work on rhythm in the psychoanalytic clinic, which systematizes the invisible contribution of rhythm to the intersubjective experience and the rhythmic elements of a transformation that will eventually be apprehended as the passage from one discreet state into another.

Arrhythmia of care

Baby at the driving wheel. Red Suzuki. The gang disembarks, machine guns in hand. Music on. Baby times them by the music, mimes singing, mimes driving, turns screen wipers on and off, and rocks to the music. The gang inside the bank fire their guns to the ceiling; he watches; police sirens in the background; he mouths the words of the song and when it finishes: "Thank you very much ladies and gentlemen, the famous Bellbottoms!" The bank's alarm goes off; the gang scrambles to the car; demonic car chase through red lights, pile-up behind. Baby is calm and focused; the police throw a chain of spikes in his path; he swerves and pushes it to the side with the wheel; police car tires burst; more cars in the chase. Baby spots two red cars on the other side of the road; U-turn, pitches his car between them and slides into the slip road, police helicopter duped; inside the car park; end of chase; calm.

At the warehouse, Doc presents the team with a big street map spread on the table, with toy cars to demonstrate the route. Doc speaks but Baby seems not to be paying attention; he is wearing dark glasses and has his earphones on. "Is he retarded?" asks Buddy, obviously annoyed with Baby's indifference. "Retarded means slow, is he slow?" remarks Doc. "He is a good kid and a devil behind the wheel, what else do you need to know?" Doc asks Baby what he was just talking about. Baby repeats it verbatim. "That's my baby!" exclaims Doc.

Baby does not respond to words, taunts, or aggression. The others make fun of him: "baby has not said his first words." Buddy approaches him and runs a toy car off the table; Baby still does not respond: "So you are a mute, baby?" snarls Buddy and yanks his earphones off. Baby replies: "No." Buddy is getting angrier and demands to know what Baby is listening to: "music," he responds calmly. Buddy snatches off Baby's glasses and demands to know "what goes on in this mind." Baby says he is listening to Egyptian reggae and pulls another pair of glasses from his pocket. Buddy throws a punch but stops in mid-air. Doc splits the money, and all head for the elevator. Buddy and his girlfriend kiss passionately: "Mummy and daddy are getting on"—his last words to Baby.

The opening sequences of *The Beat That My Heart* establish Thomas as a low-life criminal. Fragmented scenes of Parisian bars at nighttime, brawl, men shoving each other out of the bar, Thomas escorting a drunk laughing woman into a taxi. In the next scene, a friend tells how his aging dad became feeble and how he nursed him until his death. Thomas drinks and says nothing. Cut into the Parisian night again, Thomas driving, fuzzy lights. Daytime: Thomas negotiating a deal with a business associate. Nighttime: Thomas and friends release a sack full of rats into a block of flats to scare the tenants. Cut to another Parisian bar: Thomas and friends get embroiled in a brawl and are kicked out. Daylight: Thomas arriving at a block of flats just occupied by homeless migrants. To him they are squatters. When an advocate for the group explains that if the apartments have facilities, then occupants "get rights," Thomas and his friends trash the interior so that the flats are uninhabitable. Cut to a night scene, Thomas driving in his car, alone, beat music on headphones, looking calm, almost content. The drumbeat, as it turns out, punctuates his days, when he tries to decompress.

Thomas meeting with father at a restaurant. The old man he looks tired, worn out. Thomas arrives, headphones on, and tries to interest dad in his music. Father is not impressed with electronica. He tells Thomas he is getting married to a beauty and describes her body in lurid detail; when the fiancée, Christine, arrives, Thomas takes an instant dislike to her, insults Christine, and gets up to leave; outside the restaurant, he tells dad he is marrying a whore. Dad needs Thomas. He is dad's strong man. Dad asks Thomas to scare a tenant to paying back the rent he owns. He invites Thomas to a restaurant, days after the meeting with Christine, a place, as it happens, opposite the shop that owes him rent. Thomas dares his father to sort out his own affairs but when he tries, he is beaten and thrown out of the shop. Thomas enters the premises by the back door, lures the manager into the kitchen, beats him up brutally, and extracts dad's money. All dad has to say is: "You see, it was not that difficult!" Cut to Thomas driving alone in the car, beat music on.

The aim of this section is to show that rhythm holds together the fragmented lives of the two young men, linking disparate elements, aporias, and lacunae. Bachelard links rhythm to habit, duration, and action. Duration is a multiple ordering of actions, and rhythms constitute habit, both conscious and unconscious (Bachelard, *Intuition of the Instant* 41). Habit, argues Bachelard, invites us to follow the rhythms of well-ordered acts, which "is ultimately experienced as an imperative of quasi-rational and aesthetic nature" (*Intuition of the Instant* 43). This, in turn, allows Bachelard to suggest that the individual is, in fact, habit. In both films, everyday life is ordered into fine-tuned patterns. Criminal life has its regularities.

The two young men seem to be effective and professional, at ease with their misery, or safe in a state of chronic collapse (Eigen 725). Fragmentation and catastrophe in the past are superseded by highly territorialized activities which veil loneliness and a generalized lack of care. Rhythms, we might propose, conceal an arrhythmia of care—by the Other who does not respond to the son's desire or only tends to their own jouissance. Rhythm accompanies near-muteness and exclusion from language, invisibility, and isolation.

Habitual rhythms compose the individual and the milieu: Baby has no life outside of them but does not inhabit them either. Thomas is and is not part of the paternal milieu. Baby and Thomas are inscribed in the thievery machine for their asset, their "hands": the hands of the driver or the thug are "alpha hands," as Eigen would say, necessary to the Other. In an assemblage of profit and exploitation, the hand conjoins man to car, to drive, to reward for doing one's job well: a cut or a share in the paternal loot but not in his affection. In this assemblage, one gets to be the father's phallus—a logical surplus and a meaningless excess. The lacuna on the level of the subject's own desire (the fundamental *what am I in the field of the Other*?) is papered over by rhythmic habit and only becomes apparent as a beat. The beat marks the locus of a lacuna in the thievery assemblage, the black hole to which one is trying to fix a center at any price. "Sometimes," Deleuze and Guattari comment, "one organizes around that point a calm and stable 'pace' (rather than a form); the black hole has become a home. Sometimes one grafts onto that pace a breakaway from the black hole" (Deleuze and Guattari 344). For now, the young man is a (missing) beat, a recurrent beat, and an interminable attempt to escape. The beat is a comforting counterpoise to the chaos within and the lawlessness outside, to the extremely well-organized rhythm of thuggery.

In such an assemblage, the child is always a paradox. Baby is a paradox; a deaf-mute who speaks and a slow man who thinks and drives fast. Baby-ness alludes to the pre-linguistic or primal provenance of rhythms, and to infancy as a state at which one lacks the material framework to handle distress. The latter may spiral to infinity (Eigen 723), giving rise to nameless dread and an oscillation between helplessness and omnipotence (Eigen 724). Thus, Baby remains the missing link between the mother and the father, and an ineffective link between incompatible and unintegrated realms, such as the parents, material possessions, and the city grid. Baby is not deaf or mute but not in language either, he is *in rhythm* and in the limited structure or phrases that speak (to/for) him.

Baby and Thomas inhabit a static time of well-rehearsed moves. Civitarese argues that repetition ensures that life and death are controlled on an existential level, and mimesis normally serves that purpose. Does not Baby always *mime* the consummate performance he will give ahead of driving the getaway car, and does not Thomas always perform the same duties with accuracy? To repeat oneself means to bear, to sustain. Mimesis is the aesthetic way of regulating the world (Civitarese 896). As repetition it causes the specter of death to vanish, allowing the child to alternate between help-lessness and omnipotence, making not oneself but the world appear and disappear on cue. Duration is marked by recurrence: Successive robberies, hide and seek, and the ebb and flow of thuggery. In response to this arrhythmia of care one needs to become e-motional again, to begin to move and metabolize nothingness, escaping the same. One needs to inflect and inhabit time instead of living in discontinuity. Let us call this discontinuity, a cut. This cut is another paradox: a cesura of being, a deep psychic wound, an injury that the deft hand cannot afford, a material reward or share in the paternal dividend, in other words, the surplus skimmed off from the relationship between system and chaos—a metonymy of the subject itself. It works well until *something* precipitates the re-awakening of memory and the body, undoing of the temporal ordering of convenience.

Movement, stasis, nothing

The dead mother complements the indifferent father. In both films, the mother is musically inclined, a singer and a concert pianist respectively. Maternal musical memories are preserved intact in recordings of her voice. Rhythm imprisoned in sound boxes, notes Bachelard, invites us to consider the nature of duration, temporality, and materiality (Bachelard, *The Dialectic of Duration* 67). In the two films, the son is a witness of death. Flashback memories immobilize the body. Baby stands in the middle of a scrapyard, making sure a getaway car is crushed to an unrecognizable metal heap. The crushing of the car reminds him of himself watching and listening mummy recording a song in a studio booth. Cut to a happy scene, where the parents are giving him an early iPod as a present. Cut to the three of them in a car, first laughter, then quarrelling, then crush. Whilst remembering, he is immobilized, transfixed.

When Thomas begins to reconnect with music, he brings out old tapes of his mother's rehearsals. Sonia is heard saying: "Not good," and then: "I cannot focus, my heart is beating too hard," and soon afterwards: "The emotion is not very generous." Thomas is shifting through sheets of music until he finds her favorite Bach Toccata in F# minor. He begins to play hesitantly, with many errors, body tense, frustrated. Mother eludes him.

The preservation of the maternal memories suggests a deep and unfinished mourning, a catastrophe survived but not overcome. This is also evidenced by the inflexible way in which Baby treats music—it always must be the right kind for the right job—and in Thomas's claim of knowing music despite his mediocre skills. "A mistake in the speed, rhythm, or harmony would be catastrophic." note Deleuze and Guattari, "because it would bring back the forces of chaos" (Deleuze and Guattari 343). When Thomas approaches a conservatoire maestro to coach him to a professional level, he candidly tells the maestro what he does for a living and admits having abandoned the piano. The maestro cannot conceal his amusement and points out that Thomas may be a bit too old to start again. The latter confidently states: "But I know about it" (music).

Standing just outside the scene of death, having survived the fatal accident or outlived the mother, the child is fixed in an impossible position. Bachelard notes that the other's death veils the disquiet of one's own, and the fixing of memories, versus the regular rhythms of life, creates a temporal enjambment of deferred action (Bachelard, *The Dialectic of Duration* 44, 50). Deferred action, in turn, creates a void or, in the language of the two films, *the skipped beat*, that is the child, a cesura of being inside the arrhythmia of paternal indifference. For Lacoue-Labarthe the role of rhythm in relation to death, life, and representation lies in its kinship to the inside and outside of language in the topological imaginary of Lacan, Derrida, and others. I do not aim at exhausting the range of philosophical expressions of rhythm but to sketch out what is relevant to psychoanalysis in Lacoue-Labarthe's concept of the subject's suspension or desistance. Moving beyond inscribing the suspension of movement characteristic of death into the order of life necessitates a transition to relationality, in which going outside (*e-moi*) does not tend toward death but toward the other.

Lacoue-Labarthe discusses rhythm with close reference to Reik's autobiographical account and the latter's obsession with a melody of Mahler's which began with Karl Abraham's death. The melody haunts Reik, just as maternal music does the two protagonists of our films. In Reik's autobiography, the persistence of the melody over a number of years is coupled with serious difficulties in writing and producing intellectual work, and prompts Reik to analyze his feelings, his unfulfilled musical inclination, his intellectual debt to Freud and Abraham, and "to theorize and confess" (Aviram 212).

As a post-structuralist, Lacoue-Labarthe considers the self as a continual process of self-composition and self-writing, the disruption of which might turn into decomposition, even madness: "What am I? Anything I say in answer to this question is what I make of myself *at the moment*" (Aviram 208). Thus, Reik's obsession with the haunting melody registers a continuous attempt, even a compulsion of self-writing, and a failure to do so (Aviram 211). In discussing Reik's case, Lacoue-Labarthe acknowledges the importance of the Oedipal identification with a paternal figure (Lacoue-Labarthe 169), as per Lacan's mirror stage, and a rivalry with the father, which suggests that beneath mourning, in Reik's case at least, there is guilt and ambivalence (Lacoue-Labarthe 159). However, he is not interested in what the mirror of the imaginary can accomplish but what happens when it fails, pursuing the theme of death to the point where the specular self becomes unstable: "One can imagine," writes Aviram, "not only Reik looking in to the mirror—or into Mahler or Abraham—who serve as mirrors, but Reik himself holding himself up as another mirror, with the result that there is an endless series of reflections back and forth, in which *the self itself gets lost*" (Aviram 213, emphasis added). In this loss, the subject does not entirely vanish but *desists*, stands "outside-me" (e-moi). Death or loss is imperceptible. It is (de)constitution, "a muffled breakdown of the imaginary and of the resources of the imaginary" (Lacoue-Labarthe 174). Again, the important conclusion is not that (one's own) death must be imagined for the dialectic of recognition to function, but the fact that there is no unity or stability of the figural to permanently absorb it, since "the imago has no fixity or proper being" (Lacoue-Labarthe 175). The imaginary, notes Lacoue-Labarthes, destroys as much as it helps to construct (175). The moment where the subject begins to lose itself is the moment at which music comes to fill the gap (Aviram 214).

Lacoue-Labarthe emplaces desistance and rhythm within the horizon of figural ontology, considering death as discord that no speculation can dialectize (Lacoue-Labarthe 172, 174). This further allows him to posit music as an expression of mood (*Stimmung*) and affect (happy and unhappy) in an "unthinkable passage from chaos to figure" (186). Rhythm in this context is *the condition of possibility of the subject* (Aviram 217), simultaneously supporting figuration and pointing to *the abyss* of the subject, an impossible originary identification with originary suffering from which the subject is formed (Lacoue-Labarthe 186). Music both engulfs the subject and offers consolation through emotional discharge but "without losing [oneself] irretrievably." Finally, rhythm has priority over the visual register: "Rhythm," Lacoue-Labarthe writes, "of a specifically musical (acoustic) essence here, is prior to the figure of the visible schema, whose appearance, as such—its very possibility of being perceived—it conditions" (194).

Two important observations can be made at this point. The first is theoretical and concerns the *outside* of language. Lacoue-Labarthe ignores the dimension of the Real in Lacan's work, the outside of language par excellence, despite positing music as belonging neither to the register of the visual-imaginary nor to the symbolic as law, language, and custom, as a "sort of gap between two orders" (Aviram 211). Nor does he refer to the existence of the subject, which indexes the foundational lack and its alienation in the Other. Lacan discusses the impossibility of one's own death in *The Other Side of Psychoanalysis* where he considers the myth of the father's murder as told by Freud in *Totem and Taboo* to be a convenient *énoncé* (articulation) of the impossible (Grigg 59). The dead father presents us with the sign of *the impossible itself*, the Real of our own death as a category radically distinguished from the Imaginary and the Symbolic. Lacan writes: "No one knows, no living being in any case, what death is. It is remarkable that spontaneous productions formulated at the level of the unconscious are stated on the basis of this, that, for anyone, death is properly speaking unknowable" (Lacan 123). An experience that evokes death, then, is "a first step into nothingness" (Grigg 52, 53–58), always referring back to the Real and the constitution of the subject in language.

Of course, we can only speculate as to whether the oversight concerning the Lacanian Real is deliberate or not, but Lacoue-Labarthe does choose to stay within the bounds of consciousness and experience. Like the song of Deleuze and Guattari's child in the dark, rhythm becomes the accompaniment of the subject, a kind of mourning for one's own death, but, most importance, a marker of the *non-coincidence* with oneself as the founding condition of the subject. However, the drama that links repetition to the impossibility of one's own death and the possibility of life cannot be resolved; it can only ever be *performed and experienced.*

Verhaeghe notes that the novelty of the Mirror stage in Lacan lies in how it sums up ontology and man's relation to nature as one of *dehiscence* at the heart of the organism, a primordial discord: "The subject is always divided between something that it neither is nor has and something it will never be or have" (Verhaeghe 86). This division corroborates the *homology* between the structures of the body, the drive, the unconscious, and the subject. Lacan focuses on how this fundamental lack, which recurs on all levels of the subject, aims to restitute an older order (as drive and jouissance) and supports signification (87). Lacoue-Labarthe, then, seems to prioritize rhythm over the signifier (and desistance over *dehiscence*) at a very *special* moment, a moment of (symbolic) *destitution* in which lack and the collapse of the Other (including language) overpower the subject. One cannot inhabit that place forever and must return into the fold of The Other via rhythm—or risk permanent exclusion, in madness or in death.

Reik's musical obsession can also be understood in temporal terms. The temporality that interests Lacan in the clinic comprises three times, the instant of the glace, the time for comprehending, and the moment of concluding. The process of psychoanalysis effects a complete reconstitution of one's history as the analysand retroactively signifies sequences of events (Castagna 162). In Lacanian terms, then, the haunting melody conjoins two times, *the instant of the glance*, the first occurrence of the subject's "ignored' attribute (161), and *the time for comprehending*, in which the subject, unable to deal with its own lack, enters into reciprocal relations with others, transposing itself and "observing in the others the same experience of absence from which his desire for understanding begun" (161). We could say that Lacoue-Labarthe's definition of rhythm describes both the first gap of knowledge with which the subject "arises" in its symptom and the long stretch of time, the reality of the lengthy biographical experience.

Might we then propose that exploring how rhythms inhabits the multiple passages between instance and duration, allows us to create a more elaborate overview of experience over time? The Lacanian subject calls into question linear time and causality, since it is "interruption [temps d'arret]," rather than smooth flow of meaning, that determines the chain of events as "signifying" (Castagna 161). Lacan refers to sensed action rather than simple physical movement: doubt, haste, reasoning, choice, in a few words, the time of the subject's consciousness (161). The trajectory from ignorance to moments of concluding passes through discontinuity and interruption. In a very similar linguistic manner, Bachelard notes that failure, fear, curiosity, loss of interest, slowing down (Bachelard, *The Dialectic of Duration* 31), paralysis of action, and hesitation (*The Dialectic of Duration* 33) indicate that everything is experienced as discontinuity (36). Our temporal hesitation, adds Bachelard, is ontological and the positive experience of nothingness can help us clarify our experience of succession, knots, and duration in multiple ordering. Behind the temporal experience, lies a total failure that would shutter the subject (18) and, inversely, the constant recreation of being by itself (19). At the very heart of it, the rhythm of creation and destruction, work, and repose always refer to the dialectic of being and nothingness (21).

We could suggest that both Lacoue-Labarthe and Bachelard recognize rhythmic possibilities in the subject's experience of temporality which are, admittedly, only nascent in Lacan, but not incompatible with the signifier. Just like the signifier, rhythm may affect working through and work toward interpretation. It can certainly inhabit the longtime of comprehending. In the vein of an interpretation, Bachelard links invites us to appreciate what a backward glance—hypothetical, unavailable but not dissimilar to the Lacanian interpretation—could afford: a unique perspective into potentiality. Bachelard writes,

> If we had the wisdom to listen to the harmony of the possible within ourselves, we could recognize that the myriad rhythms of instants come to us bearing realities so precisely interrelated that we should understand the ultimately rational character of the pains and joys that reside at the source of being. Suffering, then, is always linked to redemption, joy always linked to intellectual effort. (Bachelard, *The Dialectic of Duration* 53)

In the Lacanian clinic, knowledge and interpretation can be affected by the analyst's manipulation of the length of the sessions. This form of punctuation segments the analysand's discourse into significative semantic modules (Castagna 163), and the *cutting* operates as discontinuous transformation (164). In culture, the inter-subjective encounter with many *others* provides a wide variety of intersecting rhythms and cuts which inflect subjects *with*-in their environments. In. Of course, the re-configuration of subjectivity and temporality in living assemblages cannot be compared to a clinical intervention. Deleuze and Guattari study their transformation with minimal attention to subjects through the concept of the refrain. The refrain sums up the relative stability of certain living rhythms as well as the forces transformation. Purely temporal in its inception, it describes assemblage and disassemblage, but above all, vital *movement*. Below, we consider how individuals change dynamically with their environments.

Passage through the imperceptible

If between the dead mother and the indifferent father the subject has nothing else to hang on to apart from their own rhythmic desistance, how does change occur? How does rhythm, refrain, and e-moi allow one to (re) gain access to *living* time? Bachelard writes, "A mechanism, [is] waiting to be set in motion by a future coincidence" (Bachelard, *The Dialectic of Duration* 53). For Civitarese becoming e-motional "can happen only within a new affective experience that is both lasting and profound" (Civitarese 902), like *becoming-child* in the hands of the lover, we might add, or becoming-musical. As process philosophers Deleuze and Guattari consider *movement* as the typical condition of being-becoming, a constant passage from milieu to milieu and territory to territory, and a creation of new assemblages when certain elements gain independence, converge, intensify, or acquire density. Movement supports a constant process of transcoding or transduction, "the manner in which one milieu serves as the basis for another, dissipates in it or is constituted in it" (Deleuze and Guattari 356). Not only does the living thing pass from one milieu into another, but "the milieus pass into one another [. . .]. In this in-between chaos becomes rhythm" (356).

In this flexible landscape, a refrain is defined as the creative inflection of expression and form: "We call a refrain any aggregate of matters of expression that draws a territory and develops into territorial motifs and landscapes" (Deleuze and Guattari 356). In Bartok's music, for instance, the refrain sums up the creative transformation of Hungarian folklore tunes into Bartok's own melodies. Transcoding requires a first type of refrain, which can be seen as a territorial or assemblage refrain (the folk melody), for one to transform it from within, deterritorialize it, producing a refrain of the second type as the end of music (385). At the same time, the refrain retains its agility, as motifs may take on variable speed and articulation, become mobile and opening routes toward other territories. Refrains are therefore classified as territorial; territorialized (like the lover's refrain, the lullaby, professional refrains, or when they mark new assemblages, or pass into new ones); and, finally, refrains that collect or gather forces at the heart of a territory or to go outside, departures that sometimes "bring on a movement of absolute deterritorialization" (360). In every case, the refrain is not imposed structure, only oscillations and passages from center (of an assemblage or territory) to exteriority and back (362). By the same token, rhythm is not a secondary attribute of temporal transformation but the very characteristic of every passage, even in drying up, death, or intrusion (345).

The temporal character of the refrain and the importance of rhythm are further revealed in the way they connect interiority to exteriority and past to present. The refrain is said to be catalytic, like a protein or a seed whose internal structure has two essential aspects: augmentations and diminutions, additions and withdrawals, amplifications, and eliminations. It is further characterized by *a retrograde motion* running from center to extremes and back, in "the strange retrograde motion of the Joke" (Deleuze and Guattari 384). If interiority and exteriority conjure images of centripetal and centrifugal forces gathering at the periphery or the center, it is because the refrain creates time. Deleuze and Guattari argue time is not an a priori form, the refrain is the apriori form of time "which, in each case, fabricates new times [temps: also "metres," "tempos"]" (385). While the fabrication of time is always in the present, it looks back to the past:

> Childhood scenes, children's games: the starting point of a childlike refrain, but the child has wings already, he becomes celestial. The becoming-child of the musician is coupled with a becoming-aerial of the child, in a non-decomposable block. The memory of an angel or the becoming of a cosmos. (386)

Deleuze and Guattari disperse the subject in the assemblage, leaving little room for its appearance. However, we might observe that rhythm defined as the pure time potentiality that resonates with a mnemic trace might not be incompatible with the psychoanalytic suggestion that rhythm is encrypted in the infant's body, providing an inter-corporeal link with that which lies on the side of the *un*mentalized and the primordial bond with an object "before there is really a subject;" a fantasy of the body which remains somatic, semiotic, pre- or sub-categorical "in fact, on the axis of ontogenesis the rhythmic/sensory/implicit/semiotic precedes the semantic/representational" (Civitarese 904)—ready to arise, we might add, under the right circumstances. In some cases, this vital transformation may be cut short and stasis may prevail; closures instead of the becoming-child of the musician, "paralysis of the finger and auditory hallucinations, Schumman's madness, cosmic forces gone bad, *a note that pursues you, a sound that transfixes you*" (Deleuze and Guattari 386). In the present chapter, we have encountered notes that transfix and melodies that immobilize, or even prevent music (331). However, a melody which indexes desistance or a cesura of being may well keep alive the umbilical connection between rhythm and nothingness (chaos).

Adopting a Bionian approach to rhythm as embryonic poetry and its ability to re-animate the body, Civitarese argues that rhythm (the basic pleasure and un-pleasure) is older than trauma (Civitarese 886), and draws attention to its significance in the trans-individual constitution of the subject. For Civitarese, rhythm must be understood as an organizing action in relation to chaotic life, and symbolization at a most basic level (906). As prior to trauma, rhythm may refer to the coincidence of pain and pleasure in Freud's reading of the *fort/da* but goes well beyond it. In a passage which chimes with Deleuze, as well as Lacoue-Labarthe, Civitarese writes: "From another point of view (other to the fort/da), this coinciding could also be called a constitutive non-coinciding of the subject with itself" (907). This difference is particularly relevant to sadomasochism as a composite movement which "destroys" the object while transforming it into no-thing, "thereby avoiding its turning into a noughtness" (908). We might then propose that the Deleuzian "prevention of music" finds its equivalent in a sadomasochistic movement which is commensurate with "the distance that the subject succeeds in placing between himself and the horror of the void" (908). It is, in fact, a rhythmic way of keeping the chaos at bay.

In Deleuze and Guattari, transformation is affected by a change of intensities, which operate in a rhizomatic way (Deleuze and Guattari 361), with no form or "correct" structure imposed from without or above; just an articulation from within, "as if oscillating molecules passed from one heterogeneous centre to another" (362). Processes of consolidation takes place but there is no beginning from which a linear sequence can derive, only densifications, intensifications, reinforcements, injections, and intercalary events. These are accompanied by "a superimposition of disparate rhythms, an articulation from within of an interrhythmicity, with no imposition of metre or cadence" (362). We come across a similar emphasis on movement in Bachelard, who argues that change has a temporal structure and is kaleidoscopic and discontinuous (Bachelard, *The Dialectic of Duration* 68). Movement creates a sense of duration out of what we usually experience in terms of continuities and discontinuities. "At the very most" notes Bachelard, "the apparently continuous duration of the subordinate psyche, consolidates the more broken form of intelligent thoughts and actions, broken by all its lacunae" (*The Dialectic of Duration* 78). This ploy is contrasted to the imperative of opening immanent time, which can be set in motion through particular rhythms of transitive time (95). Again, as in Deleuze and Guattari, there is no beginning per se, only intervals, superimposition of disparate rhythms, intrercalations, and inter-rhythmicity. The beginning always happens in-between, in the intermezzo.

In psychoanalytic terms, change is subtended by the human capacity to transform pain into pleasure. Linking with others in the Other (Civitarese 907) extends the work of the symbolic but ever neglected *string* in the *fort/ da* game. Civitarese not only elevates the role of the string but also links it directly to love:

> the Italian word *filarino*, which derives from *filo* (string) and *filare* (to form a sequence, to make sense), means "perfect love," and denotes a pair of lovers who have a perfect understanding. *Filare*, however, also stands for *amoreggiare* (to flirt). (896–97)

To that he adds: "Would not the first memories we can imagine take the form of *ordered rhythms* of sensations inscribed in the body?" (897, emphasis added). The string maintains contact between sensations, rhythmic memory, and the Other, providing a foundation for linking-with (legare) the other, territorializing sexuality, as Deleuze would put it with reference to the lover's refrain, opening infinite possibilities. Becoming emotional, venturing into the o/Other effects a passage from dissonance to linking and from dissonance to harmony. Falling in love, as we will see below, effects and is affected by a change in cadence and rhythm as new alliances are being formed, gather pace, and jar with the old ones.

Everything starts by chance in *The Beat That My Heart Skipped* (*De battre mon cœur s'est arrêté.*). Driving past a Parisian concert hall, Thomas comes across his mother's old manager. The latter assumes that Thomas is a professional pianist by now and invites him to an audition. Thomas is caught up in the dream of becoming a pianist. Through a Chinese student at the conservatoire, he finds himself a piano teacher, Miao Lin, to coach him for the audition. Miao Lin is a Chinese scholarship student and speaks no French. The piano lessons take place in her small flat, introducing a new rhythm, a new regularity. Miao Lin sets boundaries: She does not allow Thomas to smoke in the flat. The lack of linguistic communication means they focus on gestures, music, and the body. Thomas is tense as he plays. Miao Lin gestures to him to relax his wrists. Thomas obeys and begins again, until nerves and errors overcome him. Again and again Miao Lin's calm instruction links music to body and emotion to music. Thomas gets self-conscious and cannot play while she is watching. He asks Miao Lin to turn his back to him and look out of the window. She only turns toward him when she needs to intervene, to instruct. Miao Lin is patient with Thomas's errors; she corrects him gently, again and again, but explodes in an angry tirade in Chinese when he is disobedient and rude. Miao Lin can stand her ground. Thomas is taken aback and obeys. Gradually, familiarity creates a small space of reciprocity: she teaches him the piano, he teaches her French words for everyday objects. This brief scene is repeated in the film.

Miao Lin is not interested in Thomas, only in the music. She curates the melody, which is born slowly, grafted on the hands and the body. Their interaction segments time and produces new regularities, a new rhythm of visits and a new regime of inter-acting. Something (rather than someone) cuts and segments, repurposing the hands and re-programming the day. A new territory with a rhythmic pattern begins to establish itself. We could say that within this territory the (maternal) melody and the child are being nested or inscribed. Such a territory is not someone's direct doing. Surely, Thomas does not know how to be a concert pianist, and the viewer might consider his clumsy attempts with compassion, but this new assemblage is the assemblage of becoming (new, experimental, naive) as opposed to the one-off doing-knowing.

The new rhythm begins to *invade* the thuggery assemblage, introducing disruptions into that orderly life. Audiard stages these disruptions by setting up a rhythmic regularity of fast cutting between scenes in Miao Lin's flat and Thomas with friends, counter-posing the rhythms of the piano lessons to those of business, and melody to beat. For example, Thomas is seen alone in his flat; cut into a piano lesson; cut into Thomas running late to a meet with his associates; cut into another piano lesson; cut into the associates complaining that he is becoming soft, "Did you tell your dad?" and "What's in it [piano lessons] for us?" A recurring motif (a refrain of practicing fingers) invades the thuggery assemblage: Thomas practicing finger movements on different surfaces: the breakfast table, the bar, the dashboard, at home alone; hands now moving to a tune that does not belong to thuggery. Beat versus melody: the dealings with the father and the work associates are still punctuated by beat music when emotions run high or Thomas is left angry, but another rhythm runs ahead of-with the subject in pursuit of an elusive ideal, allowing the deficient ego to care of itself or to follow a line of flight grounded in a new temporality. Repeated cutting and passing augments the duration of the emerging assemblage until a new territory (becoming-music) is being established. We could even say that what used to de-sits now ex-sists: Thomas literally becoming part of *another scene* (pianist) while moving in and out of both.

Baby sits at the café where his mother used to work. Looking out of the window, his reflection merges with the passing traffic. Music drifts in and a young woman, Debora, walks through the door headphones on, singing a melody that sounds like an old Ronettes song: "b-a-be my baby." Baby in captivated by the sound and records her voice. He looks on as Debora vanishes through the kitchen doors. He takes his glasses off and plays the recording as she approaches to wait at his table. She pretends to be dismayed at being "monitored for quality purposes" but is smiling. Confused, Baby pretends to study the menu without realizing it is reading the kids' menu. Debora flips it over and asks him what he does for a living. He replies that he drives. "When was the last time you hit the road just for fun?" she asks. "Yesterday," Baby replies. All Debora wants is to head west on the 20 in a car she can't afford, "Just me and my music." When Baby pays her a compliment, she goes away singing "b-a-be my baby." Again, he turns.

The rhythms of courtship and flirtation are visually represented by circular or semi-circular camera movements in juxtaposition of rapid, linear, vectoral scenes of Baby's gang life. For example, after a badly executed robbery attempt, Baby is running on foot chased by policemen. He enters a mall, glasses on, one lens missing. He puts on a jacket and new glasses as camouflage, runs down the escalator and through an alarmed door, and so on. A meeting with Debora has a very different *mise en scène*. In a Laundromat, they sit next to each other, feet keeping time in unison to the beat of music in their headphones. "You are from here, you like music, you do not talk too much" says Debora. "I have spoken to you more today than I did in a year," Baby replies. They stand up and appear to be dancing around each other as they chat about their dead parents and how nothing ties them to the city anymore. They arrange to meet again. The scene fades away as a close up of the tumble dryer turning comes into focus, superimposed by a turning vinyl record. Basic though this visual metaphor is, it indexes the superimposition of affect, experience and memories, new and old rhythms.

Rhythm re-segments and regulates, adding a sustained link-link-link to the cut-cut-cut of rapid change, the "responsiveness and recognition without verbalized symbolization" (Knoblauch 425). De-intensifications, intervals, and superimpositions, slowing down and producing variable speeds halfway between stillness and frantic movement, cause the subject to be carried ahead and carried away, first in rhythm, ahead of itself, in an interval, in-between assemblages. Rhythm ties critical moments ensures the passing from one milieu to another. These moments can be retrospectively systematized in sequences of conscious actions, where the *I* seems to have triumphed over adversity, but in the fluid present they always repeat, letting oneself be interpreted by what one is repeating (see Civitarese 909; Aviram 208).

Again, it is not the "miracle of love" that we are talking about when we are arguing in favor of rhythm but its *catalytic* potential, better seen when we focus on the contours of communication and the weave of interlacing possibilities. The analyst-analysand dyad illustrates the point. In language that almost chimes with Deleuze and Guattari's, Knoblauch speaks of multiple levels of dialogic rhythm, "each of which, as well as the interaction of which, constructs a wash of heterogeneous affective possibilities and meaning" (Knoblauch 424). He further envisages the space opened by rhythm as filled by "a form of 'language' [. . .] communicating meaningful affective state and state of change, a communication that is not possible to articulate in the language of words at this point" (422). A communication in rhythm, Knoblauch continues, "catalyzes a shift in the affective/cognitive/kinesthetic blending that now is transforming into a new polyrhythmicity" (422). Opacities, previously camouflaged by habitual patterns and cultural tropes of power and status, are being challenged, effecting "a powerful mutative emotional metamorphosis" (423). Analyst and analysand do not merge in the process, and meanings remain different to each one, yet related by the rhythmic flows created by both (ibid.). Such a catalytic effect is the gist of Deleuze and Guattari's description of the refrain as catalyst, glass harmonica, or a prism which "acts upon that which surrounds it, sound, and light, extracting from the various vibrations, or decompositions, projections, or transformations" (Deleuze and Guattari 384).

Rhythm binds, holds, and liberates. Courtship and flirtation as rhythmic events transmute the string of memory into an amorous motif: becoming child, relaxing the hands, accepting helplessness (*hilflosigkeit*), being abandoned in the hands of the lover. In-toning the body, containing frustration, harnessing the too-muchness of self-control, loosening up and failing, constitute working from and, gradually, *through* the black hole and the chaos. To be clear, nothing positivizes the void of loss. If psychoanalysis incorporates block, shock, and disability into a larger rhythm of decimation and flow (Eigen 722), the movement between blockage and flow, trauma and new beginning, breakdown and recovery always constitutes a rhythmic possibility of Eros as pro-tension toward an ambiguous future.

Re-configuration and ambiguity

This chapter explores rhythm at the junction between psychoanalysis and certain strands of European philosophy. My guiding light was the resonance between Oedipal formations of desire and rhythmic forces that contribute to their unclasping, dissolution, or resolution in ways that allow one to move on or leave their assemblage behind (Deleuze and Guattari 359). With reference to the two films, our starting point was the two young men's attempt to fix a fragile point as center in the middle of chaos, to answer the difficult question of the Other's desire (what am I in the Other?), and to bear a psychic stagnation similar to being dead or frozen in the middle of a busy life (Am I dead or alive?). Negotiating the passage between desisting and existing, as I hope to have shown, is a rhythmic undertaking which exceeds the conscious subject and its capacity to act at will. Bachelard offers a good perspective for this endeavor when saying that to think, live, and feel we need to bring order into our actions "by holding instants together through the reliability of rhythm, and by uniting reasons for coming to a vital conviction" (Bachelard, *The Dialectic of Duration* 29). Ordering by rhythm affords a sense of interpreting and acting, which, in turn, creates a sense of duration (*The Dialectic of Duration* 45), despite the fact that we ultimately fail to command duration (47). One is carried along by rhythms but may also grasp and alter them. Various forms of psychic suffering are characterized by Bachelard as temporal upheavals that shutter lives: "We die of an absurdity," Bachelard writes (29). Perhaps, we might add, we desist in somnambulistic living.

Change is rhythmic, as is moving between organized fields of libidinal ties and power relations, territories, and assemblages, which may be strengthened and weakened and which one inhabits, leaves behind, or is imprisoned by. But there is always movement. Taking movement out of the living scene, all we are left with is absolute stillness, still life. Making it identical with the repetitive *fort/da* game, we run the risk of missing the very potentiality of rhythm as com-possibility of being-becoming. In that sense, the question *am I dead or alive* is always addressed obliquely. Living inside-outside, in the de-centeredness this peculiar topological shift between interiority and exteriority, affords an openness of being and co-existing in different movements: instinctual, individual, cultural, and epochal.

An assemblage, note Deleuze and Guattari, should always open up to cosmic forces (Deleuze and Guattari 386). At this point, we might be allowed to offer a crude correspondence between refrains as organized rhythms and psychic orders; between forces of chaos and trauma or loss; territorialized forces and the symbolic or the structures of capitalism; cosmic forces and the processual; and the virtual and the real (345). Inhabiting these multiple rhythms, a young thief and a would-be pianist move between the (missing) symphony-harmony and cacophony, caught up in the cross-secting forces that turn the latter into the former. In the end, the apparent triumph of love, of the Other, shows what is at stake: the lover's refrain as a glass harmonium or prism defracts the rhythmic pattern of reciprocity and loss on different levels. As passage into the Other, we might argue, it allows for a moment of *interpretation* (reinforced by faith into the Other and fidelity) which ensures that this lover's refrain can be carried into the future (but always harks back to being lost and contained). Natality, argue Deleuze and Guattari, is insepa-rable from the movement of decoding and passing to the margins of the code (366). Natality is also the ambiguity between the territory and deterritoriali-zation (359). It might, therefore, be argued that natality may refer to the pas-sage from unclasping of restrictive bonds, to the transformation, if not death, of the father and the mother and the openness-contingency of the Other. In fact, to assemble anything means to assemble what destroys one (Eigen 735).

Deleuze and Guattari argue that whenever there is transcoding, we can be sure that there is not a simple addition, but the constitution of *a new plane*, as of a *surplus value*. A melodic or rhythmic plane, surplus value of passage or bridging. The two cases, however, are not pure; they are in reality mixed. It is quite possible and, indeed, tempting to see the accommodation of the subject in this new formation, as the re-absorption of the surplus into a dif-ferent or higher order, for example, of the thief as surplus paternal-phallus into the order of love. Here, jouissance is reclaimed by assuming the posi-tion of the *object a* in a new sinthomatic formation. On every level, including the level of the cosmic (the thief and the thug as capitalist instantiations), something is lost and recuperated, and rhythm allows one to see oneself as something else, making bearable the periodic evanescence of the I, while becoming incidental, adjunct, invisible, and unique. Circulating in that way can be compared to being in the long circuits of Lacan's graph of desire.

We can further refine this position with reference to Lacan and Deleuze and Guattari if we turn to the definitions of the place of organization and the plane of consistency in the latter. The two planes do not compete with or cancel each other out but constitute alternative geometries. Deleuze and Guattari describe the plane of organization (or development) as structural or genetic; a hidden structure necessary for forms, a teleological plan(e), a design, and a mental principle (293). The plane of consistency (or composi-tion), on the other hand, is permeated by

> relations of movement and rest, speed and slowness between unformed elements, or at lease elements that are relatively unformed, molecules and particles of all kinds. [. . .] Nothing subjectifies, but haecceities form according to compositions of nonsubjectified powers or affects. (294)

This geometrical plane is not tied to a mental design but to an abstract design, in which "form is constantly being dissolved, freeing time and space" (294). We could propose that the organization of desire after the model of lack (and Thing, *object a*) and rhythm might relate to one another as plane of organization to plane of consistency in Deleuzian philosophy (for a similar argument, see Voela and Esin).

As an element of the plane of consistence rhythm assumes an intermediary role inscribing several things happening simultaneously: foray into the unknown, becoming, holding, pretensions of mastery. We are in a better position now to appreciate the fundamental question expressing how rhythm responds to the question *am I dead or alive?* by complementing the cesura (of being) with linking (with the other). Silence or rhythm (rhythm and skipped beat, I and not-I). The challenge is how *to be the link*, not the cesura (as equivalent to silence, aporia, the black hole), how to respond to being the opening of (a basic) rhythm to the possibilities of external forces. Indeed, this is neither imaginary nor symbolic; neither pre-linguistic nor maternal; it is infra-symbolic and composition-al.

So let us bring this argument back to Lacan: Rhythm, and by extension the refrain as a territorialized set of rhythms, is not the same as the signifying chain and not the same as the death drive. Verhaeghe argues that the subject is not split but quartered, ex-tended between the pulsating substance of the living organism (life), the signifier, the drive, and the complexity of gender. These levels are held together loosely, in a relationship of homology to one another. One could argue that movement and rhythm conjoin the four levels of being in Verhaeghe's description, always moving "Towards [as] self-movement of expressive qualities and variable speeds independent of the drives they combine or neutralize" (Deleuze and Guattari 350). Evidently, ordinary lives embrace speed and movement as (external) characteristics of their milieu. And it is at certain junctions that we glimpse ways in which individual and epochal symptoms coalesce or fall apart, creating the volatile conditions upon which new sinthomatic formations might emerge, or provide opportunities to either *run through* or *work through* the predicaments of one's modern life.

What happens in the end? Let's return to Baby and Thomas one last time, as they finally break away from the parental assemblage. New possibilities open with a different kind of vulnerability which echoes losses through libidinal linkages that make the world habitable. The two film endings are appropriately ambiguous.

In *Baby Driver*, wanted for robbery, Baby runs away with Debora, but the law finally catches up with them on a narrow bridge. Blocked in both directions by police cars, Baby checks his surroundings for possible escape routes. Not wanting to endanger Debora's life, he surrenders. In prison, they think he is dumb. A doctor examines his ears and certifies that his hearing is fine. Baby gets a 25-year sentence, and he is eligible for parole in five, due to good behavior and witnesses testifying about his consideration for human life in the last robbery. Debora sends him retro postcards of big automobiles in coastal landscapes. Baby sticks them on the mirror. "I can't get use to the fact that your real name is Miles," Debora writes. Baby looks at himself (and the cards) in the mirror. He daydreams of Debora waiting outside in a classic car. The scene is black and white at first but then fades into color.

Toward the end of *The Beat That My Heart Skipped*, Thomas's father is murdered by a business associate, Minskof, whom he threatened to expose. In the final scene, two years after this event, Thomas is driving Miao Lin to a concert hall for a performance. On the way he reassures her that she will give a great performance and talks to her about housekeeping matters and forthcoming events in London and New York. We gather he is now her husband and agent. Thomas drops Miao Lin off at the front of the concert hall and promises to be with her soon after parking the car. In the men's restroom he chances upon Minskof who is formally dressed and obviously attending the event. Minskof does not know him. Thomas beats him badly, possibly to death. Then he enters the auditorium, a bit disheveled and with a blood stain on his shirt, but no one seems to notice. He sinks in his seat from which he has a clear view of Miao Lin playing on stage. He fixes her eyes on her with a strange, contented smile following the piano melody with his fingers.

Works cited

Audiard, Jacques, et al. *The Beat That My Heart Skipped*. Why Not Productions, Sédif Productions, France 3 Cinéma, 2005.

Aviram, Amittai F. *Telling Rhythm: Body and Meaning in Poetry*. University of Michigan Press, 1994.

Bachelard, Gaston. *Intuition of the Instant*. Translated by Eileen Rizo-Patron, Northwestern University Press, 2013.

——. *The Dialectic of Duration*. Translated by Mary McAllester Jones, Clinamen Press Ltd., 2000.

Castagna, Marco. "Psychoanalysis at the Test of Time: Jacques Lacan's Teaching." *The Concept of Time in Early Twentieth-Century Philosophy*, edited by Flavia Santoianni, vol. 24, Springer International Publishing, 2016, pp. 157–66, http://link.springer.com/10.1007/978-3-319-24895-0_18.

Civitarese, Giuseppe. "Masochism and Its Rhythm." *Journal of the American Psychoanalytic Association*, vol. 64, no. 5, Oct. 2016, pp. 885–916, https://doi.org/10.1177/0003065116674442.

Deleuze, Gilles, and Félix Guattari. *A Thousand Plateaus: Capitalism and Schizophrenia*. Continuum, 2008.

Eigen, Michael. "A Basic Rhythm." *The Psychoanalytic Review*, vol. 89, no. 5, Oct. 2002, pp. 721–40, https://doi.org/10.1521/prev.89.5.721.22103.

Gentile, Katie. "Generating Subjectivity through the Creation of Time." *Psychoanalytic Psychology*, vol. 33, no. 2, 2016, pp. 264–83, https://doi.org/10.1037/a0038519.

Grigg, Russell. "3 Beyond the Oedipus Complex." *Jacques Lacan and the Other Side of Psychoanalysis*, edited by Justin Clemens and Russell Grigg, Duke University Press, 2020, pp. 50–68, https://www.degruyter.com/document/doi/10.1515/9780822387602-004/html.

Knoblauch, Steven H. "Contextualizing Attunement within the Polyrhythmic Weave: The Psychoanalytic Samba." *Psychoanalytic Dialogues*, vol. 21, no. 4, July 2011, pp. 414–27, https://doi.org/10.1080/10481885.2011.595322.

Lacan, Jacques. *The Other Side of Psychoanalysis*. Translated by Russell Grigg, W.W Norton & Company, 2007.

Lacoue-Labarthe, Philippe. *Typography: Mimesis, Philosophy, Politics*. Edited by Christopher Fynsk, Stanford University Press, 1998.

Rajchman, John. *Truth and Eros: Foucault, Lacan and the Question of Ethics*. Routledge, 2013.

Verhaeghe, Paul. *Beyond Gender: From Subject to Drive*. Other Press, 2001.

Voela, Angie, and Cigdem Esin. "Movement, Embrace: Adriana Cavarero with Bracha Lichtenberg Ettinger (and the Death Drive)." *Hypatia*, vol. 36, no. 1, 2021, pp. 101–19, https://doi.org/10.1017/hyp.2020.49.

Wright, Edgar, et al. *Baby Driver*. TriStar Pictures, Media Rights Capital (MRC), Working Title Films, 2017.

Chapter 6

Burning

Afterburn and Lawlessness in the Anthropocene

Jessica Datema and Manya Steinkoler

Lee Chang Dong's *Burning* (Lee, Ah-in, et al.) shows how fire is a manifestation of contemporary societal imbalance, destabilization, and compartmentalization. These cultural pressures are symptoms of degeneration in the Anthropocene that threatens nature and our whole ecosystem. The film shows this degeneration through the class differences and smoldering social ties of three young South Korean characters. Their triangular tryst burns boundaries, ignites fires, and eventually extinguishes everyone but the main character, Jong-su. The film is entitled *Burning* to show the literal and figurative fires that are accelerating and scorching global communities, families, and cultures, in this case, North and South Korea.

Burning is an adaptation of a short story by Haruki Murakami (Murakami, "Barn Burning"), who, in turn, based it on William Faulkner's famous short story "Barn Burning" (Faulkner). The film's protagonist is Jong-su, whose antagonist is Ben, a Korean Gatsby figure and con artist who burns women after using them, rendering their bodies and his crimes untraceable. The fiery interaction of the characters exemplifies the symptoms of our time: income inequality, imaginary rivalry, tribalism, political division, and narcissistic exceptionalism. Fire is emblematic not only of the serial killer Ben but also of the burning which results from political and social tumult. The adaptations make evident how countries like Korea, and the United States, continue to foment cultural divisions and natural devastations instead of sustainability. *Burning* shows how globalization fans the unruly flames of an afterburn caused by the foreclosure of law, which ignites social relations.

Truth and lies are virtually indistinguishable in Lee Chang Dong's film,[1] a parable of the corruption and excess of our contemporary world and a summons to meaningful action therein. The film is set at the South Korean border with excursions to Africa and TV clips of Trump in America proclaiming the need for a border wall. The setting underlines a wearied anxiety concerning the decline, abuse, and spreading destruction of social relations. *Burning* shows how an accelerated global society does not serve to unite citizens in difference, but divides and endangers nations, laws, individuals, as well as our planet.

DOI: 10.4324/9781003194033-9

The film exposes how communities have become a seething cauldron of endless panic. This is because society and desire no longer organize around sustainability and a sacrifice that concerns *philia*. Community fails as citizens forgo balanced rituals and shared undertakings, the original sacrifices that served as an impetus toward civilization. Instead, community is a fire where citizens are reduced to consumerism through accelerated rhetoric and technology, the unwitting partner of the death drive. With the lack of shared cultural activities, there is only *jouissance* acting out (*passage à l'acte*) and provocation. The symbolic breakdown of language into abbreviations, tweets, following, unfriending, canceling, and propaganda accompanies the breakdown of the social realm and shared histories. Fake news, fascist rhetoric and the perverse enjoyment that sustains them are the smoke screen that both covers and reveals the *in flagrante delicto* of what is really going on: the incineration of truth by inflamed rhetoric.

Burning shows how globalization affects communities and creates blank characters unaware of the symbolic history that has determined their position. We see this even in the film's title that evokes the fire of the drive, overwhelming language, undermining the possibility of a word that could bind. The foreclosure of history, law, and memory is the afterburn that continually overrides cooperative dialogue, subjugating it, and reducing it to ashes. Reasonable discourse can no longer be relied upon or taken for granted.

In this regard, the film's protagonist is significantly named Jong-su, also spelled Jeong-soo or Jeng-su, a Korean name that means upright, outstanding, virtuous, and chaste. Over the course of the film, as a kind of critique of the world we have just described, Jong-su lives up to his name as a symbolic mandate by putting an end to Ben's serial burning. As he fathoms Ben's monstrosity, Jong-su begins to realize that he will never learn the truth from him. Nor will he ever finally have proof of what he knows about the disappearance of his beloved Haemi, namely that she was murdered, and her remains were burned and discarded. In the end, Jong-su must believe and act on what he unconsciously detects more than what he can prove.

Jong-su's act can be thought of as a hard-boiled instantiation of Dupin's letter, illustrating Poe's opening Senecan epithet, *nil sapientiae acuminate minio*, "Nothing is more hateful to wisdom than cunning" (Poe 192). In the story, Minister D forces Dupin to act; he forces the arm of the law to catch him (Muller and Richardson 91). At the same time without evidence, Dupin can act undetected; his clever deduction shows that the law can be protected by logical deduction itself. This is no longer the case today. Ben's flagrant burning, his murdering of women, his amassing of wealth, his provocative behavior is the letter on the table that goes unpunished, forcing Jong-su to arrest Ben's monstrous *jouissance*.

Ben taunts or even seduces Jong-su with the suggestion that he is the murderer, putting him on a discovery mission to find out the truth. In this sense, the film recalls Poe's "Purloined Letter" in that the murdered woman is like the letter on the table, there to be seen if one can read what is in front of one's eyes. Around the to-be-murdered-woman, a Poe-like triangulation fuels both the criminal murderer, a man who dares all things, as well as the protagonist, who ultimately executes the criminal to reestablish the law. While murder is a provocation of the law, Jong-su's act is an execution of the law. The lawless seduction and provocation of Jong-su by Ben for the entire film requires that he answer, and he does.

Jong-su does detective work on Ben not only to eliminate the serial crim-inal, but also to make the narrative that becomes the film. *Burning* creates and resolves the crime that is the film's narrative, which mirrors the social and political discourse of wrongdoing and negligence that rules culture today. The end of Ben's burning is the beginning of Jong-su's story and the filmic narrative itself. Here, fire becomes the principal metaphor as trans-formative, allowing language and art to rise out of its destructive wake. As Lacan tells us in *Seminar XV*, the psychoanalytic act, there is an absence of contradiction between Saint John's "In the beginning was the Word," and Goethe's "In the beginning was the action" (Lacan). In the film, the end contains the act that makes the narrative a film. *Burning* is a *mise en scene* of this marriage between word and act.

Presciently writing three quarters of a century ago and critiquing the positivism of Freud's *Woll es War, soll ich werden,*[2] Maurice Blanchot remarked, "All speech is violence" (Blanchot, *The Writing of the Disaster* 42). The force of the drives resides at the end(s) of speech. This force can be channeled by *Eros*, or, as we see more often today, inflicted on self or other by *Thanatos*. Ben's provocative silence, fast driving, and bragging about burning are a manifestation of the death drive in overdrive. While a killer, Ben is also a product of the one percent as the spoiled limit-less child of excessive wealth. In contrast, Jong-su stands for the dignity of every man and possibilities of phoenix-like restitution via aesthetic engagement. He ennobles the working class with his care for reading, writing, language, and love, which propels him to act. After multiple provocations, Jong-su initiates a new narrative in the final scene, putting an end to Ben's criminal burning of women.

A serial murderer, Ben is bereft of symbolic castration. It is notable that there is not a lot of dialogue in *Burning*, rather, the film depicts a world in which dialogue has broken down and violence emerges. As perverse, Ben murders the women he dates by burning them in green houses, then brag-ging about his crimes euphemistically. In this way, Ben is the literal mani-festation of the death drive of capitalism, making life into death. Ben is so bold as to taunt Jong-su. Yet, the literate working class Jong-su calls Ben the Korean Gatsby. He hears Ben in a way that the serial killer could not have imagined and responds by executing him. In the end, Jong-su's murder of Ben is both a literal and figurative essential act that creates the filmic narrative and curbs the burning.

The end of the film features Jong-su making a real separation between life and death by executing Ben by fire. Jong-su displays his own manhood in this gesture that contrasts with Ben, who becomes the very woman he was attempting to separate from by way of his serial killing. Given that for the pervert, separation can only occur in the real, Jong-su realizes the futility of any symbolic cut. His execution is a real act that creates lack. The act makes the execution into a new story that is the culmination of the film and a comment on society. It is as if *Burning* admonishes all of us to rise up and act in the name of the law, the earth, and the future, and to do away with those strong-arm leaders that are hailing the end of democracy. Ben is a wealthy and shifty con like current day fascists Kim Jong-Un and Donald Trump. They reign as tyrants, caring for no one, scorching global communities, and leaving barrenness in their wake.

The film underlines our current day political reality where society is operating without any shared history. Ideals once helped to occlude the real, but now ignite and combust the subject. The lack of ideals is portrayed as both an external social and internal psychic reality in the film, which reflects our world today. Modifying the short stories of William Faulkner and Haruki Murakami, the filmmaker weaves a tale where art, creation, and even acting are crucial for witnessing and retelling history. Director Lee Chang Dong finds a kind of double in his protagonist, the aspirational writer, Jong-su, who composes a narrative and enacts an execution to reestablish the law. By way of both his writing and the execution, Jong-su engages in action where law fails. As such, the film promotes investigated engagement in the face of impotence and passivity, a stasis that is precisely the source of our current anxiety.

Burning shows that the perverse enjoyment and speed of global capital threatens the fragility of justice which is bulldozed in its wake. Ben flies from Korean to Africa and back, speeds across the Korean border, and scorches natural and cultural relations with ease. This monstrous *jouissance* involves the magnification of division in society. Moreover, the film shows how the historic divisions in North and South Korea are not dissimilar to those between the American South and North during the Civil War as Faulkner references. In Korea, the Communist North is split from the rest of the country by a demilitarized zone.

Similar divisions still haunt the United States, fomenting the current political divisions. Southern reactionaries wish for a return to the past with fascist leaders who would bring back the master. Such extremism is on the ascent today, as seen in the wish for the "South to rise again" in the name of a kind of pre-symbolic idealized utopia. This regressive and nostalgic erasure of history and symbolic difference uses propaganda and *jouissance* to replace communal ambivalence and complexity, which are foreclosed. Extremists call to storm the capital, reinstall walls, and revive national boundaries as monumental substitutes for history, merely mark symbolic failure and the foreclosure of law. Electric fences and steel walls only exhibit a lack of mobility, cultural divisions, and a collapsed paternal metaphor.

After the American Civil and Korean wars, these countries were split—either officially and unofficially—with rhetoric, divisions, or walls between the North and South. Walls are an attempt to mitigate and foreclose the afterburn of political and psychological trauma, difficult memories of national historic events. Korea, unlike the American South, was unified after the Civil War, yet Lincoln's assassination weakened reconstruction which led to Jim Crow. The film shows how unresolved past political traumas return in present day divisive social interactions, as with Ben, Jong-su, and Haemi who lack a shared discourse.

Society and desire are no longer organized by discourse or a shared history but through objects of enjoyment. This inability to mourn or make a narrative out of symbolic and historic losses affects everyone as the afterburn of historic amnesia:

> In France the word "history" has disappeared from the curriculum, to be replaced by the expression "situate yourself in time" and the bundling together of events with no reference to chronology. It is the tomb of Lavisse and the way given to the mourners of guilt. Paradoxically however, history returns where we did not expect it: in the event, real. (Brousse)

Moral or legal losses and concerns are being replaced by the fetishization of consumption, and the hybridization of desire into self-segregating narcissistic and cowardly culture wars.

Fake news, toxic tribalism, alternative facts, and disinformation are causing more fires as Brousse describes: "On Saturday 1 December Paris was burning, according to headlines around the world." The "yellow vest" protests of 2018 were just the beginning. Looting riots and fires followed in 2020, America's first summer of the pandemic. Discourse has been hybridized and unanchored such that, "We have passed to an open dictatorship of the surplus-*jouissance*" (Brousse). Without limits, the rioters beget fire and violence. Their looting exhibits the lack of lack, or any link to the other, a split between meaning and the real. Without an understanding of history, the past will return in the real.

In this manner, the fragility of justice that results from the failed name of the father is shown throughout the film as well as from the stories from which it was adapted. In both the film and Faulkner's story, the fathers of the protagonists are on trial for crimes; in Faulkner's story, Snopes, the vagrant father, is burning the barns of his social superiors, and in *Burning*, Jong-su's father commits obstruction of justice and is sentenced to jail. Both Jong-su's jailed father, who exemplifies North Korean leaders, and Snopes, who exemplifies the Confederate father, aid and abet the foreclosure of history.

Snopes, like Ben, consumes the earth and the economy. In addition to horse trading, Snopes is a sharecropper for the landowners during reconstruction who were familiar with profiting off free labor from slavery. In Faulkner's tale as in the film, class resentment abounds due to the political fallout after a Civil War, as manifest in the burning.

In *Burning*, the class conflict escalates after Jong-su warns his girlfriend Haemi that Ben is a modern-day Korean Gatsby. Ben's wealth is decadent and of uncertain origin like the plantation owners during Reconstruction who had to reinvent themselves to retain their money. Ben, like Snopes, is unwilling and unable to take care of anything or participate in any social bond, except provocation and destruction. When Jong-su asks Ben what he does, he claims to be involved in the import-export business, which "does this and that, you wouldn't understand even if I told you, I play. Work is play." Toward the end of the film after murdering their mutual girlfriend, we see Ben hinting at "burning" while reading Faulkner in front of Jong-su. This is the film's suggestion that Jong-su writes Ben out as the murderous villain, even though he, like Snopes or Trump, fancies himself as star.

Significantly, filmic scenes in a court of law never include Ben. *Burning* includes court appearances with Jong-su as with Snopes' son in Faulkner's short story. "Barn Burning" begins in a court that smells of moldy cheese, suggesting that the law has turned rotten. In both the film and in Faulkner's story, the son is at once witness and inheritor of a corrupt and bereft father. After having served their governments, both fathers believe their country is criminal, doubting the law and provoking their own sons. The sons are in the position of repairing a malignant inheritance yet most of them, like Ben, just act out like the primal father.

As an exception, Jong-su served in the military. He tells Haemi this while showing her pictures of him as a soldier at his home. Still, she is not impressed and falls for Ben, whose jet setting lifestyle is more appealing. A lawyer at his father's trial asks Jong-su whether he is finished with college and why he hasn't found a job yet. After hearing that Jong-su wants to be a writer, the barrister tries persuading him to craft a petition on behalf of his father. The story of the petition only underscores a theme of the film, namely how any act is initiated after the foreclosure of law. Jong-su's petition is a mode of ritual engagement that leads to participation, rather than a reinstatement of the foreclosed law. At the same time, it allows Jong-su to defend his community, farm, and father through an appeal. This act inspires him to later defend Haemi's memory and put a stop to Ben's crimes, including his evasion of justice.

In Faulkner's story, the collapse of the father forces Snopes' son, just like Jong-su, to expose the truth of a rotten paternal inheritance. Jong-su writes not only about the burning regarding Ben's women, but also, importantly, about his own mother's disappearance when he was a boy. We see that disappearing women is part of Jong-su's traumatic history. In both Faulkner's story and the film, sons are put into the position of upholding truth and law after the paternal function breaks down and is unable to provide any legal or paternal support; indeed, far worse, the sons must act within and as a direct result of its total failure. Because of this lack, sustaining the paternal function becomes more impossible yet more necessary. Instead of reinstalling the paternal metaphor, *Burning* suggests a bold enactment that revives an understanding of history and concern for nature as related to femininity, and in this case disappearing women.

At the end of Faulkner's "Barn Burning," the son betrays his father and upholds the law by warning the landowners that Snopes has just set fire to their barn (Faulkner 24). In alerting the landowners, the son severs ties with his father's bad inheritance and engages in an enactment. This act severs him from Snopes, whose motto is "wood and hay kin burn." In this phrase, "can" sounds the same as "kin" due to Snopes' Southern accent, at the same time underlining the destruction of inheritance and paternity. What is burning inside of Snopes is his confederate legacy and vengeance for being humiliated. By way of the warning, the son not only saves the landowners from their barn burning but he also acts to sever ties with his own kin by "betraying" his Confederate father.

The collapse of the paternal function forces both Snopes' son and Jong-su to become men by crossing the Rubicon, acting in ways that sever their past to create a new future. For Ben and the children of the one percent, their inheritance just foments passivity and the death drive through entitlement. While *Burning* could be considered a crime story, Ben's crime, like the crimes in our current political environment, are sustained, grave and flagrant all the while remaining undiscovered. The film highlights the way cultural divides and geographical boundaries are an attempt to mitigate and cover over grave crimes. The film shows once again how everyday life is the afterburn of unresolved rifts. "Fire feels like family," is a quote from Murakami's "Landscape with Flatiron," a reworking of Faulkner's story, "Barn Burning" (Murakami, "Landscape with Flatiron") that exemplifies how every facet of cultural ties are scorched.

While there is no mention of the Japanese colonization of Korea, Haruki Murakami's "Barn Burning" shifts the political situation to disturbing and subtle social interactions. In Murakami's "Barn Burning," the narrator's casual girlfriend's latest boyfriend, an apparent businessman, reveals to the narrator that he has a secret penchant for setting fire to barns, and then the girlfriend disappears (Murakami, "Barn Burning"). While not overt, the story appears to allude to the stifled historic fact of missing Korean women due to Japanese internment before World War II. Likewise, in the film, Jong-su's mother and girlfriend Haemi go missing without explanation. He is left, like the mixed babies from before the war that were half Korean and half Japanese alone ostracized. No one cared for the babies or recorded what happened to these "comfort women." *Burning* is about what no one sees or records, even state sanctioned crimes like separating the refugee children from their families at America's borders.

Fire also appears in a later Murakami story, included in *After the Quake* (2000) (Murakami, "Landscape with Flatiron"). This collection is, indeed, about characters suffering from the fall out of the real Great Hanshin Kobe earthquake that happened on January 17, 1995, in Kobe, Japan when 50,000 buildings were destroyed and 300,000 were left homeless. Murakami refines his story "Barn Burning" in this later story "Landscape with Flatiron," which features not only a missing girl but also another male character named Miyake who is displaced by the uncanny quake and builds fires. In that story, the quake victim makes bonfires to control the afterburn from the Kobe Quake. The fire becomes a symbol of renewal after political and social upheavals, a force that divides and displaces cultures but can still warm.

What there is of the concealed crime story in *Burning* becomes Jong-su's narrative. The film shows how there is no legal arbitration on the national or global level that protects the neighbor, woman, citizen, or environment. Instead, there is only fuming propaganda and unrelenting hostility, as portrayed with the blaring propaganda from a North Korean loudspeaker in the demilitarized zone near Jong-su's house.

"Fire feels like family" also refers to the uncanny homelessness of the characters in *Burning*. Jong-su is living in the aftermath of political and social dissolution when he returns home to his abandoned country house after serving as a South Korean soldier. His Paju home on the border of North and South Korea is blitzed by loud propaganda broadcasts. The country house is barren save a lone calf. The animal is a metaphor for Jong-su as the sacrificial son.

Throughout the film the phone rings, but no one speaks when Jong-su answers. Since Jong-su's mother abandoned the family when he was young; she calls but doesn't say anything to hear his voice. After she left, Jong-su's father forced him to burn all her clothes, symbolically destroying her. Flashbacks to this primal heart-wrenching scene occur when Jong-su realizes that his girlfriend, Haemi, has been burned, that is, murdered by Ben. In the end, Jong-su's vengeance upon Ben exorcises the early abandonment by and destruction of his mother.

Significantly, this burning of the mother's memory occurs in the context of global and national schisms, with the feminine connected to the earth's demise in the current trend of global warming. *Burning* shows the disappearance and destruction of femininity and the natural world through many cinematic motifs, including the extinguished greenhouses, Jong-su's abandoned home, and Haemi's cat. The cat is enigmatic and only visible at the end of the film even though earlier Haemi asks Jong-su to watch it while she travels to Africa. As such, Jong-su becomes the keeper of the feminine space. Haemi exclaims, "a cat should not be moved from its house" even while she strays to another country. Significantly, the "cat" is named Boil, indicating her boiling displacement and eventual disappearance, that is, the burning of Haemi. While Haemi is traveling, the litter box shows evidence of the cat, but Jong-su never sees Boil, who disappears like Haemi. This shows that what is at stake is the destruction and the feminine, the animal, and the natural world.

The cat, like Haemi, is the lost object that the pervert Ben uses to provoke the symbolic. Boil suspiciously ends up in Ben's apartment after Haemi dies, along with the objects of all his girlfriend's, including Haemi's watch. Haemi herself had given this watch to Jong-su at the beginning of the film and he gave it back to her. Yet, Jong-su's attempts to keep Haemi in symbolic reality, in time, are foiled by Ben, who murders her and puts the watch in his drawer, and her cat in his apartment, trophies of his victory. The watch in his drawer is a provocation to Jong-su to watch. To Ben, the women are animals that threaten the phallic nature of his perverse reality. On the side of death against death against life, Ben murders the women before they can become mothers. He burns the seductresses before they can ever bear fruit, rendering them the scorched earth of unregulated capital.

In the same vein, Jong-su's uncanny abandoned house represents the destruction of domesticity as tied to unhomeliness, to the end of farming and fertility. Burning represents the supernatural arson of our earth as our first home, that is, the womb. Greenhouses are the graveyard for the women Ben murders; they are where he claims to deposit their remains. In actuality, woman is a stand-in for land and society which is being scorched by the one-percenters like Ben who are incapable of making a home. Instead, Ben is always on the move; he parties, travels, and murders.

Greenhouses are normally a symbol of fecund life, but in the film, they appear without cultivation as empty husks, abandoned enshrouded casings. After Ben tells Jong-su that he burns them down from time to time and intends to torch one near Jong-su's country home, Jong-su tries to identify in which greenhouse Ben buries the burned women. This futile search ultimately leads Jong-su to realize that Ben was just bragging about serial murder, not actually torching greenhouses. Ben, like the perverse leaders who are torching the earth on a globalized scale, scorches women as the bearers of life, attacking the possibility of future and generational transmission.

Proliferating perverse figures like Ben aggressively burn the life force or eros in service of a monstrous *Thanatos*. Like Ben's serial murders, they show the global economy's unwillingness or inability to address and repair damage incurred to the environment. The film presents contentious and incendiary politics as concomitant with an abandoning of concern for our earth. The lack of concern for scientific data about global warming is like the lack of respect and concern toward women and the vulnerable. Research and development to deal with global warming should be vibrant, but like the abandoned mausoleum-like greenhouses in *Burning*, it is being diminished and destroyed. In *Burning*, greenhouses are a symbol of the world's unwillingness or inability to adapt to our enfeebled planet, to take care of the earth and its fragile economy in new ways. Scientific facts are foreclosed in favor of grandiloquent crowd kindling, 1% tax cuts, and building a wall to keep the bad other out.

Globalization is the partner of the Anthropocene accelerating global destruction. In Faulkner's short story, the barn is the womb, a site of Southern vulnerability after the Civil War when the economy shifts. In Lee Chang-Dong's *Burning*, the barn becomes the greenhouse and a symbol of serial murder, alerting us to a modern situation just as critical as the aftermath of the American Civil War. Not only are we not caring for our country, but we are also not taking care of the planet, of women, or of our social realm due to the afterburn of history, manifest as political inaction and apathy. Our future is in jeopardy. Our garbage traps the heat that would have escaped; we're turning our planet into a mausoleum greenhouse, destroying the rainforests, eradicating the ozone and our atmosphere.

At one moment, looking to discover Ben's crimes, Jong-su sees his own reflection in the greenhouse fabric, and almost burns it himself, but stops. This is the kind of break, or limit to identification with the mirror image which inspires Jong-su to act in a way that stops the burning; this is exactly the kind of active concern we need from the law and our social realm today.

Fire as uncanny desire has always described the force of the drives which both builds up and breaks down civilization. Prometheus used fire as a vehicle of culture, to civilize, an act for which he was punished by the 1% Olympians. The film shows how the threat of *Burning* is both the internalization of political divisions and social conflicts, as well as the very real external threat of our world burning down. There is a global turn away from taking care of our planet as a vulnerable ecological system. Correlatively, there is a turning away from the vulnerable other, from Haemi, while conflict, divisions, and political walls multiply. Our whole ecology is becoming uncanny as the greenhouse effect suffocates and burns. The afterburn of political and social history will eventually raze our civilization unless we curb the uncanny speed of fire, the very ignition that marked *Homo Sapiens* rise to dominance.

Burning underlines the anxiety and horror of our present moment, where our constitutional and human rights are being torched as the world watches, fascinated and paralyzed. It shows how we live benumbed, anxiously hoping to act to put a stop to the destruction of democracy and our sweltering planet. Jong-su is a writer looking for sense in this world filled with intentionally unresolved mysteries. In the film's slow, lengthy, and beautiful scenes, *Burning* makes the audience feel the political tension and fires that pertain to the post-law perverted greenhouse society in which we live.

This tension represents our moment where we must cease being stunned and paralyzed by the demise of basic values, not to mention the planet, and act. Jong-su's story involves an act that is not accomplished in the Murakami text from which this film was derived. Jong-su's execution of Ben is like Snopes' son who informs on his father; both young men enact justice after the failed father. A half a century ago, Tennessee Williams wrote in *The Milk Train Doesn't Stop Here Anymore*, "We all live in a house on fire" (Williams 107). *Burning* adapts these stories to wake us up visually and show that we must fight the fires that go unchecked in our public realm before they destroy our planet. While we were writing this, Notre Dame was burning.

Notes

1 Chang-dong Lee's other films include *Secret Sunshine* and *Poetry* (Lee, Do-yeon, et al.; Lee, Jeong-hie, et al.), which examine extremism as the other side of the banality of evil.
2 While Freud describes the installation of the unconscious as driving speaking being (Freud), Blanchot describes violence as constituting an end to discourse.

Works Cited

Blanchot, Maurice. *The Infinite Conversation*. University of Minnesota Press, 1993.
——. *The Writing of the Disaster*. Translated by Ann Smock, University of Nebraska Press, 1995.
Brousse, Marie-Hélène. "The Triumph of Objects." *The Lacanian Review*, 8 Dec. 2018, https://www.thelacanianreviews.com/the-triumph-of-objects/.
Faulkner, William. "Barn Burning." *Selected Short Stories of William Faulkner*, Random House, 2012, pp. 3–26.
Freud, Sigmund. *The Future of an Illusion*. Translated by James Strachey, Standard ed, Norton, 1989.
Lacan, Jacques. *The Psychoanalytic Act: 1967–1968, Book XV*. Translated by Cormac Gallagher, 1968, http://www.lacanianworks.net/?p=5924.
Lee, Chang-dong, Yoo Ah-in, et al. *Beoning*. Pine House Film, NHK, Now Films, 2018.
Lee, Chang-dong, Jeon Do-yeon, et al. *Milyang*. CJ Entertainment, Cinema Service, Pine House Film, 2010.
Lee, Chang-dong, Yun Jeong-hie, et al. *Shi*. UniKorea Pictures, Pine House Film, Diaphana Films, 2011.
Muller, John P., and William J. Richardson, editors. *The Purloined Poe: Lacan, Derrida & Psychoanalytic Reading*. Johns Hopkins University Press, 1988.
Murakami, Haruki. "Barn Burning." *The Elephant Vanishes: Stories*, translated by Jay Rubin, Knopf Doubleday, 2010, pp. 131–50.
——. "Landscape with Flatiron." *The Elephant Vanishes*, Vintage Books, 1994, pp. 25–46.
Poe, Edgar Allan. *Edgar Allan Poe: Selected Tales; with The Narrative of Arthur Gordon Pym*. Edited by Diane Johnson, Library of America, 2009.
Williams, Tennessee. *The Theatre of Tennessee Williams. 5: The Milk Train Doesn't Stop Here Anymore. Kingdom of Earth (the Seven Descents of Myrtle). Small Craft Warnings. The Two-Character Play*. New Directions Publ. Corp, 1990.

Part III

Slowness

Chapter 7

"I repeated the routine"

The Lacanian Drive in Ling Ma's
Severance and COVID-19

Erica D. Galioto

The novel *Severance* (2018) by Ling Ma eerily prefigures the COVID-19 pandemic of 2020 in terms of its initial outbreak, rapid contagion, and worldwide devastation. Candace Chen, the novel's protagonist, tells her story in sections that alternate between the Beginning and After the End. The Beginning is the near past reality of the year 2011 in New York City, where Candace lives with her boyfriend Jonathan as they follow predictable rhythms of repetition in their work and leisure. After the End is her present-day reality where she is pregnant and apart from Jonathan but instead with eight other Shen Fever survivors as they attempt to escape the devastating death sentence that accompanies the fictional pandemic. The End, of course, is the traumatic intrusion of the Shen Fever pandemic into a world unprepared for its catastrophic effects.

Woven within these alternating sections are ruminations on the multiple meanings of severance as a concept. Severance figures prominently in the novel as the large sum of money that Candace will receive if she continues to work despite the dangerous conditions of Shen Fever. Severance also describes Candace's absolute isolation from authentic meaning in her daily life. She has broken ties with significant relationships, denied her cultural heritage, and abandoned necessary self-care prior to the End. Severance also connotes the abolishment of difference between East and West in service to the required homogeneity of consumerism. Ma's Shen Fever exposes these variations of severance as a concept, and its application to the economy, psychic life, and difference calls into question the causes and effects of severance from others and the self. Severance relies on the constant movement keeping Candace separate from attachment, and this continued movement is making her physically and psychically ill.

Reading *Severance* alongside our continued escalation of COVID-19 on the cusp of 2021 conjures provocative questions about the fictional reality that Ma envisions and its adjacence to our own traumatic reality. In Ma's prescient fiction, the Asian Shen Fever she imagines is caused by a host of environmental factors and eventually "results in a fatal loss of consciousness" (Ma 149). To read *Severance* in 2020 and beyond occasions urgent

DOI: 10.4324/9781003194033-11

introspection in the crosshairs of psychic life, speed, and infection: What are the environmental factors leading to disease in *Severance*? Are these explanatory causes fact or fiction? How does COVID-19 bear the traces of these same factors? And more urgently, how does severance from authentic pleasure in the service of capitalism affect both the novel and our present-day existence?

As a contemporary writer, Ma offers us a chilling reflection of how disease may stem from unchecked global capitalism and American consumerism, and she offers us new ways, albeit discomfiting, to engage in our present cultural and personal moment. Ultimately, I would like to contemplate the proximity between Ma's fictional Shen Fever and our global reality of COVID-19. Candace risks fever until the date of her promised severance package by living in her workspace and continuing to meet the demands of nonstop acceleration though she is alone and starving. Eventually she too flees a decimated New York City to camp in an abandoned mall with a small group of unfevered individuals attempting survival with cheap commodities. As Ma writes in Candace's perspective,

> Memories beget memories. Shen Fever being a disease of remembering, the fevered are trapped indefinitely in their memories. But what is the difference between the fevered and us? Because I remember too, I remember perfectly. My memories replay, unprompted, on repeat. And our days, like theirs, continue in infinite loop. We drive, we sleep, we drive some more. (Ma 160)

Following the question of the preceding passage, *But what is the difference between the fevered and us?* this chapter uses psychoanalysis to explore how the distinction between the fevered and the unfevered might be nothing at all, merely only a diagnosis away. Ma's novel suggests that this new fever stems from the pace of everyday life: the Lacanian drive circuit, explicitly articulated in the concluding sentence above, as an endless repetition aiming to install a lack that has never been permitted. The 21st century's refusal of lack encircles this constitutive absence but does not engender it unless psychic revolt forces a confrontation with lack as a necessary presence. *Severance* ultimately illustrates that opting out occasions this confrontation and entails abandoning both the perpetual present and the nostalgic past to the destabilizing unknown future of the unconscious. Like Shen Fever, COVID-19 also prompts an engagement with psychoanalytic lack as a transformative potentiality.

I

Though *Severance* was published in 2018, Ma's imagined Shen Fever and COVID-19 share many common qualities. Perhaps the most destabilizing similarity is that for both, as novel protagonist Candace thinks, "The

End begins before you are ever aware of it. It passes as ordinary" (Ma 9). In early 2020, like Candace a decade earlier based on the timeline of Ma's novel, most of us were insulated in our own protective existences until the loss of innocence on or around Friday, March 13, 2020 that heralded the stoppage of life as we knew it. Like Candace, we scoured the internet for information and were presented with FAQ's similar to those she locates on Shen Fever in terms of the known details, "The first case of Shen Fever was reported in Shenzhen, China in May 2011" (Ma 148), symptoms, "Because these symptoms are often mistaken for the common cold, patients are often unaware they have contracted Shen Fever" (148), and transmission, "Shen Fever is contracted by breathing in microscopic spores in the air…however, the infection is not contagious between people" (149). Like COVID-19, Shen Fever is invisible to the naked eye, yet strongly aggressive in individual bodies that are infected and among collaborations of social bodies in densely populated areas like New York City, which was an early epicenter for both diseases.

Due to the ambiguous natures of Shen Fever and COVID-19, it is often difficult to detect who has it, and therefore how one gets it. Symptoms may rapidly shift from allergy-like congestion to inability to breathe and eventually, as we now know, death, despite assertive medical intervention. While both diseases are initially treated lightly as occasions for humor, especially through their early civilian mandates of hospital-grade personal protective equipment, such as "an N95 respirator [that] may be worn to reduce the chance of transmission," both had almost immediate effects on working conditions, urban life, and interpersonal contact with others (Ma 149). Our quarantine experiences have made Ma's projected reality fact, for her fiction in *Severance* portrays how Shen Fever-directed stay-at-home orders moved work and school to previously unknown virtual platforms, as well as pushed many inhabitants out of urban centers and forced the seclusion of individuals within pods who typically only include immediate family members. These fevers prompt reflection on the way we live now, and our responsive changes in relation to the possibility of contagion make us contemplate authentic and deliberate existence from psychic, physical, and social perspectives. It is perhaps most notable that in both cases, it is common that those afflicted with Shen Fever and COVID-19 have no recognizable symptoms and can continue to function asymptomatically, while potentially affecting others. The nature of affliction and its nearly seamless overlap with daily life must then be problematized, through the lens of Ma's *Severance*, as well as our own destabilized reality.

In *Severance*, the "fevered" reach their state of blank oblivion prior to death through the devastating incarnation of Jonathan Crary's *24/7: Late Capitalism and the Ends of Sleep* (2013), where he argues that the present capitalist demand for 24/7 production and consumption erodes human subjectivity, autonomy, relationality, and meaning. In his words, "There is no possible harmonization between actual living beings and the demands of 24/7 capitalism, but there are countless inducements to delusionally suspend or obscure some of the humiliating limitations of lived experience, whether emotional or biological" (Crary 100). The encroachment of the 24/7 economy on our last frontier of resistance, sleep, is the most dangerous strategy currently being used to force human subjects into a sleep-deprived automaton state where these aforementioned "delusional suspensions" and "obscurings" are more likely to effectively separate us from the necessary respites, acknowledged limitations, and distinctions of time now "being effaced by the monotonous indistinction of 24/7" (Crary 30). In *Severance*, as in the world today, individuals in compliance with the continuous functioning of the 24/7 economy and those afflicted with a fever that seeps into people through "invisible spores in the air" are indistinguishable from each other (Ma 149). "They," or the fevered for Ma, "may appear functional and are still able to execute rote, everyday tasks" (148). This indistinguishability between health and disease, between being awake and being asleep, resonates with Crary's project to expose the encroachment of demands for use and consumption on the last sacred space of sleep.

In Ma's novel, those afflicted with Shen Fever remain trapped in the continuous functioning of daily working life in their severance from others and the self, and their meaningless work is the endlessly looping capitalist system that reproduces nothing but cheap simulacrum. Candace risks fever for the promise of her enormous severance package by living in her workspace and going through the empty motions of work, though there is little to do; we, during COVID-19-inspired work-from-home, teach-from-home, learn-from-home orders, work more, not less, eager to clock more hours of productivity now that commutes and distractions and social gatherings are gone. Working in tandem, Ma's *Severance* and Crary's *24/7* illustrate that there are three significant factors that contribute to our nonstop unquestioned injunctions to work and spend: (1) our unprotected inundation of technology; (2) our flattening of time to an elastic perpetual present encumbered by nostalgia for the past; and (3) our superegoic commands to "Enjoy!," despite the absence of authentic pleasure.

Ma, in her fiction, and Crary, in his philosophy, both illustrate how capitalism has warped the demarcations of time through nonstop immersion of technology in daily life that urges us to partake in the production and consumption of empty enjoyment. Each highlights the psychic rewiring that occurs due to the confluence of these three factors and implicitly suggests that this psychic penetration makes us unwell. Ma accelerates this disease through her elaboration of the fictional Shen Fever, and she anchors the disease in the materiality of time in a way that explicitly resonates with Crary's dystopic reality that has encroached on our biological need for sleep. Shen Fever, it bears repeating, is "a disease of remembering, [where] the fevered are trapped indefinitely in their memories" (Ma 160). Time and again, in

Severance the characters reach a point of no return with Shen Fever when they go back to the past, typically a past associated with childhood or adolescence. Suburban hometowns, childhood homes, adolescent hangouts; rather than holding forth as wistful reminiscences of carefree times, these memories of the past shackle the diseased to eventual death. "It's like nostalgia has something to do with it," Candace muses when considering why Ashley, an apparent survivor, devolves into unrelenting Shen Fever upon a return to her childhood home (143). Another survivor, Evan, rejects Candace's interpretation with "I'm pretty sure it's not because of memories," though it is quite obvious that the relationship to time plays a major role in one's experience of Shen Fever and that early symptoms trigger a return to the past that accelerates a coincidence with death (144).

Ma, in accordance with Crary, insinuates that technology has exacerbated the manipulation of time in haywire directions. In the 2011 realism of *Severance*, as in our current reality, distinctions of time have become obsolete due to our absolute inundation with imperatives to live a technologically-driven virtual life, where human subjects feel the demand to consume, create, and reproduce digital content without cessation. Bob, another apparent survivor in *Severance*, describes the confluence of time and technology like this:

> The internet is the flattening of time. It is the place where the past and the present exist on one single plane. But proportionally, because the present calcifies into the past, even now, even as we speak, perhaps it is more accurate to say that the internet almost wholly consists of the past. It is the place we go to commune with the past. (Ma 114)

Bob's sermon on the internet and time prompts further realizations from the group of survivors of which Candace is part. One by one, each of the as yet unfevered individuals contributes a detail that adds to Bob's notions. Echoes of "All those archives of news articles" and "I never totally forget the past because I'm seeing it on my Facebook wall every day" quickly pass through the group (115). "Our eyes have become nearsighted with nostalgia, staring at our computer screen. Because being online is the equivalent to living in the past," Bob further concludes (115).

Time in *Severance* has become irrevocably skewed, as Crary summarizes with "no moment, place, or situation now exists in which one can *not* shop, consume, or exploit networked resources, there is a relentless incursion of the non-time of 24/7 into every aspect of social or personal life" (30). Perhaps, then, it is not memories or nostalgia that worsens Shen Fever, but rather our inability to manage our relationship to time in healthy and meaningful ways. On the one hand, those afflicted with Shen Fever are indistinguishable from their unfevered counterparts because they merely continue their work-based rote tasks in an unchanging perpetual present, labeled "non-time" by Crary (30). On the other hand, Shen Fever worsens when sick individuals feel the pull of the past and return to places and relationships they can never leave and where they ultimately perish.

Technology and its imbrication in the continuous functioning of the 24/7 economy is ensnared in both deviations of time. Its ubiquitous availability flattens the natural evolution of time to a uniform experience of insipid dull monotony, while synchronously it erects the same fixed present into a monument of already-lived recent past in a fossilized timeline. Neither free to live authentically in the present, nor prepared to endure the working-through the past requires, we are trapped and unwell whether we continue the endlessly repeating rat race or float backward on the retroactive idealization of nostalgia. We cannot walk away from the timeline and instead get stuck in its striated sedimentation. As Crary emphasizes, "Instead of a formulaic sequence of places and events associated with family, work, and relationships, the main thread of one's lifestory now is the electronic commodities and media services through which all experience has been filtered, recorded, or constructed" (58–59). Temporary fabricated virtual normalizations dominate our relationship to time and memory and loss, yet we push to embed ourselves even further in these networks for the promise of satisfaction they fail to grant. As such, the interminable demands of the super-egoic pressure to enjoy cement us even deeper into this troubling relationship with time and technology. In the words of Candace, she sums up this uninspiring pleasureless pleasure before the End as "I was enjoying myself, but it was an insulated enjoyment. I was alone inside of it" (Ma 54). Here, Candace describes the homogenization of her experience as well as the paradoxical relationship between repetition and stasis: an acceleration leading nowhere for no meaningful purpose, the "infinite loop" shared by fevered and unfevered alike (160). This paradox is the Lacanian drive, and it is very clearly at work in the adjacent realities of Shen Fever and COVID-19.

2

Candace's pleasureless pleasure distinctly resonates with the conception of the Lacanian drive circuit, as "a constant force" following the Freudian definition and its malfunction in capitalist society today (Lacan, *The Four Fundamental Concepts of Psychoanalysis* 164). The cyclic repetition of the Lacanian drive encourages a psychoanalytic reading of *Severance* that likewise bears an immediate synchrony in our experience of COVID-19. The constant thrust of the drive allows us to relate the perpetual present of continuous movement to the capitalist imperative of consumption and enjoyment and ultimately to the failed satisfaction enunciated by Candace above. Candace makes this connection herself when she thinks, "The past is a black hole, cut into the present day like a wound, and if you come too close, you can get sucked in. You have to keep moving" (Ma 120). The necessity to "keep moving" is the push and pull of drive, the unrelenting pattern of repetition that creates the illusion of forward momentum but really just maps a circular outline around that "black hole" of lack or absence.

The psychoanalytic drive as the endless repetition of circuity aiming to install a lack that has never been permitted reinforces Crary's argument in *24/7* and leads us to similarly acknowledge that this nonstop functioning aims toward the deliberate disavowal of lack in present-day society. Unlike desire, which leads subjects to pursue the filling of an absence that is eclipsed temporarily to bring the brief satisfaction of *jouissance*, the Lacanian drive circuit describes the refusal of lack that pushes subjects to follow an unending cycle of acquisition that has reached a bloated dimension with the ever-increasing omnipresence of capitalism in daily life. In this dizzying spinning top, time marches on without us, though it relies on our compliance with the system to continue. "The future just wants more consumers," Jonathan, Candace's boyfriend, states as he projects the elastic continuance of capitalist drive executed in and through the human subjects on which it depends (Ma 13). Drive never satiates and thus requires more bodies and more possessions for its unfulfilled promises of consumption and completion, and therefore its effects are often rendered shallow and empty rather than enjoyable. The symbolic fevered employee in the flagship Juicy Couture store endlessly folding and refolding unneeded sweaters in Ma's *Severance* conjures the intersecting vacuity of mindless work and unnecessary spending of the psychic drive in the time of late capitalism (258). "By snatching at its object," Lacan famously states, "the drive learns in a sense that this is precisely not the way it will be satisfied" (Lacan, *The Four Fundamental Concepts of Psychoanalysis* 167). The object, we know, never satisfies, but the capitalist economy and the drive hinges on the possibility that the next one might.

The super-egoic cultural imperative to "Enjoy!" has turned 21st-century human subjects into amalgamations of cheap products we are constantly encouraged to throw away and replace, so we too are dissatisfied with the stagnant, lifeless, and bored commodities we have become. Candace and the Bibles she adorns with fake gemstones and then sells with "the same content repackaged a million times over, in new combinations ad infinitum," with the fictional Spectra company stand as icons to the shallow facades of our replaceable products as well as the human husks that fetishize them (Ma 23). Late capitalist imperatives make enjoyment itself a duty, but we have been barred access to a surplus enjoyment that is only available through the effect of the master signifier on the signifying chain of discourse. Working in tandem with the virtual homogenization and time warping described in the first section, this drive to be the same, consume the same products, and enjoy in the same way persists because the enjoyment is offered without limits. Compulsory all-access pleasure is not authentic pleasure, as Candace illustrates, and we unfortunately know all too well. As Ma shows in *Severance*, enjoyment based on an otherness that capitalism transforms into a reproducible, equal, and identical pleasure fails to deliver pleasure because for enjoyment to exist as the pleasure of surplus *jouissance*, it must come from an otherness that cannot be metabolized, accessed, and quantified equally among all subjects. This authentic pleasure of *jouissance* is predicated on lack, the lack encircled, yet not permitted to exert its force, in drive.

While it is true that we do not experience the authentic pleasure of *jouissance* in the constant thrust of drive, Lacan explores the crucial relationship between drive and satisfaction. Though "there is set up an extreme antinomy" between drive and satisfaction as we are well aware, we continue the cyclic patterns and loops of the drive circuit anyway and there is satisfaction to be found there (Lacan, *The Four Fundamental Concepts of Psychoanalysis* 166). Lacan explains this paradox by applying his drive concept to patients who repeat consciously unpleasant symptoms: "They satisfy something that no doubt runs counter to that which they might be satisfied, or rather, perhaps, they give satisfaction *to* something. They are not content with their state, but all the same, being in a state that gives so little content, they are content" (*The Four Fundamental Concepts of Psychoanalysis* 166). When we think of this passage through the lens of *Severance* and present-day reality, it is possible to make the same pronouncements. The repeated failure of satisfaction in drive becomes a reliable contentedness on its own. The avoidance of lack permitted through its encircling becomes predictably safe. The satisfaction we give to the capitalist machine allows its knowable continuance. The failure of drive allows us to exist in the only way we know how. Encircling loss but not engaging it produces the failure that allows the only access to pleasure, though empty, provided in the capitalist framework.

Though the drive continuously fails in its central endeavor to provide a subject with a permanent and definitive satisfaction of enjoyment, its sheer force highlights society's desperate need for the appropriate constellation of absence, prohibition, and intersubjectivity within the psyches of individuals who more and more are removed from necessary lack in daily life due to the ever-increasing demand for continuous functioning. "Make use of yourself," recalls Candace when she remembers her Chinese parents and their advice to her; "No matter what, we just want you to be of use" (Ma 190). In its removal of lack from daily life, the continuous functioning of 24/7 capitalism forces a drive economy that pulses for those necessary irregularities. Candace rarely and her boyfriend Jonathan somewhat more so only subliminally acknowledge their need for these irregularities when suddenly they are surprised by the forced space of pleasure early in the fever: "And finally, it took a force of nature to interrupt our routines. . . . We just wanted to feel flush with time to do things of no quantifiable value, our hopeful side pursuits like writing or drawing or something, something other than what we did for money" (199). Shen Fever, combined with "a category 3 hurricane, named Mathilde," urged the New Yorkers of *Severance* to take to the streets despite warnings of flood, where the mood was lively and festive

(193). "The world was exploding into a party," thinks Candace, as crisis brings spontaneous interpersonal contact rarely found in our meticulously circumscribed routinized encounters with strangers (198).

What Candace responds to here is actually *less*, the lack missing from her economy, pushing her to experience what Žižek refers to as "this failure of the symbolic fiction [that] induces the subject to cling increasingly to imaginary simulacra, to the sensual spectacles which bombard us today from all sides" (Žižek, *The Ticklish Subject* 369). It is clear that what Candace requires here is the same as what Crary advocates through sleep and that is to make lack present through self-removal from the 24/7 economy: a feat only accomplished in Ma's fiction through the coincidence of global pandemic and natural disaster. Caught in drive rather than desire, Ma's Shen Fevered zombie subjects are desperate to install a needed gap; the gap that continuous functioning refuses; the "black hole" to be avoided at all costs (Ma 120). It is only through deliberate refusal that space opens to the more of the authentic pleasure of *jouissance*. Privation—not getting satisfaction—paradoxically, brings access to an excess of pleasure, not the ineffectual consumption played in a repetitive loop of dissatisfaction. Ironically, the capitalist demand for "More!" actually stymies the enjoyment that can only be experienced through the acceptance of "less."

As Ma shows through her own critique of capitalism, despite this pervasive belief in completion and fulfillment and perfection, Candace and Jonathan are empty and dissatisfied and then Shen Fever and Hurricane Mathilde strike and lack presents itself in their enclosed reality and must be confronted. Unsurprisingly, they are quite literally dumbfounded as to how to deal with what had previously been unthinkable; the mindless repetition of drive halts, perched on a precipice to reassimilate as a new loop or unwind in response to the previously unthought traumatic intrusion into reality. Before the pandemic of Shen Fever initiates, lack was not permitted, so any possible emergence was covered over with the continuous functioning that provided the excess of late capitalism's plenty. As Lacan explains of the constitutive lack that Candace and Jonathan are finally inhabiting, "This is the hollow, the gap that no doubt a number of objects initially come and fill—objects that, in some way, are adapted in advance, designed to be used at stoppers" (Lacan, *The Other Side of Psychoanalysis* 50). Stripped of their prepackaged, replaceable fillers and the self-induced continuous functioning of work obligations, Candace and Jonathan confront the lack engendered by Shen Fever and diverge in their response.

Jonathan enacts his own refusal and tries to convince Candace to leave New York City with him. In their final conversation, he articulates the mind-numbing monotony of their lives. "I don't want to hustle 24/7 just to make rent," he asserts (Ma 200). And he directly questions her with, "Why do you want to work a job you don't really even believe in? What's the end-game of that? Your time is worth more than that" (201). Deaf to his entreaties despite her pregnant state, which she has never revealed to him, Candace stays behind to work out the time until her severance package drops into her account. Determined to continue to be of use, or possibly fevered herself, which Ma leaves open for reader interpretation, Candace remains in New York City in the monotonous repetition of printing mass-market Bibles in China, while Jonathan leaves. Abandoning his previously fetishized mouth retainer as a symbol of the sedimentation of perpetual present demanded in the 24/7 economy, he heads to the utopian country, the low-tech, unbound space of unknown future. In her defense, she silently seethes, "In this world, money is freedom. Opting out is not a real choice" (206). In their divergence, Jonathan permits his encounter with the potentiality of lack to trigger movement toward an unknown future, while Candace pauses and reconstitutes a variant of her original drive to cover over the emergence of unwanted lack.

3

Though she uses "opting out" as an impossibility locking her in place, it seems, in fact, that "opting out" is our only option to resist the 24/7 capitalist economy, the pleasureless existence that is the drive, and possibly Shen Fever and perhaps even COVID-19. Even further, the seeming impossibility of opting out only amplifies its necessity. For Lacan, the drive doubly reflects the impossible. On the one hand, the drive's complete satisfaction is always already impossible, as we have been emphasizing. But on the other hand, the real is the obstacle to satisfaction, and that realm itself is labeled as impossible. As Lacan states, "the path of the subject passes between the two walls of the impossible" (Lacan, *The Four Fundamental Concepts of Psychoanalysis* 166). Caught in the narrow gap between the impossible satisfaction of the drive and the impossible access to the real, the subject has the potential for deliberate opting out through the gap of lack that exists in between both impossibilities. Lacan calls this revolutionary response the act, and it is the potential for the act that Candace negates in her refusal to join Jonathan in his self-removal from the drive's repetition. Her refusal to leave is tantamount to a symbolic "No!" as an explicit rejection of all that opting out entails, and it is a "No!" that has also been seen in response to COVID-19 all too frequently.

In late January 2020, Žižek penned a short piece called "My Dream of Wuhan" that quickly went viral. In it, he mused on the anticipatory racist paranoia, interpersonal isolation, and world-wide trauma soon to come. More importantly, he offered explicit commentary on dead time, which aligns powerfully with Candace's early resistance to opting out. He cautions:

> There is, however, an unexpected emancipatory prospect hidden in this. . . . to live without dead time, to enjoy without obstacles. If Freud and Lacan taught us anything, it is that this formula—the supreme case

of a superego injunction since, as Lacan aptly demonstrated, superego is at its most basic a positive injunction to enjoy, not a negative act of prohibiting something—is a recipe for disaster: the urge to fill in every moment of the time allotted to us with intense engagement unavoidably ends us in a suffocating monotony. (Žižek, "My Dream of Wuhan" 2)

As Žižek writes here, early responses to our own pandemic and Candace's responses to the escalations of Shen Fever led to deeper adherence to work, to compulsive productivity, to nonstop consumption, and to unbroken daily cataloguing of time online for those who were able to work, live, and spend at home. Though there was more time, there was less engagement with disposable open time to be still and reflective and self-directed. This became "a recipe for disaster," he concludes, because the super-egoic demand to enjoy and produce expanded exponentially to accommodate newly revealed open space.

The infrastructure of work and the manipulation of time halted altogether; "there is nothing keeping us here" in the words of Candace's coworker Blythe, but the self-imposed routines and demands increased under threat of extinction (Ma 238). Necessary dead time, using Žižek's label, evaporated, and was instead filled with even more productivity, more empty purchases, more virtual, rather than actual, life. If opting out exists in the space between two impossibilities, it means deliberate disengagement from what coordinates those two fields. It means saying "No!" to the continuous functioning of the 24/7 economy, and it means saying "No!" to the trauma of the real threatening to engulf us in sickness. It means saying yes to dead time and to sleep; it means saying yes to lack and saying yes to lack means a more authentic inhabitation of the self that permits absence as a necessary presence.

Candace eventually leaves an uninhabitable New York City for an abandoned mall with a small group of unfevered individuals, and their desperate survival reflects our own absurd reliance on endlessly replaceable and disposable products, like toilet paper, that can disappear too quickly for our crippling need. Their haven is called The Facility, a hollow mall that used to be called Dear Oaks, gutted from the inside where it was believed that "We'd be close to all those retail outlets and big-box stores, most of which are still stocked, most likely with an endless amount of food and supplies. We would have access to everything we could ever need for the foreseeable future" (Ma 189). Reinstituting the prevailing imperatives of continuous functioning and super-egoic enjoyment warned against by Žižek, this small group of escapees from New York City refused the potential for dead time and instead, "In the end, we have come to the facility to work" (221). Survival becomes their work and the group takes to extreme measures called "live stalks," as opposed to our ubiquitous online Google stalks, where they approach the fevered trapped in their own homes in their mechanical daily routines and steal their remaining goods before killing them. It has to be done because, "Not working is maddening," thinks Candace when she is prevented from doing so due to her pregnancy. "Your mind goes into free fall, untethered from a routine. Time bends. You start remembering things. Past and present become indistinguishable" (221–22). More desperate than ever to forestall the unknown potentiality of lack, this small group of survivors relaunches the drive circuit anew, feeding themselves to its constant pressure and finding hollow pleasure in the repetition of its well-worn failure.

The group's intent to keep working and to align existence exclusively with working, despite the overwhelming influx of fever, is troubling in our current historical moment, as is their, and maybe our own, refusal to engage with dead time, the lack most characteristic of our pandemic. "Dead time—moments of withdrawal, of what old mystics called *Gelassenheit*, releasement—are crucial for the revitalization of our life experience," Žižek argues, yet our resistance to this necessary engagement with lack portends the kind of dead wakened state that Crary illustrates is the goal of our sleep-deprived consciousness (2). Even when we might get away with flipping our off switches, we are choosing not to, and this decision continues our hectic fever. Disengagement is revolt in this assertion, and our lives depend upon it.

Also written pre-pandemic yet likewise standing as a preemptive caution against what was to come in the ominous 2020, Jenny Odell's *How to Do Nothing: Resisting the Attention Economy* (2019) provides a cultural critique against the way we live now and offers avenues for revolt that line up with the psychoanalytic disengagement synchronous with the act in the present day. Odell first argues that "doing nothing" is the conscious decision to disengage from the nonstop demands for our attention primarily in virtual spaces that lock us in the space of perpetual present elucidated in *Severance*, and then she continues her argument by advocating for the reorientation of attention elsewhere. This purposeful devotion of attention elsewhere "is nothing less than time and space, a possibility only once we meet each other there on the level of attention" (Odell xviii). Contrasting the mindlessness of the solitary drive-based attention economy with the alive presentness of the internally transcendent attachment to intersubjective time and space, Odell persuasively argues that doing nothing not only provides human subjects with a more authentic existence but also pokes holes in the thrust of collective drive by exposing possibilities for living outside the consolidating economy. She urges us "to exit the trajectory of productive time, so that a single moment might open to infinity" (29).

Paradoxically, this finite rootedness in material time expands outward to the unknown. We inhabit our bodies more fully, yet also permit their capacity for expansion; we are more aware of the utmost importance of the present moment, yet also its proliferation into an unwritten future. When doing nothing, the "state of openness that assumes there is something new to be seen" offers a therapeutic response to the environmental conditions that are making us psychically ill, if not physically sick (Odell 112). This return to the body and time and its infinite possibilities comes through the opting out of continuous functioning and the technology inseparable from it. Odell's charge to do nothing is the Lacanian imperative to engage with lack; to chart the course between the two impossibilities of the drive and the real. Engaging nothingness through the inculcation of lack is the only horizon available for revolt, and it occurs at the level of the psyche. Though we are uncertain of Candace's future survival, Ma provides examples of this inculcation of lack that holds the potential for new encounters with time and space that might reverse psychic damage on individual and collective levels. Pregnancy, art, and religion provide avenues for Candace to apply deliberate attention after first disengaging from the routinized circuit of drive.

Though she never tells Jonathan, Candace knows she is pregnant with their child during their final conversation. As Shen Fever worsens and Candace flees to The Facility where she works to survive along with the others, it's clear that carrying future life in her body affects her own attitude toward possibility. At the same time, she frequently dreams of her mother who recently passed away from Alzheimer's disease, another illness of time and memory. The simultaneous present reality of Candace's pregnancy alongside her dreams of her mother provides her with a timeline to reconcile. As she consciously confronts the unconscious content of her dreams in her waking state, Candace experiences the universal transition from daughter to soon-to-be mother. The psychic effort required to negotiate this role shift opens Candace to her own mother/daughter relationship, as she contemplates her childhood memories and even more recent ones with what is yet to come with her own unborn daughter Luna, named for her nocturnal wakefulness as well as her gravitational pull.

Luna adds significant weight to not only Candace's body but also her goal of survival. Threading this tripartite lineage into the past, Candace's mother appears in a dream where she urges, "You should escape now," and plants the seed of stealing the keys of the survivors' car from the parking lot of The Facility (Ma 244). Luna is a present absence to Candace that forces contemplation of unknown vistas into the future. "I want something different for Luna, the child of two rootless people," Candace contemplates upon her escape from The Facility; "She will be born untethered from all family except me, without a hometown or a place of origin" (287). This line of thought shows Candace's conscious engagement with the unknown, and it significantly causes her to consider roots, the same roots that she had previously severed to fully embody the continuous functioning demanded of our 21st-century reality. Candace's desire to give Luna roots illustrates her awareness of new potential in the space of lack afforded by her pregnant state and its effects on her body, sense of time, and relationality with others.

In addition to pregnancy, which is certainly problematic as a potential cure to psychic fever, Ma also offers art and religion as possible pathways for new attention subsequent to the lack encountered through opting out. As a pregnant female Candace houses lack, while in her relationship to art, she becomes the lack that might trigger confrontation with absence in others. We learn early in *Severance* that when Candace first moved to New York she had an online photo blog called *NY Ghost*, where she posted pictures of the city from the perspective of an outsider. Over time, she became dissatisfied with the images and felt they resembled every other stock New York City image readily available from a simple online click, and so she stopped posting new shots. After a years' long lapse in posting, Shen Fever and Jonathan's encouragement inspired her to resume her hobby so that she can represent the changed landscape of urban iconography. These new silent and empty images prompt responses: "Readers wrote in asking for pictures and dispatches from their old neighborhoods, their friends' apartments, nostalgic sites" (Ma 110). Though they don't know that Candace took those photos, the other survivors at The Facility recall the blog and how "the city did not look habitable" but rather "almost empty" (110). Both pre-fever and, more importantly, post-fever, "The ghost was me," Candace remembers (41). In her inhabitation of the unseen viewer, Candace provides the scenes of empty absence that confront the viewer with strange sights that prompt contemplation of the previously unseen and unknown. The *NY Ghost* photo blog presents what the drive avoids: a reality that must be witnessed. Art, and its potential for representation and reimagination, can indeed direct purposeful attention to absence and its structural necessity in daily life and psychic experience.

Like art, religion emerges as a predictable engagement with lack, yet its precise manifestation is surprising in its newness. Candace, it must be remembered, participated in the 24/7 economy through Spectra, a company that made mass market Bibles with cheap labor and materials in China. The epitome of simulacrum and shallow belief, their Daily Grace Bible for example, "was an everyday Bible for casual use, but Three Crosses Publishing also wanted to imbue the product with the high-value feel of an heirloom" (66). These cheap Bibles reemerge during the height of Shen Fever; they are often hollowed out to contain hidden cell phones or are seen in the hands of fevered individuals who are catatonically "reading, or assuming the act of reading" them (68). Meaningless in both cases, the Bibles hold what we really worship in the cell phone or contain the drivel we no longer understand in its severance from internal belief. In sharp contrast to these vapid Spectra Bibles are the new displays of belief in the face of an unknown future plagued with the escalation of Shen Fever. In the car, Candace steals from The Facility following her dream of her dead mother, she looks out the window and "Passing underneath a highway overpass, [she's] startled to see makeshift Catholic shrines, decorated with Virgin Mary and saint iconography, strewn with burned-down candles" (285). Alters of communal living belief pepper the landscape, testifying to how lack and uncertainty propel new awareness of the need for religious mystery in the face of the unknown.

Though Ma provides pregnancy, art, and religion as new objects of attention in the face of lack, readers are unsure of Candace's short- and long-term future. Whether she is heading to the country to find Jonathan and give Luna deep roots of survival or to the city to rejoin a past she can never work through in Shen Fever's disease of remembering, we are not sure. If she survives or succumbs to fever herself seems to be based on whether she productively engages in the nothingness of psychic revolt. As shown here in *Severance*, Ma's novel suggests that Shen Fever, and by extension maybe COVID-19, stems from the pace of everyday life, the Lacanian drive circuit as an endless repetition aiming to install a lack that has never been permitted, urging us to opt out with ever-increasing strength yet also locking us in place with the constant movement that leads us nowhere. The central question remains, Why instead are we choosing to deaden ourselves even more severely? Like Candace's empty workspace, more and more we too, even during our own pandemic, resemble psychic subjects who metaphorically and actually are "entombed, blinds drawn across floor-to-ceiling windows, our cubicles small, silent sarcophagi" (Ma 192).

The physical illness of Shen Fever metaphorically resembles the Lacanian drive run amok in our late capitalist reality and the psychic severance that is its symptom. It may also be argued that COVID-19 follows the same syllogism. In both realities, the pandemic inculcates the lack that drive disallows and forces both an individual and collective confrontation with the potentiality of dead time. As COVID-19 continues to inflict unspeakable trauma, we are behind the wheel like Candace at the end of *Severance*, just before she gets out to continue on foot. Will we opt out and walk the narrow path between two impossibilities, or will we reconstitute a new drive loop in service to the demands of late capitalism? Are we alive or are we fevered?

Works Cited

Crary, Jonathan. *24/7: Late Capitalism and the Ends of Sleep.* Verso, 2013.

Lacan, Jacques. *The Four Fundamental Concepts of Psychoanalysis.* Translated by Jacques-Alain Miller, WW Norton, 1998.

——. *The Other Side of Psychoanalysis.* Translated by Russell Grigg, W.W Norton & Company, 2007.

Ma, Ling. *Severance.* First edition, Farrar, Straus and Giroux, 2018.

Odell, Jenny. *How to Do Nothing: Resisting the Attention Economy.* Melville House, 2019.

Žižek, Slavoj. "My Dream of Wuhan." *DIE WELT*, 22 Jan. 2020. www.welt.de, https://www.welt.de/kultur/article205630967/Slavoj-Zizek-My-Dream-of-Wuhan.html.

——. *The Ticklish Subject: An Essay in Political Ontology.* Verso, 1999.

Chapter 8

Richtering Rhythms
Never Look Away

Jessica Datema

Some Thing Missing

This chapter analyzes *Never Look Away*, whose original German film title is *Werk Ohne Autor*, or Work without an Author (Donnersmarck et al.) The film, directed by Florian Henckel von Donnersmarck, explores German history between 1932 and 1965 as inspired by and intersecting with the life and work of the artist Gerhard Richter. It displays biographical events in German history surrounding Richter's artworks—specifically a painting entitled *Aunt Marianne* (1965)—detailed in an article by Jurgen Schreiber. *Never Look Away* is based on facts but focuses on rhythm as a creative force that sparks rebirth in "the movement between blockage and flow, trauma and new beginnings" (Eigen 722). It is a filmic biography not reducible to the painter's life. Rather, *Never Look Away* is an *allobiography* that screens over the fluidity and drift between creator and creation to reflect "a movement at work everywhere in one form or another" (Lacoue-Labarthe 179).[1] This movement unearthed in the artwork is the Orphic rhythm of creative death and rebirth that outlasts the artist and defies representation.

The film, like Gerhard Richter's artworks, offers a different way of look-ing at history, which contrasts with past methods. In post–World War II Germany, many in both the East and the West were focused on building new societies, not reckoning. *Never Look Away* unfolds slowly over three hours as a drawn-out view of catastrophic events in German history. It unreels the bounds between life and work, fact and fiction, to echo the impasse and drift of conscious and unconscious memories. As not supporting any spe-cific statement, *Never Look Away* displays creative rebirth amidst incredible change, disaster, and loss. The film, like Richter's artwork, compels viewers to keep looking and engage uncertainty.

Never Look Away screens a different kind of communication via rhythm and the senses. It draws out the contours of inexplicable events to let viewers see through a fusion of artistic mediums. Its *allobiographic* cinema works through the rhythmic drift between moving images, documentary music, multiplicity in naming, and an indefinite genre. The film engages more than

DOI: 10.4324/9781003194033-12

represents to challenge seeing as believing, and to show an affective beat or "rhythm [that] does not appear; it is the beat of appearing insofar as appearing consists simultaneously and indissociably in the movement of coming and going of forms or presence in general. . . . " (Nancy 24). *Never Look Away* overscreens the rhythmic drift that compels dis/appearing forms as exemplified in Gerhard Richter's life and work.

Art and activism are modes of expression that construct an intermediary for reflecting through disaster. Clinical views of trauma reiterate its unyielding physical impact and its inability to be represented or remembered. Yet, art offers indirect reflection upon what eludes naming in history as one psychoanalyst notes,

> Art and political activism are the examples par excellence of how pain and trauma can be productively enlisted. . . . I am not arguing that trauma should not be respected as perimetered, individual space-but I am saying that the very registration of trauma's injuries and the ability to reflect though its paralyzing effects may make it possible for the subject to recognize that trauma is both intimate and, at times, social emanating from large-scale inequalities and structural coercions. (Saketopoulou 3)

The suggestion is that external cultural coercions connect to internal psychic structures of trauma that can be worked through via aesthetic engagement.

In *History Beyond Trauma*, Jean-Max Gaudillière and Francoise Davoine suggest that art and literature are tools for discovering erased truth of a historic madness (Gaudillière). Their most recent work *Madness and the Social Link* conceives of trauma and psychosis as standing at the crossroad of personal and world history. It firmly places individual madness within the social and political circumstances of catastrophic historic events that can be traced back through generations. *Madness and The Social Link* also argues for the role of art, literature, and psychoanalysis as uncovering "counter-historic" truths of societal madness that were expunged. The film, like Gerhard Richter's artwork, searches for these counter-factual truths to screen what was erased in past disasters. Richter's artworks are exemplary in their non-representational painted, blurry, dream-like, and cyclical images that resurface the overlooked. The view is that art, like analysis, might expose the political or societal madness that accelerated the vanishing of individuals like Marianne.

Never Look Away uses aesthetic engagement to make the other that was killed alive again—the other that the narcissism of totalitarian representation tries to annihilate. Donnersmarck's film is based on real people who lived through traumatic events. Yet, like his 2006 *The Lives of Others* (*Das Leben der Anderen*), *Never Look Away* accentuates rhythmic engagement—in painting and music—as an "interruptive aesthetic exposure, more so than the characters or plot of the film" (Datema 70). It contrasts Kurt Barnert (Tom Schilling), an artist based on the early life of Gerhard Richter, with the Nazi turned Stasi gynecologist Dr. Seeband. He (Sebastian Koch) is based on Heinrich Eufinger, who was part of an SS medical team of chief doctors and gynecologists deployed to sanitize the German female population of contaminated wombs. He became Kurt's father-in-law and is presumed responsible for giving the order to exterminate his aunt. *Never Look Away* contrasts the perverse Nazi gynecologist that destroys the womb, as emblematic of life, to the painter who siphons trauma into artistic rebirth.

The film is inspired by director interviews with Gerhard Richter and an article by Jürgen Schreiber, journalist, and Berlin-based author. Schreiber's writing exposes how Gerhard Richter's aunt was marked for death by his father-in-law, a high-ranking gynecologist in the SS. A newspaper excerpt notes how Richter "painted Aunt Marianne, he painted his future father-in-law Eufinger, [and] he became the messenger of the German drama without being aware of it" (Schreiber 2).[2] Schreiber writes that all this happened outside Richter's conscious knowledge. His article entitled "The Painter's Secrets" describes actual historic truths hidden in the artist's works about which the artist remains silent in life.

When Schreiber's work came out, Richter became consciously aware of the link between his father in-law's crimes, the authorization to euthanize his aunt, and his painting. *Tante Marianne* (1965) is based on a photograph of the artist as a boy on his aunt's lap. Not long after the photo, Marianne was taken to a psychiatric unit in Arnsdor near Dresden. There she was given unsuccessful shock treatments, which for the SS was tantamount to a death sentence. Ten years later, she was forcibly sterilized then euthanized. No longer a child, Gerhard Richter overpaints a family photo of himself on Aunt Marianne's lap that makes a haunting visual echo of real events.[3] In an interview with Schreiber, Richter finally sees the date scrawled on the back of that photo and the real-life connection. The artist works through historic disasters by avoiding discussion of them and letting the paintings say what happened. The film explores how artworks, like Richter's *Tante Marianne*, screen erased truths of political and cultural madness.

As with Richter's paintings, *Never Look Away* does not directly represent or explain the facts. Rather it reflects enigmas opened by his artworks. The film shows how the artist's childhood was riven by catastrophes, including the Dresden bombings[4] and the tragedy of his Aunt Marianne Schönfelder who

> was a delicate, attractive girl, [but] who, by the *time* she was twenty had been institutionalized with a diagnosis of schizophrenia. Mental illness was a dangerous label to wear in Nazi Germany. Mentally ill or physically and intellectually disabled women were subjected to forced sterilization and in 1940 the government established a medical

murder program, with sex execution centers [in hospitals] equipped with "showers," to destroy them. By 1941, when Hitler shut the gassing program down some thirty-five thousand women had been killed. (Goodyear 38)

Unspoken and erased traumas—like the extermination of Marianne—haunted not only Richter but also the entire German population.

Never Look Away explores how the artist had the foresight but not all the facts to paint the now famous uncanny *Tante Marianne* (1965). Both Kurt and Dr. Seeband are compelled by an uncastrated acephalic drive that does not repress the real. The drive of a pervert or psychotic[5] is different from the artist's drive, as Marie-Hélène Brousse notes,

> The opposition between art as production of object and art as fiction and operative of truth, in order to be valid cannot be reduced to the opposition between neurosis and psychosis. In effect, it is by depriving himself that the poet of courtly love produces a woman object.... this woman object is presented as an impossible or as a non-human partner. .... Where the signifying function creates a void, art presents itself as organizing this void through an [impossible] object. (Brousse 69)

The artist's position toward drive satisfaction is organized around truth as love of the void. This contrasts with Dr. Seeband's knowledge, which is driven by the destructive certitude of *Thanatos*. The other that Dr. Seeband exterminates becomes the impossible partner to which Kurt is bound in painting as a praxis of artistic rebirth. This scaffolding is the alpha and omega that allows the artist to love, work through trauma, and artistically resurrect his aunt.

Blue Wombs: Paintings Mini Cages

Never Look Away shows how free expression is considered insanity for citizens residing under an autocratic rule. During Gerhard Richter's lifetime, German citizens were forced into fearful silence or worse. The film portrays Gerhard Richter's Aunt Marianne as a likeness of Kurt's Aunt Elizabeth who, despite her appearance and citizenship, fails to politically conform. As a boy, Kurt becomes agonized after witnessing Elizabeth arrested and starts to fill the non-apparent void with drawing. She is arrested for disregarding a fascist ordering of the world where "appearances are not merely deceptive but doomed to be incomplete..." (Lane and Brody 72). Even though she was tall, blonde, and not infertile—a model Nazi poster girl—Elizabeth's free expression led her to be labeled mentally ill and sterilized. Elizabeth is a rebellious, beautiful creature, like the artwork and ephemeral sensory expression her nephew eventually paints.

From the beginning, Elizabeth exposes Kurt to art and shows him how to engage the senses. On a trip to the Dresden Art Museum with his aunt, Kurt is lectured by a Nazi museum guide who claims even a child could paint Kandinsky. This guide critiques modern and expressionist paintings by Picasso, Mondrian, Otto Dix, and Rene Magritte as examples of the degenerate New Objectivity Movement (*Neue Sachlichkeit*). Memories of the museum trip with his aunt impress the boy, who later enrolls at Dresden Art Academy in East Germany. There Kurt hears an anti-communist speech on art like the Nazi lecture that prohibits "Modernist and Expressionist artworks which is vain and stupid, disrespects the proletariat and contaminates the viewer with mysticism, pornography, and narcissism—'*ich, ich, ich*'" (Donnersmarck et al.). Both Nazi and Communist institutions espouse the regressive view that art should convey a message and serve an institution. Incidentally, neither the boy nor his aunt buy the "message."

After participating in a Nazi parade, Elizabeth breaks a plate on her head and plays the piano naked in front of her young nephew. This snap is perhaps a hysteric channeling of the mass cultural psychosis demonstrated at the march. As mentioned in *History Beyond Trauma*, the cause of her madness appears connected to catastrophic socio-historic events (Gaudillière 211). Kurt uses art as a tool for unintentionally reflecting through erased truths about his aunt connected to disasters in World War II Germany. The artist's response to Elizabeth differs from her family who, unable to resist or shift perspective, cave under Nazi pressure, and eventually report her to the authorities.

Elizabeth's disappearance makes a void and bodily sensed muse for Kurt's drawing. He sketches her many times after the parade, piano, and plate scenes. These renderings multiply as the artist develops a devotion to drawing which crosses every realm of life and art. This devotion shows up later in Kurt's first love interest who—like the real-life painter—has the exact same name (Marianne/Elizabeth) as his departed aunt. Nicknames allow the painter to maintain a distance, while simultaneously keeping the muse close. Gerhard Richter called his first wife "Ema," short for her full name, which was Marianne Eufinger. Likewise, in the film Kurt calls his girlfriend "Elly," short for Aunt Elizabeth. Using a variable muse to reflect through trauma, the artist begins creatively multiplying, negating, and playing with representation.

This practice of play with language and non-representational symbols escalates and continues in the artist's painting. *Never Look Away* screens the artwork as communicating a truth not based on identification. This type of expression relates to Lacan's later seminars that rethink the "Name of the Father" as only one way to organize symbolic psychic structures. In both the film and real life, the artist uses neologism, negation, and auto-poesis to create through a "saying (*dire*) that is behind all that is said (*dit*) -which is something that arises in historical actuality" (Lacan, "On Psychoanalytic

Discourse"). Kurt inadvertently turns to an artistic ritual to survive, speak, and remain mobile despite cultural oppressors that Joyce so well describes:

> I will tell you what I will do and what I will not do. I will not serve that in which I no longer believe whether it calls itself my home, my fatherland, or my church and I will try to express myself in some mode of life or art as freely as I can and as wholly as I can, using for my defense the only arms I allow--silence, exile and cunning. (Joyce 247)

As a cinematic art of saying (*l'act dire*), *Never Look Away* screens over Gerhard Richter's praxis of painting by renaming (dire) the artist as Kurt, overpainting, and rhythmic negation.

On the challenge of depicting fluctuation in form, Gerhard Richter says,

> Pictures which are interpretable, and which contain meaning are bad pictures. A good picture takes away our certainty because it deprives a thing of its meaning and its name. It shows us the thing in all the manifold significance and infinite variety that preclude the emergence of any single meaning and view. (Tallman 4)

A good picture displays variability in negation by scraping the canvas of its meaning and name. The film redoubles the picture by screening over the painter's life and work to show it as a relation of manifold uncertain "Things."

The first part of *Never Look Away* is set in East Germany between 1932 and 1945 and full of lengthy, dark, and opulent historic images, which like Gerhard Richter's artworks look at the overlooked. It contains a plethora of blue scenes that indicate loss and foreshadow catastrophe. When Elizabeth invites Kurt to accompany her at the Dresden art museum, he is impressed by his aunt's candid speech and sensory embrace of the ephemeral aesthetic. Unlike the artist's real mother, Elizabeth becomes a muse for Kurt's painting through beats, pulses, and strokes, which like Joyce's "*saint-homme . . .* [take] his art to the point of excess" (Lacan, "Joyce the Symptom II" 3). Arhythmic noise resounds at a bus depot during their ride home when Elizabeth asks every driver to honk in sync. Blue saturates this scene where camera pans follow her circling to buses blaring, which signal that the whole society is out of tune.

Kurt's fascination only increases after seeing his aunt spin around hands out to siren sounds, looking like "whatever deserves to live through melody" (Lacan, *The Sinthome* 34). Yet, blue lights cast a dead pallor on her skin that foreshadows her untimely death. This scene presages the parade where Elizabeth's clear calm blue eyes follow a passing Nazi train, and she passes Hitler flowers. As the camera loops backs to the parking lot, a blue twilight settles on the two young people, holding hands, dazed as if hit by a whirlwind. This camera shift is repeated later when Kurt returns to the bus depot without his aunt and repeats the scene. All this circular movement and clamor signals a societal madness that the artist later exposes in a praxis of painting after Elizabeth vanishes.

On their way home from the museum, his aunt whispers in Kurt's ear, "the truth is, don't tell anyone but I like painting," then adds "your father is very strong to defy the Nazis" (Donnersmarck et al.). Her expressions are not spoken loudly. Neither Elizabeth nor Kurt's father exhibit the proper zeal for Nazi politics. When Kurt's father loses his teaching job, most of the family vilifies him. Contrarily, Elizabeth articulates his father's courage. The painter never turns away from her haunting words, which become emblematic of other erased voices in history.

Elizabeth's whispers stay with Kurt even after his father and aunt are dead. When Elizabeth is driven away to an asylum, she mouths the words "never look away" through the bus window. He reads her lips, takes these unspoken words to heart, and makes Elizabeth "the woman object [who] is presented as impossible or as a non-human partner. The analysand's work [like the artist's] is well situated in this place, the public having never become a partner for him" (Brousse 69). Elizabeth becomes the artist's non-human partner in painting as an artistic act of silent saying (*l'act dire*).

This artistic expression of what cannot be said publicly connects to "the splendor of Antigone" in Lacan's *Seminar VII. Never Look Away* depicts Kurt's Nazi father-in-law, like Creon, as an advocate of an unjust law that is eventually exposed. The painter in *Never Look Away*, like Antigone, engages in a performative act of silent saying that counters official history and law. In burying her brother Polyneices, Antigone stages negation and inverts symbolic law. Both Kurt and Antigone upend the trauma of war by resurfacing a family member or ancestor effaced by an insane political rule. Antigone's act—like Kurt's art—is a tragic engagement of the truth regarding the dead relative whose name and cultural history are erased. This truth is not expressed through direct communication but through a performance where the artistic actor situates themself as both within and outside a symbolic frame.

Lacan discusses Antigone's act of burial, like the artist's painting, as a performative expression of *Emoi* (Lacan, *The Ethics of Psychoanalysis, 1959–1960, Book VII* 249). *Emoi* is a sensory expression of an erased truth and void, which, like a parallax view, is outside the frame of representational reality as what is spoken. It translates from the French into English as a tumult, sensation, or agitated movement that is *frisson*. Further, *Emoi* "has nothing to do with emotion nor with being moved. . . . In any case [it stages] a question of power . . . involved in the sphere of your power relations; it is notably something that makes you lose them" (Lacan, *The Ethics of Psychoanalysis, 1959–1960, Book VII* 249). The painter like Antigone accedes to *Emoi* instead of force to show a painful performative truth beyond recognition and naming. In surrendering to *Emoi*, the artist envisions their own death and exclusion from symbolic reality to witness to the "madness" of law. *Antigone* like Gerhard Richter's *Tante Marianne* is a tragic artwork whose splendor comes from its performative and parallax view. It emerges below the belt, so to speak, as an unintentional artistic act that shows an erased history.

What Lacan calls *Emoi* is akin to what Deleuze describes as the "logic of the sensation." In his book on Paul Cezanne, Gilles Deleuze describes painting and other art forms as enactments driven by sensation, agitation, and rhythm. As the unique pulse of artistic appearing, rhythm is what

> the painter would thus make visible . . . a "logic of the senses," as Cézanne said, which is neither rational nor cerebral. What is ultimate is thus the relation between sensation and rhythm, which places in each sensation the levels and domains through which it passes this rhythm runs through a painting just as it runs through a piece of music. It is diastolic-systolic: the world that seizes me by closing in around me, the self that opens itself to the world, and opens the world itself. (Deleuze, *Francis Bacon* 37)

As the beat driving all appearance, rhythm is only seen indirectly but organizes all formation. It is felt as what compels the creative process through *Emoi* as an agitated opening or closing of sensations. Deleuze notes that rhythm's control of sensation is usually repressed except by the artist who bodily performs and cultivates a "logic of the senses."

Kurt's auto-poesis is a submission to affective rhythmic sensations—what Lacan calls *Émoi* and Deleuze calls the "logic of sensation"—that are not sublime. The artist's painting process involves an exhausting ritual of variable gestures, brush strokes, blurs, scrapes, and rhythms of the body. Aunt Elizabeth's disappearance condemns Kurt to this aesthetic bodily praxis. His painting—like Gerhard Richter's—is an all-encompassing, physically taxing life-long performance of revivifying what vanishes via rhythm. As the filmmaker Corinna Belz notes,

> There's a physicality to these pictures, because he really works the paint on the canvas; the layers and movements of color are so beautiful. And Richter himself has a strong physical presence when he's painting. The way he works with the squeegee the elegant sweeping motion, his assessment of the paintings—we could capture all that better with the and-held camera.[6]

Part III of the film, between 1955 and 1965, shows the painter's first exhibit with *Tante Marianne* (1965), which inaugurates the artist's career in the West. Its melancholic hues echo the film's initial use of blue, which has been associated with aristocracy or eugenicist ideology. Yet, blue appears throughout *Never Look Away* as a sign of extreme vulnerability, death, beauty, sadness, and political failure. The film's blue shades portend the aunt's spiral into death but also the artist's long-term praxis of creative transformation through disaster and loss. Blue is analogous for a mourning that Jacques Lacan relates to the lost object, which is excluded from representation but persists in the unconscious. Yet, the artist is not "blue" or in mourning. Rather, he has lost track of loss and looks into the void of the muse via arrhythmic aesthetic engagement.

Never Look Away displays a melancholic beauty akin to Gerhard Richter's paintings, especially *Tante Marianne* (1965). While not even knowing the history or name of that woman, countless riveted viewers never look away. As a character only briefly seen, Elizabeth is a ghost whose appearance is also a disappearance that compels a look back. The film, like Richter's art, facilitates what Kaja Silverman calls a "retro-vision" of traumatic memories by facilitating reflection through what resists naming (Beckman 3). The artist, like the melancholic, does not remember, except via performing the rhythmic ritual of painting through trauma and disaster. Silverman suggests that Gerhard Richter's paintings help viewers work through disasters that are diminished in news briefs or not recorded in history. Richter's artworks engage the viewer without trying to categorize, explain, or measure the immeasurable.

Retro-vision is not about a material loss of reality like what Jacques Lacan calls the lost *object a*. Rather, it reflects an immaterial real pulsation, whose appearance is simultaneously its disappearance, like the mythic Eurydice. The film, like Richter's art, screens this overlooked or uncertain beat of history that eludes representation. Silverman notes how Richter's art changes over time from "feminizing death and attributing violence to the state he aligned with into transforming his horror into grief" (Silverman 211). In this way, Richter's paintings exemplify retro-vision as a way of reflecting through shared trauma. Their staged strokes are not simply personal and pulsate with counter-historic truths of a collective madness erased by official history.

Silverman's retro-vision, like Jacques Lacan's idea of *après-coup*, involves an Orphic look back at a traumatic pre-symbolic realm not reducible to symbolic naming. Reflections on this realm happen as a shock or agitation that echoes the primary cut of speaking being. This cut occurs as the voluntary castration of *being* required for identification and speaking. Civitarese notes that Freud's

> cotton -reel game tells us that any trauma is experienced unconsciously as a detachment from the maternal body. . . . The concept of rhythm would not emphasize a purely economic factor in the variation of the body's tension—a mere mechanics of hydraulics of the drives, so to speak—but a variation that is closely linked to the qualities of the object

and to the earlies phases of the relationship with the object, to its capacity for love by means of physical action and reverie. (Civitarese 906–07)

Speaking being unconsciously senses rhythm via this *fort-da* play of the cut and being a child negotiating the loss of their earliest love object.

Never Look Away screens the artist's aunt as this beat, the muse or hole in signification which contrasts with object *a*. This void compels the artist's praxis of painting via variable sensation around a primordial negation. In an unwitting look back, artists and activists play with what precedes a signifying system through variable driven sensations. Their work goes back to the sensory arrhythmic play of a child first sensing the power in speaking that punctures being. Unlike speaking beings who represses driven sensation, the artist taps into this play as rhythmic "contagion and transport of the muses" (Nancy 24). As exhibited in the film and painting, this arhythmic muse is not consciously accessed except indirectly via aesthetic engagements.

The first two parts of the film unfold from 1945 to 1955 and move between minimalist blue and color hues that indicate the artist's sensory development across a spectrum of movement, time, and place. At the end of Part I, the film cuts from the artists hometown of Dresden burning down in 1945 to blue shades of his aunt falling dead on the gas chamber floor. Tin foil drops from the dark blue and black sky while houses burn. The young painter and his family run outside to watch the fires then flee the exploding bombs. In real life, Gerhard Richter was born in Dresden and witnessed the destruction of his hometown of Waltersdorf. The Richter family moved to the now Polish town after his father was released as a World War II prisoner of war.

The second part of *Never Look Away* features pale yellow scenes of fields after the family moves to the country in 1948. There Kurt runs through a blowing wheat pasture and climbs a tree to panoramically view the whole scene. Reflecting upon the earth, sky and straw tips moving in the wind Kurt has an epiphany and realizes that *alles miteinander verbunden* (everything is connected). After surviving World War II, the bombing of Dresden, and the loss of his beloved aunt during childhood, the painter vows to paint the transient movement inherent to all creation. While his parents think he is crazy, Kurt is transformed by this epiphany that everything—like Elizabeth's whispers—is ephemeral. Moreover, he realizes that non-apparent movement is what animates and sustains all life. Thereafter, the artist paints the transient invisible rhythms that are everywhere but not always visible.

Sigmund Freud's 1915 essay "On Transience" describes the artist's unique connection to transience and their ability to express the ephemerality of all things (Freud).[7] On a walk with Freud, and Lou Andreas-Salomé, the poet Rainer-Marie Rilke becomes overwhelmed by immanent war. He proclaims that all the beauty they see on the walk—of the landscape and pre–world war German culture—will be swiftly destroyed. Freud does not see things with the same bleakness as Rilke, but the analyst admits that artists are able to convey the truth of transience. The painter, like the poet, vows to paint transience after presciently envisaging its disaster. By artistically preserving a transient landscape the artwork helps us remember what is erased.

Colors begin to amplify at the end of Part II when the family moves back to Dresden in 1951 and Kurt leaves East Germany right before the wall is erected in 1961. This corresponds to Gerhard Richter's artistic career, which was launched after leaving East Germany. In 1961, Gerhard Richter quit the Dresden Art Academy, emigrated to the West, and enrolled at Düsseldorf Art Academy. It was in Düsseldorf that Richter studied with Joseph Beuys, a professor and founder of the Fluxus movement. It was also in West Germany that Richter finally enjoyed a circle of friends and future artistic collaborators, including Sigmar Polke, Konrad Fischer, and Blinky Palermo. There, the artist was able to engage a vibrant community of artists, exhibitions, and events—not least of which was the ZERO group founded by Otto Piene and Heinz Mach in 1957. In the 1970s, Gerhard Richter continued making pictural sculptures from photos, including color landscapes, misty skulls, and illusory windows revealing the influences of Vermeer and Velazquez.

While *Never Look Away* ends with Kurt's first exhibition in Dusseldorf, that was just the beginning of Gerhard Richter's career. His artwork has flourished globally after the fall of the Berlin Wall (*Die Wende*). In 2007, Richter settled in Cologne, and in 1983 when being made an honorary citizen, he created a stained-glass window consisting of 11,500 pixel-like squares. Richter's *Cologne Cathedral Window* has been likened to his color square style of paintings. The window installation is synergistic and based on the colors of natural light, as one critic notes:

> In theory, [it] a reprise—its approximately 11,500 color squares were arranged by algorithm and tweaked by the artist to remove any suggestion of symbols or ciphers—the experience it provides is utterly distinct. The squares are made of glass using medieval recipes, they rise collectively some seventy-five feet, and are part of a gothic cathedral. When the sun shines through and paints floors, walls and people with moving color, the effect is aleatoric, agnostic, and otherworldly. (Tallman 4)

There is nothing square or static about Richter's stained-glass windows. It casts a contingent play of light that goes beyond the windowpane as a square framed object. The *Cologne Cathedral Window* mediates, intwines, and connects the rhythmic flow of the people, light, and noise that are both outside and within.

The huge, oblique, and slanted window throws variable moving colors that reflect through the cathedral. The window's intensity comes from its linking of rhythms outside and within, for example, the sun rising or falling that casts a shadow within, noises outside that join the elevated hush of prayers. In 2020, Richter gave a separate set of stained-glass windows to the oldest working abbey in Germany. This abbey is home to 12 Benedictine monks and is situated in tranquil green hills near the borders of France and Luxembourg. An article in *The Times* notes that "in brief comments reported by the German press agency DPA on Wednesday, Mr. Richter said the Tholey windows might be the last entry in the official catalog of his works, which begins with the 1962 painting *Table*" (Hickley C2). As only three artworks away from 1,000 at the time of this article, Richter's artistic output seemed prodigious and infinitely enduring. Yet, the color-saturated Tholey Window is a final gift, which, as the artist notes, will reflect the ephemeral rhythms of life long after Richter's catalogued works and life end.

Too Spectacular: Parallax Screens

Traumatic events or a violent political legacy often exceed perspective such that, as W.G. Sebald says, "When we turn to take a retrospective view, particularly of the years 1930 to 1950, we are always looking and looking away at the same time" (Sebald viii–ix). *Never Look Away* screens over Richter's technique of overpainting to both "look and look away" from representational history like the artist. Overpainting involves an indirect perspective like what Slavoj Žižek calls a "parallax view." *Tante Marianne* (1965) is one of the first paintings that utilizes a parallax view to paint over a photograph on canvas, animate, and bring inverted images to life. This perspective first appears in *Never Look Away* when the artist as a young child uses four fingers to form and flip a "V/ ∧" frame around his eyes. The redoubled V frame makes an "X" that allows the Kurt to keep looking when his aunt is taken away and later to paint through traumatic events. This parallax perspective enables the artist to both look and not look, as situated both inside and outside a visual frame.

A parallax view inverts the symbolic to expose the antagonism between object *a* and the void. The artist uses this view to look past appearance: "The standard definition of parallax is the apparent displacement of an object (the shift of its position against a background) caused by a change in observational position that provides a new line of sight" (Žižek 17). Kurt uses the flipped double "V/ ∧" frame to invert and contrast a lost object, that is, Elizabeth as object *a*, with a primary void. The artist adopts this gaze after his aunt's whispers that he "never look away."

Speaking being avoids the parallax view to focus on object *a*. It tries to avoid ever seeing the void that is repressed after mirror identification. The initial mirror connection occurs when a child watching itself in the mirror identifies with the specular "haste, thrust and forward movement" (Lacan, *The Four Fundamental Concepts of Psychoanalysis* 118). This movement is sutured with the *fascinum* after identification occurs and being acquiesces to speaking. Yet, subjectivity is not entirely reducible to the image, name, or representational identification. Jacques Lacan notes how the artist, and specifically the painter, uses the gaze and bodily gestures to render the non-representational movement of being.

In layman's terms, visual art and painting uses a parallax view to show the transient moment one sees that they were not seeing. Lacan describes Merleau-Ponty's method of painting as an example of " . . . *trompe-l'oeil.* For it appears at that moment as something other than it seemed or rather it now seems to be that something else" (*The Four Fundamental Concepts of Psychoanalysis* 112). Like the *trompe l'oeil*, a parallax view allows the viewer to see "something else" beside mimetic forms. Kurt's technique of inverting, blurring, and eviscerating a painted image follows Gerhard Richter in facilitating parallax reflection. This type of artwork shows that what we are seeing depends upon the way we are looking. Žižek notes, "What characterizes some of Gerhard Richter's paintings is the sudden passage from (slightly transposed/blurred, true) photographic realism to a pure abstraction of color stains . . . as if, all of the sudden, we found ourselves on the opposite side of a Moebius strip" (Žižek 152).

A parallax view contrasts two opposing ontological views, for example, appearances with the non-apparent, a lost object with a primary loss. Žižek explains how "the *object a* is the very cause of the parallax gap, that unfathomable X which forever eludes symbolic. . . . Another name for the parallax gap is therefore minimal difference, a pure' difference which cannot be grounded in positive substantial properties" (Žižek 18). The painter renders this minimal difference as a contrast between pre-symbolic movement and symbolic identification. After flipping his fingers "V" up and down "∧" over his eyes, Kurt does not incessantly paint his aunt, that is, the lost object. Rather, he uses a parallax "X" to paint the void and reflect through real traumatic or transient events.

Lacan's *Seminar XI: The Four Fundamental Concepts of Psychoanalysis* analyzes the scopic as a paradigm for all the other drives since it exposes a variable stain in representation. Lacan notes how Cézanne contrasts two mutually exclusive arcs of driven movement on the canvas. This is done through oscillating attunement to the antagonism of symbolic reality and the ticklish real. A parallax view happens unintentionally through sensory exposure to the agitation outside representation. Likewise, when Kurt is asked to explain his painting technique to critics, he repeats Elizabeth's words that "everything that is true is beautiful" (Donnersmarck et al.). His response conveys how art is not intentional but an attunement to variable sensory repetition.

Philosophers before Žižek, like Kant, describe the parallax view as the aporia of the *noumenal* thing-in-itself (*Ding an sich*) and *phenomenal* object realm. Kant explores reflective judgment as a method for aesthetically approaching this unbridgeable gap in his third *Critique*. Reflective judgment relates to Žižek s idea of a parallax view where "the roles are reversed (with regard to the standard notion of the active subject working on the passive object): the subject is defined by a fundamental passivity, and it is the object from which movement comes, i.e., which does the tickling" (Žižek 17).[8] Unlike Kant's elevating sublime, a parallax view is not active or uplifting, but a passive and plummeting exposure to variable ticklish sensations.

A parallax view engages an arrhythmic ticklish agitation, which guides the artist. The artist realizes ontological difference through this agitation that is an attunement to an ontological dehiscence within being, as Žižek notes via Heidegger: "The attitude of *Gelassenheit* (openness)" . . . [to the tickling that] "is a symptomal 'point of torsion,' the 'impossible' intersection of the two officially opposed discourses . . . what Heidegger calls being as active resoluteness, the extreme effort of willing, and the passive attunement to the world" (Žižek 279). As a sensorily open and engaged dis/position, a parallax view allows the painter to explore the "torsion" between ontological (real, imaginary, and symbolic) registers.

The painter's parallax view contrasts the "X" of Being/being by working through the "terminal time of the gaze, . . . which completes the gesture. . . . The gaze in itself not only terminates the movement, it freezes it. Take those dances I mentioned—they are always punctuated by a series of times of arrest" (Lacan, *The Four Fundamental Concepts of Psychoanalysis* 117–18). The painter marks the "X" that contrasts the tickling void and dancing intervals of pre-symbolic being with mirror identification. Playing with visual limits, the painter (Cézanne, Richter, Kurt) puts the dance and tickling movement back into the picture but as reflectively redoubled and left out.

Painters use the gaze to render real movement that is usually left out of mimetic screens that saturate everyday life. Mirrors, computers, phones, and machines all communicate and connect spectators, but also facilitate imaginary capture. The artwork foregrounds the narcissistic entrapment that goes unnoticed in a fetishized mimetic screen by inverting the "conjunction of the imaginary and the symbolic, and it is taken up again in a dialectic, . . . which is concluded in the *fascinum*, which is what arrests movement and kills non-representational life" (Lacan, *The Four Fundamental Concepts of Psychoanalysis* 118). The painter reopens the dialectic to expose the movement of non-representational being via the *fascinum*.

A parallax screen incorporates its own blind spot or specular limits. Gerhard Richter's artwork is a tireless engagement of institutional, physical, and psychic limits, including genre. In this sense, his technique might also be compared to what the Romantics called negative capability, as one critic notes, "his soft-focus landscapes and portraits channel both the *Sturm am und Drang* of German Romanticism and the cool distance of contemporary photography. Uncertain terms were Richter's métier, and critics simply did not know what to do with it" (Tallman 4–5). His style avoids genre classification by incorporating uncertainty in representing. Richter has spent a lifetime evading and multiplying classifications. His multivalent shifting styles and inversion of rules in painting only magnify his fame.

Gerhard Richter's parallax painting involves an arrhythmic negation, pulverization, and proliferation of signifying images. His experiments with technique range across a tremendous set of performative gestures. Glenn D. Lowry, the director of the museum, wrote in a catalog of a 2002 retrospective of Richter's work at the Museum of Modern Art in New York City:

> No artist of the postwar era has placed more intriguing and rigorous demands upon specialists, interpreters, followers, and average viewers alike—nor upon himself. In Richter's work . . . there is a demonstration of the way in which painting's resources are constantly replenished by the very problems it seems to pose, both for the painter and viewer. (Storr et al. 7)

Richter's abstract, scrubbed, or squeegeed strokes allow the viewer to see movement in the picture. It uses a parallax view and process approach to contrast a transient non-apparent real with the spectacle of modern-day "virtual reality"—social media platforms, personalized screens, and political and cultural rhetoric. As inverting symbolic and imaginary registers, Richter's artworks suspend extremist rigidity in all forms, including online rhetoric.

Never Look Away cinematically redoubles the Richters in a parallax view that reflects through, rather than chronologically mirroring history and cultural events. It screens over the real artist's earliest traumatic experiences, including the Dresden bombings, the Stasi painting period, and family entanglements with Nazi officials. For example, war is a feature of the film and so many of Richter's paintings, not only *Aunt Marianne* but also the later series *Stripes WTC* (2006), which depicts the American tragedy of 9/11. This series of linked pictures moves from clear photos of the towers getting hit to indecipherable monochromatic gray and blue screens. Richter's sequence of pictures goes from representative to abstract images of burgeoning steel haze which simulate the incomprehension of that disastrous day. This process is redoubled but not imitated in the film, which screens war alongside uncertain intervals in the painter's life and work.

Many of Richter's artworks, including *September*, the *WTC* series, and the Baader-Meinhof series, make an open-ended inversion of a dominant viewpoint in history. His works spark reflection upon war and traumatic events like 9/11 as not reducible to one *instant* but part of an *interval*. Each contrasting picture in the *Stripes/Steifen, WTC* 2006 series echoes a real transient, traumatic, and horrific moment as one part of a cultural, political, and artistic interval. Clearer depictions of the twin towers simulate viewers trying to find, keep, and preserve an image that explains what is happening.

Less clear images simulate the instants after the bombings where dark blue and gray dust clouds all vision. Each picture in the series echoes the uncertainty happening on the ground, on TV, and in the media that day. Finally, the last pictures in the *WTC* sequence where colors bleed conveys the total obliteration of vision and apprehension that occurs in war. These images culminate in a parallax and inverted view from the ruins underneath the rubble. The last images take on the perspective of being under the collapsing towers and seeing their shaky and fragile structures finally fall. Richter's paintings invert the viewer's gaze to reflect upon that disturbing instant—which emerges as quickly as it disappears—as part of a larger interval.

Painting often engages an historic instant but in the classic tradition. History painting is a genre of the 17th, 18th, and 19th century, for example, *The Raft of the Medusa* (1819) by Thèodore Géricault. Traditionally, history painting celebrates and symbolizes a grand powerful figure or event. Richter's *September* and *WTC* series reverse this tradition by depicting an instant in partial mimetic form then dissipating its grandiosity into ambiguity. This technique requests history be viewed differently, as one critic notes,

> *September* exemplifies one possible mode of activated viewership vis-à-vis media images of international conflict, such as those associated with 9/11 . . . the viewer herself, emerges not as a passive media con sumer but as exemplifying an emerging form of citizenship, one that challenges preconceived notions of what national belonging is. In this view, the power of the citizen lies not only in the expression of her voice but also on the right to see—and crucially to see differently. This right is precisely what ambiguous artworks such as September, which interrupts and expands predominant historic and political narratives without guiding the viewer toward a specific direction, encourages. (Dâmaso 169–70)

Richter's doing and undoing of an historic instant, particularly his images of terrorism, war, and disaster, do not celebrate or interpret a moment. Rather, they allow viewers to affectively and reflectively keep looking at violent and traumatic events as part of a larger symbolic war waged in history.

Richter parallaxes the tradition of history paintings in artworks that span over a half century from World War II to the Iraq War. Both *Aunt Marianne* and the *WTC* series invert and complicate triumphant or nostalgic images of history. His parallax process of overpainting and unpainting stretches the bounds of time and the instant to elicit a more activated spectator.

Similarly, the film makes an interval by screening uncertain instants both within and beyond the bounds of official history to activate spectatorship. One example is when Dr. Seeband goes to Kurt's studio and sees himself and his Nazi associates as scary through the penetrating gaze of the paintings. Like Gerhard Richter, Kurt paints over a whole sequence of family photos and newsclips which Seeband eerily recognizes and tries to repress. In this scene, the painter uses the gaze to invert mimetic certainty, interrupt an official perspective, put history into question, and present a counter-history.

The painter's parallax view relates to what Gerhard Richter says about his artistic approach in a 2004 interview: "My approach is very simple. Whatever is real is so unlimited and unshaped that we have to summarize it. The more dramatic events are, the more important the form. . . . Form is all we have to help us cope with fundamentally chaotic facts and assaults" (Thorn-Prikker 26). It is ironic that Richter describes his artistic techniques—including painting over a photo—as simple. There is nothing simple about the artist's parallax process that breaks down an "assault of fundamentally chaotic facts" to expose a transient real.

Screening over Richter's parallax praxis, *Never Look Away* reopens questions regarding past events in German history adjoining the artworks. Instead of confirming facts for the viewer, the film makes a variable speculative and sensory screen. From its inception, cinema has followed physiological rhythms of the body like human breathe. As it is a reel unity of moving images, Reneé Clair declared film an "orchestration of images and rhythms" (Henriques et al. 10). It is an art form, like music and painting, that incorporates a rhythmic reel to open reflection. *Never Look Away* engages a sensory reel to show how "everything [*tout*] changes from one to the other. On the other hand, the movement-image include intervals" (Deleuze, *Cinema 2: The Time-Image* 29). The film engages its own visual limits in a word play with official names, naming, and documentary music to stress a rhythmic real outside the screen.

Never Look Away features two artists with the same last name Richter, who are very different. In addition to Gerhard Richter—the renowned painter—the film score features music by the remarkable composer Max Richter. His post-minimalist modern classical music compositions are exemplary of documentary musical form. Max Richter's music documents the lives of notable artists, politicians, wars, and other historic events. In addition to filmic scores, Max Richter composes for stage, opera, ballet, and theater. His first album (2002) entitled *Memoryhouse* (2002) echoes the aftermath of the Kosovo conflict (Richter). Max Richter's other albums aurally document the lives and works of notable politician or artists, namely Franz Kafka, Eleanor Roosevelt, Virginia Woolf, and Czeslaw Milosz. Like the film, documentary composition is a non-mimetic rhythmic expression that musically tells the story of historic lives and moments.

Each track on Max Richter's recent album *Exiles* is a carefully curated expression about the outbreak of war in Iraq.[9] On his own musical process, Richter says: "I think creativity by its nature is activism," he says. "It's about meaning, it's about experiment, it's about the unknown, it's about discovery" (Lister).

Max Richter's idea of documentary music and creativity as activism is echoed in *Never Look Away*'s musical score. The film engages all the "richters" as layers of an artistic screen that engage the

> body with its great intelligence . . . [it] seeks with the eyes of the senses, it also listens with the ears of the spirit. . . . Behind your thoughts and feelings, my brother, stands a mighty ruler, an unknown sage—it is called the subconscious self; it dwells in your body, it is your body. (Voigt, "The Great Reason of the Body")

Never Look Away encourages viewers to see with their ears or hear with their eyes. Its sensory play with the name "Richter" exemplifies the film's redoubling of representation into a rhythmic play, not only with the painter and musician, but also with many of characters whose names are fictive doubles of well-known German citizens.

The German word *richter* means to make right or judge. In English, it refers to measures of velocity or ripple effects after an earthquake. Yet, the film does not judge the artists or German history. Rather, it overscreens the rhythms that follow traumatic events as sensory expressions that elicit reflective judgment. These variable rhythms, like vibrations on the Richter Scale, activate the spectator as not reducible to any specific memory or message. A seismograph, like a parallax screen, exposes sensory pre-inscriptions of earthshaking traumatic events. These eruptions cannot be seen directly or fully explained by social media, dominant historic narratives, or law. *Never Look Away* multiplies artistic forms of engagement to parallax the cinematic screen into "richtering rhythms." It inverts official names and facts—Donnersmarck, Kurt, Gerhard, Max, and Richter—to echo real seismic, transient, and traumatic vibrations in creation.

State Owned Womb: Blood Mirrors

Werk Ohne Autor (Work without an Author) is the film's original German title and the literal phrase that art critics used to discuss Richter's work in the seventies. This was due to Richter's refusal to disclose any biographical material and the artworks' seeming lack of subjectivity. While the film eschews direct correlation, it is cast from exchanges between the artist and Donnersmarck. The director began filming after reading an investigative journalism piece by Jürgen Schreiber in 2004 on Richter's father-in-law. It reports that Heinrich Eufinger was an infamous SS gynecologist and responsible for thousands of women being forcibly sterilized and gassed, including Richter's aunt. The artist's famous painting that contains his aunt's name, *Tante Marianne* (1965) is now directly linked to his life. Donnersmarck interviewed Richter for hours, recording retorts like "my paintings know more than I do." These interchanges were friendly and even led to declare

Richter not only a "master of visual representation" but also a "master of narrative" (Goodyear 34).

Jürgen Schreiber's article exposed Gerhard Richter's father-in-law as the Nazi doctor and renowned gynecologist Heinrich Eufinger, who was a notorious Nazi ob-gyn who ordered the sterilization of incalculable women, including Richter's own Aunt Marianne. After World War II, the Nazi doctor was never taken to court or tried for his horrible crimes, including sterilization, euthanasia, and genocide. Indeed, until the recent article by Schreiber, Heinrich Eufinger was honored and memorialized in a portrait at the gynecology hospital in Dresden. In the film, Eufinger is played by the actor Sebastian Koch and called Dr. Carl Seeband.[10] Like Eufinger, Seeband was part of a team of SS Medical Corp. hospital officers and doctors deployed to sterilize and relieve crazy, handicapped, or infertile women of their "meaningless existence." The SS Medical Corp. eventually turned into the more ominous Waffen-SS, which was a formation of Nazi professional doctors who provided medical services to the state first.

In totalitarian governments where law is foreclosed or lack disavowed, citizens suffer under an arbitrary yet inflexible rule. *Never Look Away* portrays fascist leaders as uncastrated phallic fathers who arrest and pervert *jouissance*; this contrasts with the painter who nurtures creative expression against fascist ideologies. Dr. Seeband is not separated by phallic lack but still tied to the primordial womb. The film is fueled by an impasse between Kurt and Carl, the pervert versus the painter, as a position of *jouissance*. In disavowing the failure of law, Seeband exerts a perverse power over the womb to determine the true population of Germany. Contrarily, Kurt finds a parallax method of creative rebirth in painting. Their positions regarding *jouissance*, as Lacan says, entail "a distinction between the true and the real . . . the true is what gives pleasure, and this is just what distinguishes it from the real, which does not necessarily give pleasure . . . enjoyment [*jouissance*] is the real" (Lacan, *The Sinthome* 36). Kurt uses *jouissance* to provide visual pleasure and paint the truth, while Dr. Seeband hurts women with the hard real of medical purification.

After World War II, the film cuts to 1956 East Germany, which was when the Soviet Union took over Czechoslovakia, and many Germans started doubting that Communism was any better than what they lived through in the Third Reich. Kurt enrolls at the Dresden Art Academy, and he meets his future wife, and this is when the painter and the perverse gynecologist meet. After a short courtship, blue light settles over Ellie and Kurt in bed. Hearing her father return, dogs start barking as Kurt escapes, dropping naked from a tree out of a window. He lands right in front of Ellie's mother who doesn't reveal her daughter's secret and agrees to house Kurt as a tenant. Ellie's father, the former SS doctor now turned Communist gynecologist, Dr. Seeband, loathes the idea of anyone else controlling his daughter's womb. Without even knowing that Kurt's aunt was Elizabeth—a woman he marked for death—Dr. Seeband hates Kurt and starts a rumor that he is partially paralyzed.

While the artist siphons transient *jouissance* into painting, Dr. Seeband uses a perverse gaze to slice and slay women deemed unfit for motherhood—including his own daughter—by the state. As his name suggests, Dr. "See-band" puts a "vice or ban" on seeing as distinguishing by injuring, restraining, and shrouding the womb. Dr. Seeband originally appears in the film as a Nazi gynecologist who literally, physically, and politically controls the movement of femininity and fertility for the benefit of the state. In Nazi and extremist governments where there is no lack or Name of the Father, the phallic becomes maternal and perverse. This fascist leader exerts the most devastating form of institutional control disavowing lack and sadistically applying law without grace. Dr. Seeband enjoys using official diagnosis to control the maternal body and future German population.

Throughout the Dresden World War II bombing and into the Stasi occupation, Seeband's uncanny mansion stays beautiful and intact. The house, like the doctor himself, has no limits or distinctions between inside and out, public or private, personal or official. The Seebands host perpetual dance school classes on their first floor where people are waltzing constantly in motion but do not see anything that happens. In addition to aborting his daughter's child upstairs, Dr. Seeband surgically and speedily clenches every womb in his house. The conception of Kurt and Ellie's child is cinematically juxtaposed with Seeband and his secretary having mechanical sex. The Dr.'s enjoyment of assaulting wombs is not limited to his professional life and gets personal when his daughter becomes pregnant with Kurt's child out of wedlock. Seeband intuits her condition, including the month and date of the infant in utero with eerie precision, and aborts the child in the family home.

As with Kurt's aunt, Dr. Seeband labels Ellie's womb defective and eventually terminates the pregnancy. When she first tells Kurt, he quietly and clumsily proclaims his love, "well then you belong totally *to me—with me*—I mean." For a while they are happy until out of the blue, Dr. Seeband realizes his loss of control over Ellie and puts a vice grip on the couple. On a walk with the family, Dr. Seeband justifies the abortion to Kurt by lying about Ellie having a vaginal infection when she was a girl. After the baby is excised by her own father in their childhood home, Ellie starts disclosing more about her father's past as a Nazi doctor to Kurt. She recalls how during World War II, Seeband would narcissistically stand in front of a full-length mirror in uniformed Nazi regalia for hours admiring himself and practicing salutes.

Kurt's relationship is full of creative stops and starts in the studio and with Ellie that lead her to proclaim, "your pictures will have to be our children." After Dr. Seeband extinguishes their child, the young couple immigrate to the West and Elizabeth loses another baby. A doctor there says there was no infection, but that Seeband's abortion made her cervix insufficient to hold a pregnancy. Eventually, Elizabeth gets pregnant. The film includes this pregnancy, which is not a result of surgery, medicine, or her infertility being fixed. Rather, it is an artistic and mythical rebirth, an ordeal imagined in *Never Look Away* that is in no way verifiable as part of Gerhard Richter's life.

The film connects the artist's prolix with his personal life in a culminating scene of Barnert's first art exhibition. This exhibit includes the painting that eventually exposes Dr. Seeband, and a painting of Elizabeth that is a homage to Duchamp's "Nude Descending Staircase." In real life, Richter's painting is entitled "Ema (Nude Descending a Staircase)" and is based "mainly on photographs, which I received and then turned into paintings" (Richter et al. 262). The film adds another speculative dimension when it imagines that Kurt's paintings convict his father-in-law and aid the artist's rebirth out of Seeband's sterile and authoritarian grip.

In the film, Kurt's paintings eventually expose his father-in-law's crimes as part of a Nazi team of Waffen-SS doctors. While not arrested like the actual Nazi doctor Heinrich Eufinger, Dr. Seeband is stricken and doubles over, panicked, after being convicted by the gaze of Kurt's paintings. As part of the Nazi charge, Dr. Seeband regulates bare life and the womb with an immobilizing grip that continues beyond World War II. He enjoys the title of Professor after helping an occupying Russian Stasi officer's wife give birth. Yet when the Russian occupation ends, Dr. Seeband is eventually forced to flee Germany, like the real Dr. Eufinger, who survives reputation enact until Schreiber's article. Meanwhile Kurt, like Gerhard Richter, survives by immigrating with his first wife to West Germany where he is finally able to paint freely outside a fascistic regime. In these juxtapositions, *Never Look Away* contrasts the crime of creative expression with cultural and political crimes never officially sentenced or adjudicated by law.

Today, the enemies of creativity are ideologies of security and safety that view free expression as dangerous. Military intelligence and social media play a dominant role in policing privacy and controlling creative expression. Whistle blowers, social media critics, and uncategorizable voices are deemed unsafe or treated with suspicion. Jacques-Alain Miller describes how art or analysis is non-conformist in that

> The very thing that is forbidden in usual life becomes allowed in analysis; you are invited to speak your unspeakable desire, and if you don't, your dreams will speak for you. So . . . according to Freud everyone is a criminal in the Unconscious. . . . There is some permissiveness in analysis and in that sense psychoanalysis is anti-social . . . you will obtain what I could define as a capacity to dialogue with your Unconscious, to put it at use, to work with it. That would be the 'true promise of psychoanalysis. (Miller 211–12)

Art, like psychoanalysis—is committed to the "criminal" unconscious and "unsafe" dialogue that cannot be controlled by any platform, institution, or ideology. Its vow is to free associative expression as a vehicle for working through immobilizing representation.

Never Look Away runs for almost three hours and covers almost 30 years of German history, between when Gerhard Richter was born in 1932, and ends in the 1960s at the time of his first exhibition. Over the course of Gerhard Richter's life, the crisis of representation and explosion of extremist rhetoric has only multiplied while everyone assumes to "know" what they are seeing. *Never Look Away* parodies the extremism of both late capital and communist rhetoric that reduces art and creative movement to a political message. The desire to reduce art or analysis to interpretation is not unique to fascist Germany and exists in America today. Politicians use social media, technology, and advertising to twist facts and control cultural expression.

Extremist governments attempt to clamp down on any sort of creative life pulse, especially the womb. The fascist state declares the womb monstrous, an overwhelming *Das Ding* in the absence of castration. Given the perfect is the enemy of the good, Dr, Seeband and his team swiftly sterilize and euthanize to perfect the future German population through diagnosis. In disavowing a lack of a cure, Freud himself imposed a forced diagnosis and closed the Wolf Man case out prematurely. Schneiderman says Freud injured the Wolf Man by affixing a cure on the *jouissance* of his melancholia. (Schneiderman 124). While the Freudian diagnosis is not equivalent culturally or politically to Nazi crimes, doctors in both cases hastily imposed a diagnosis that stopped free expression, which is the aim of art and analysis.

After the film's release, Gerhard Richter expressed unhappiness to one critic, stating,

> To recall all the events, I had a look into the quite hefty folder regarding the case von Donnersmarck. Unfortunately, this visualization of all the facts caused such bad feelings and my dislike of both the movie and the person grew so much again...With best regards, Gerhard Richter. (Goodyear 35)

Richer, on the side of analysand, ultimately refused that position and deemed Donnersmarck's film a diagnosis too rigid. His dismay emerged after countless interviews with Richter in which the director claimed: "He told me everything—truly everything—about his life and was amazingly open." Donnersmarck added, "I ended up staying for one month and recording this stuff, which really I think makes any biography of his completely obsolete" (34).

After all their interactions, both Donnersmarck and Gerhard Richter stopped talking to let the film allobiographically speak. The painter and director fell out because the film is not "a psychoanalytic study of the creator and the creation, using the work or the biography of the artist. It is a matter of an interrogation of the enigma sublimation has for the artist himself" (Brousse 68).[11] The only part of their encounters that was pleasurable for both was the style of interview, which touched Gerhard Richter deeply enough to say; "He [Donnersmark] was like a psychoanalyst" (Goodyear 41).

Atlas: OverScreening

After immigrating to the West months before the erection of the Berlin Wall, Gerhard Richter enrolled at the Düsseldorf Art Academy where Fluxus flourished. Historic ideas of rhythm saturated the Fluxus movement, which, in turn, impacted the paintings of Gerhard Richter. As a post-war network of artists affirming creative power, Fluxus opposed the fixture of existing cultural and political extremism. It is no accident that the Fluxus movement ignited in the 1960s, exactly as the DDR wall was erected and Stasi communism replaced Nazi fascism. True to its name, Fluxus was not a static or clearly defined movement but networks of associated artists that were fluid in both membership and form. While not strictly adhering to any artistic creed or affiliation, Fluxus commonly staged transient uncertainty to disrupt a rigid system. One art historian notes how a multiplicity of "early Fluxus performance festivals developed throughout Western Europe beginning in 1962 with a series of Fluxus concerts held in Wiesbaden, Copenhagen and Paris, followed by the seminal Festum Fluxorum Fluxus at the Dusseldorf Art Academy in 1963" (Sherer 5). In Dusseldorf during the 1960s, Richter connected with other artists who were also disillusioned by extremist politics and the creeping conformity of mass consumption.

Postwar Germany was a country trying to rehabilitate its identity. Cleverly, Fluxus underscored that the problem was viewing political, cultural, and even human identity as a fixed category at all. The movement used the performative and plastic arts to critique subjective and political stasis. Exposing the spectator to ambiguity, Fluxus art is a "construct of different realities different forms of common sense—that is to say, different spatio-temporal systems, different communities of words and things, forms and meanings" (Rancière 102). Active looking is one common thread in Fluxus art which embraces transience as a performative non-ground in creating. It is no accident then that Gerhard Richter's artworks eschew fixed artistic, philosophical, or political categories.

Richter artwork is discernably linked to the influence of Fluxus as a performative staging of earthly, bodily, and cultural movements or *Zeitgeists*. In 1963 with Konrad Lueg, Richter staged a demonstration entitled "Living with Pop" where the two artists hung their work and presented themselves alongside furniture showcased on pedestals with these words: "We presented ourselves not as artist, but as sculptures. I wanted to display myself as an occupant, as a member of the *petit bourgeoisie*, with this pathetic blanket on the sofa" (*1961–1964*). As a parody of *bourgeoisie* and analytic stasis, the artists made an inverse stage of the immobile couch-potato and analytic session.

The German term *Hauptström* means "mainstream, power line, or principle current" and it refers to a pull in vision or cultural norms.[12] As a founder of Fluxus, Joseph Beuys' art stresses performative repetition and the body as a vehicle for change, resistance, and reinvention. Beuys produced a series of artworks in the 1960s that included the word *Hauptström* stamped on a postcard to parody the senseless flow of bureaucratic and official communication. His artwork repeats the word and stages the postcard as a vehicle of language[13] in motion to show a "'joyfully grasped, albeit pre-Freudian energy unit that doesn't give a damn whether it is expressed or can be applied in a socially negative positive, harmful or useful way, runs throughout history, throwing off new forms each time." The postcards use the variably repeated word—*Hauptström*—to invert the movement of fixed messages that economically drives the mainstream into fluctuating uncertainty.

Historically, there are many false dichotomies in philosophy and art that both over- and underdetermine fluxion as an ontological or metaphysical category. Early German culture fetishized the idea of rhythm. Lines were drawn in an ontological split over the value of rhythm as linked to dull or vibrant personhood. Predating Fluxus, German *Körperkulter* of the 1920s fixated upon rhythm as a way of "overcoming the malaise of technological civilization through communal participation, ritual, and connection with nature (something that later became the core of fascists' politics in the 1930s)" (Henriques et al. 7). Weimar Germany had an exaggerated optimism about rhythm as an animator of nature, technology, and society. This led to dark politics and racist ideas about intrinsic syncopation as an indicator of childishness or inferiority in being.

Given its inception well after World War II, Fluxus was a transformative reaction to essentialist ideologies like Nazi and Stasi totalitarianism. It also began a critique of capitalist overdrive and the European shift into commodification. Contrary to capitalist fetishization of material objects, Fluxus stages being as transient intervals not reducible to material things. Fluxus' view of ephemerality as the basis of creation makes it the progeny of philosophers like the pre-Socratic Heraclitus whose fragment—one can never step in the same river twice—could be their anthem.

Fluxus engages an array of philosophical points of view and is not bound to any fixed ideology. Art historians including Hannah Higgens point out other theoretical and philosophical influences on Fluxus, such as the aesthetic theory of John Dewey and Maurice Merleau-Ponty (Higgins). *Das Autopoietische Subjekt* (2016) describes the influence of Friedrich Nietzsche's performative theory on Joseph Beuys (Voigt, *Friedrich Nietzsche und Joseph Beuys*). Beuys rejects his metaphysics but adopts and adapts Nietzschean ideas of identity and meaning as a fluid, performative, and auto-poetic bodily task. His performative sculptures work through the body and its sensations as not reducible to substance but as a vehicle of rebirth and change. Like Nietzsche, Beuys' happenings stage being as bound by variable bodily and untimely world repetitions. Unlike Nietzsche, Beuys' stage is non-transcendent. As mothers of Fluxus, these philosophical expressions presage and are a portend of Richter's painted rhythms.

Beuys' performative artworks expose rhythm as a force at work everywhere not only in the change and vulnerability of the body but in all life. Beuys stages subjectivity as the painful and performative task of being in the world.[14] The body—as political, subjective, and earthly— is not prearranged but must be shaped by potentially sculpting oneself through creative acts. In his reading of Nietzsche, Beuys left a question mark and a large "N" over a passage from "The Case of Wagner" (1888) where he [Nietzsche] writes: "All that is good is easy everything divine runs with light feet: this is the first principle of my aesthetics" (Voight 5). Here, Beuys' "N" mark appears to negate and disagree with Nietzsche's reflection.

This inversion perfectly reflects Beuys' aesthetics, where "almost nothing in his work is running on 'light feet'—it is mostly not about what is divine but what is human. His work focuses on hurt, weighted, disabled, or isolated feet, shown for example in the action *Wie Man dem toten Hasen die Bilder erklarärt* (How to Explain Pictures to a Dead Hare) or in *Eurasienstab* (Eurasian Staff). In these performances, Beuys strapped an iron sole under his right foot and climbed a room to work fat into the corners (Voigt, "The Great Reason of the Body" 15). Beuys' performative artworks never illustrate Nietzsche but invert and break down his ideas.

Likewise, when enrolled at Dusseldorf Art Academy during Beuys' tenure, Gerhard Richter parallaxes but does not imitate Beuys. The last part of *Never Look Away* in the 1960s reimagines interactions between Gerhard Richter and Joseph Beuys in scenes of Kurt studying under a Professor Antonius Van Verten at the Düsseldorf Art Academy. After visiting Kurt's studio one day, Prof. Van Verten instructs the artist to paint "what is real and home." Then instead of giving Kurt specific advice, Van Verten tells a story about how he became an artist not dissimilar to the mythology surrounding Beuys' life and work. Scenes between the Düsseldorf Professor and Kurt are embellished but provide context on the process of Fluxus and rhythmic rebirth.

The professor says that during World War II he was a Nazi pilot and radio operator whose plane was shot down. Nomad peasants pulled him out of what was left of the fiery wreckage, rubbed grease upon his formidable wounds, and wrapped him in felt velvet. This convalescence lasted a year until the war was over. Through performance art, Van Verten became a professor, and continued the rhythmic ritual of applying grease and felt on his skin. Before his brush with death, Van Verten said his life was uneventful: "I had no artistic talent." In the end, the Professor implores Kurt to search out and repeat whatever performative acts sensorily evoke what is "real and home." Heeding the Professor's words, Kurt begins painting over clips from suggestive news articles and childhood photographs. This becomes an artistic practice of ritualistically negating representation in photographs and painting.

Richter's artworks incorporate a variable flux but avoid the metaphysical and shamanistic tendencies of his colleague, Joseph Beuys. In works like *Erster Blick* (2000), *Graphit* (2005), and the mural *Strontium* (2004), the painter incorporates nanotech images only apprehended with a microscope. These artworks amplify transient aspects of nature only detected through unnatural machines to show,

> the loss of aura inherent in its photographic destruction [which] is to be encountered predominantly in Richter's landscape series, in which the paramount examples of the sublime, namely mountain ranges and seascapes, are transformed via montage into mere serial analogies. It is the seascapes most of all that make use of the stock of montage and retouching techniques in order to deny the existence of aura, or rather to smuggle it in through the back door. (Koch 138–39)

Inverting the sublime, Richter's "landscapes" avoid fetishizing nature by magnifying its uncertainty, ugliness, and volatility.

As one of the world's most well-known living painters, Gerhard Richter's artworks suspend the barrage of "information" that crowds out reflective judgment in modern culture. His painterly technique of negation, evacuation, and overpainting allows the spectator to slowly reflect through variable rhythmic strokes. His multisensory artworks are a detox from the prison of spectacle and surface representation. Their uncertainty provokes a recovery of the senses and a realization of limits in perception. They hook the viewer into transient and untimely truths that counter official history.

For this, Gerhardt Richter has rightly been called "contemporary art's great poet of uncertainty; his work sets the will to believe and the obligation to doubt in perfect oscillation" (Tallman 4). His gray photo-paintings, many prints, facsimiles, and artist books are spin-offs of paintings and part of an atlas of objects that multiply creative movement. For example, the monumental painting sextet *Cage* (2006) started out as photo-paintings of scientific images of atoms (resembling fuzzy photographs). These images of particle behavior were committed to canvas in black and white, then color, then painted, and scratched out. At the end of four months, the atom array appeared only as an

> inherited rhythm with the complex accretion of paint. In its grandeur of agitation and resolution, *Cage* may be as close to the sublime as contemporary painting can get. Perhaps it was to knock the dust off that

sublimity that Richter followed up with two facsimile editions, breaking Cage 6 into sixteen parts that can be carried in a flight case and hung in any configuration that suits the owner. (Tallman 7–8)

Combining the techniques of capital realism, mechanical reproduction, post-minimal modernism, and Fluxus, Richter doesn't abandon or elevate representation. Rather, his artwork inverts and breaks down the mimetic into variable configurations.

As cataloging and foregrounding blind spots in his own creation, Richter's artworks are not precious and often split into many different shapes. They make a counter-history that Richter finds, keeps, and constructs into a multisensory archival Atlas.[15] This archive includes newspaper stories, media clips, and other paraphernalia that are collected and made into a library of mis/representational lost objects, clippings scraps, and memorabilia. As Tallman notes,

> Richter began keeping photographs, clippings, and sketches of potential source material that would become Atlas, his now career-long half-archive half-artwork of things [the artist describes as] "somewhere between art and garbage and that somehow seemed important to me and a pit to throw away". (Tallman 5)

These found objects, like Lacan's lost object *a*, spur the painting process that inverts representation to reveal a void. *Atlas* carries the weight of the Gerhard Richter world as an artistic map to and through the crossroads of personal and world histories.

Gerhard Richter's paintings push every representational frame, with a blurred brush stroke that defies mimetic representation. He does this by painting a parallax view of traumatic and transient flux that both looks and looks away at the same time. In keeping with Richter's artworks, *Never Look Away* overscreens disastrous parts of history that are blinding—even to the artist. The film shows nothing about Gerhard Richter's life after Düsseldorf in Cologne and most of the interactions between Kurt and his first wife are invented. To that extent, *Never Look Away* both represents and misrepresents the real painter's life. This is done on purpose as an artistic method of proliferating, questioning, and putting a pause on visual certainty in the arts, media, and official records of history. The film unravels around seasons of Richter's life and art to screen the "pre-inscription that sends us back to the chaos that obviously was not schematized by us so that we should appear as what we are. In this sense, perhaps 'every soul is a rhythmic knot.' We ('we') are rhythmed" (Lacoue-Labarthe 202). Unreeling around the reverberations of artistic rebirth after disaster, *Never Look Away* screens the void of traumatic memory and transient pre-inscription.

It makes an *allobiography* of "richtering rhythms" that shows how we are always both seeing and not seeing the movement of life while it is happening; Real vision is a parallax view and river of living forward by looking back *après-coup*.

Notes

1 Lacoue-Labarthe's idea of *Allobiography* explores rhythm in relation to the drift Derrida writes about as the problem of presence in biography and autobiographical writing and identity. Referring to Nietzsche's autobiographical works like "Ecce Homo," Derrida critiques the metaphysics of presence in these genres, which presuppose fixity where there is drift. *The Ear of the Other* exposes how entanglements of difference, lack, and the other eternally disrupt transparent identity in representation, as demonstrated in biography. Moreover, there is a fluidity or thin line between an artwork and its author's life, an oeuvre as a body of writing/art but also as a subject, a corpus, and actual body. This drift is a rhythm that poses the "problematic of the biographical in general and other resources, including at the very least a new analysis of the proper name and the signatures" (Derrida 5). Notably, there is no drift in the more fixated writing of psychotics. For example, the memoirs of Daniel Paul Schreber or the neologisms in Joyce are affective signs not signifiers. Hence, the autobiography/ memoir of the procreative non-neurotic does not represent but performatively enacts change via writing and artistic creation.
2 My translation from the German here "*Er malte Tante Marianne, er malte seinen späteren Schwiegervater Eufinger, er wurde der Bote des deutschen Dramas, ohne dass es ihm bewusst war.*" Jürgen Schreiber, "Das Geheimnis des Malers Gerhard Richter," *Der Tagesspiegel Online*, August 22, 2004, sec. Politik, https:// www.tagesspiegel.de/politik/das-geheimnis-des-malers-gerhard-richter/541096. html.
3 In 2006, this painting was a source of state controversy since it was sold to the Chinese but considered part of German history (Harding). Some, including Schreiber, view the painting as a German cultural relic that should stay in Germany. These citizens believe that it is a witness to how the Nazis euthanized and sterilized many women in psychiatric hospitals. Schreiber asserts that this information has been repressed and hidden from the German people who need it to be exhibited and discussed. Regardless, this painting and its history are being amply discussed across the globe thanks to Gerhard Richter.
4 Gerhard Richter's own website has biographical information about his time in Dresden, including being required to join the "Pimpfen," a mandatory organization for children that prepared them to become Hitler Youth.
5 In the late sixties, Lacan focuses his attention more and more on the drives as *acephalic*, and a headless knowing that brings satisfaction. This certainty involves no inherent relation to truth, no subjective position of enunciation or desire.
6 As a unique and rare event, Gerhard Richter agreed to let the filmmaker Corinna Belz do a series of documentary films about his painting and artistic method. One entitled "Gerhard Richter Painting" discusses the "physical dimension of how he works. You could see how the paintings changed, but you couldn't see Richter contemplating them. That's why we decided to use a hand-held camera after all, starting with the yellow paintings. That worked well-it became indispensable to me" (Belz et al.).

7   Freud describes the drive as the transience that is the basis of being.
8   In Lacanian terms, the parallax view is that the subject's gaze is always already inscribed into the perceived object itself, in the guise of its blind spot. The other is the object more than the object, the point from which the object itself returns the gaze. The parallax view is one of those meta-moments where you see the other seeing you, or when the *object petit a* comes forth as the very cause of the parallax gap. This *object a* inscribes "the difference between two positively existing objects, the minimal difference which divides one and the same object from itself" (18).
9   *Exiles* is also a reimagining of "The Haunted Ocean 1," which was the soundtrack and score for Ari Folman's animated documentary about the Lebanon war, *Waltz With Bashir*, in 2008.
10   Sebastian Koch was also in Donnersmarck's "The Lives of Others" and played a writer whose life, loves, and work are all scrutinized and subjugated under Stasi surveillance. This Oscar-winning film, like *Never Look Away*, shows the conflict between creative expression and state suppression.
11   "Marie-Hélène Brousse calls sublimation a "not very orthodox cure, and a not very well-defined concept." Yet, creativity allows the analysand to develop their own private discourse where each artwork is an index to the act, "pointed to the orientation of a decided desire" (Brousse 66).
12   In a warning against the total conflation of art and life, Jenny Odell discusses the impossibility and irresponsibility of artists who entirely drop out of society or "cancel culture." She uses the example of Swiss curator Harald Szeemann's Zurich exhibition entitled *Der Hang Zum Gesamtkunstwerk* (The Tendency Toward the Total Artwork) that included Beuys in this critique and quotes the writer Hans Miller, who notes, "the *Hauptstrom* as Beuys called it—the grand idea was still essential to energize society. *Hauptstrom* translates to something like 'mainstream,' in the sense of electrical current. And the word *Hang* in the exhibition's title . . . translates variously to 'addiction,' 'penchant,' or even 'downward slope,' implying an innate tendency in humans" (Odell 53–54). Szeemann was looking for an impulse that strained the bounds of representation and found in the difference between an artistic rhythm or pull and mainstream "*Hauptstrom*" rhythms. The task for the artist, then, is not to withdraw into creative rhythmic bliss, but to find a way to move between the avant-garde and mainstream such that one informs the other. Fluxus, and in this case Beuys, stages this aesthetic pull as a differential between mainstream language and expression in the artwork as a counter-cultural current.
13   Correlatively, in "The Origin of the Work of Art," Heidegger relates *Zug*, which is the German word for thrust or pull, to the "differential thrust and conflict" of art; "Whenever art happens—that is, whenever there is a beginning—a *thrust* [my italics] enters history" in (Heidegger 77).
14   One example of Beuys' happenings was his famous performance work in 1974 where he flew to America to spend three consecutive days with a wild coyote. This performance piece entitled "*I Like America and America Likes Me*" was one example of what he called his "social sculptures," which were actions intended to change society for the better. Beuys believed that "everyone is an artist" with the ability and agency to transform the world around them" (Mann 1). The piece performatively suggested that America is like a wild coyote, which is a symbol of the trickster as resilient and transformative but also a wild-spirited predator.
15   Gerhard Richter began to assemble *Atlas* in 1969 after leaving East Germany as a way of maintaining documents that would otherwise be politically seized, stolen, or coopted. The *Atlas*, like his earlier catalogue *raisonné*, is a numeric and

historic but not based on a linear system or chronology. It is partially based on thematic, partially taxonomic groupings, but mostly a collage and cut-up auto-biographical collage of pictorial non-equivalences. *In Forty Years of Painting* notes how it contains

> contrasts press photos of Adolf Hitler speaking or visiting with supporters—a series immediately preceded by mountain views that recall the Nazi cult of the Alps—with news photographs of a lion devouring a tourist that were the basis for Tourist (with a Lion) of 1975 and related paintings. The editorial mind at work in forming these ensembles seems as determined to disrupt patterns as to create them, as eager to draw attention to certain pictorial equivalences or disjunctions as to nestle the most personal or shocking items or clusters of items in settings that obscure their meaning to the artist and stymie interpretation based on conventional attitudes regarding intrin-sic significance. At once a vast index of primary material and a device for reviewing and rethinking the many possible relations of one image to an-other as icons of their own right, as imagin-types, or as entries in his intel-lectual and artistic autobiography, Atlas is a mechanism for simultaneously organizing and disorganizing information, a way of showing the artist's hand and of camouflaging his intimate connections ito the contents on display. (Storr et al. 29)

Works Cited

1961–1964: The Düsseldorf Academy Years "Biography" Gerhard Richter. 6 Nov. 2021, https://www.gerhard-richter.com/en/biography/19611964-the-dusseldorf-academy-years-4.

Beckman, Karen. "Review of Flesh of My Flesh." *The Art Bulletin*, vol. 92, no. 3, 2010, pp. 258–62, https://www.jstor.org/stable/29546127.

Belz, Corinna, et al. *Gerhard Richter Painting.* Zero One Film, Terz Film, Westdeutscher Rundfunk (WDR), 2012.

Brousse, Marie-Hélène. "A Sublimation at Risk..." *Lacanian Ink*, no. 24/25, 2005, pp. 64–73.

Civitarese, Giuseppe. "Masochism and Its Rhythm." *Journal of the American Psychoanalytic Association*, vol. 64, no. 5, Oct. 2016, pp. 885–916, https://doi.org/10.1177/0003065116674442.

Dâmaso, Mafalda. "Gerhard Richter's September and the Politics of Ambiv-alence." *Terror in Global Narrative: Representations of 9/11 in the Age of Late-Late Capitalism*, edited by George Fragopoulos and Liliana M. Nay-dan, Springer International Publishing, 2016, pp. 157–71, https://doi.org/10.1007/978-3-319–40654-1_9.

Datema, Jessica, and Manya Steinkoler. *Revisioning War Trauma in Cinema: Uncoming Communities.* Lexington Books, 2019.

Deleuze, Gilles. *Cinema 2: The Time-Image.* Translated by Hugh Tomlinson and Robert Galeta, University of Minnesota, 1986.

———. *Francis Bacon: The Logic of Sensation.* University of Minnesota Press, 2004.

Donnersmarck, Florian Henckel von, et al. *Werk Ohne Autor.* Pergamon Film, Wiedemann & Berg Filmproduktion, Beta Cinema, 2018.

Eigen, Michael. "A Basic Rhythm." *The Psychoanalytic Review*, vol. 89, no. 5, Oct. 2002, pp. 721–40, https://doi.org/10.1521/prev.89.5.721.22103.

Freud, Sigmund. "On Transience." *Collected Papers Vol. 5*, translated by James Strachey, Hogarth, 1950, pp. 79–82.

Gaudillière, Jean-Max. *Madness and the Social Link: The Jean-Max Gaudillière Seminars 1985–2000*. Edited by Françoise Davoine, Translated by Agnès Jacob, Routledge, 2021.

Goodyear, Dana. "An Artist's Life, Refracted in Film." *The New Yorker*, Jan. 2019, pp. 32–41, https://www.newyorker.com/magazine/2019/01/21/an-artists-life-refracted-in-film.

Harding, Luke. "Dismay as German Painting Is Sold Abroad." *The Guardian*, 23 June 2006, https://www.theguardian.com/world/2006/jun/23/arts.germany.

Heidegger, Martin. *Poetry, Language, Thought*. Harper & Row, 1971.

Henriques, Julian, et al. "Rhythm Returns: Movement and Cultural Theory." *Body & Society*, vol. 20, no. 3–4, Sep. 2014, pp. 3–29, https://doi.org/10.1177/1357034X14547393.

Hickley, Catherine. "A Stained-Glass Gift, From God and Gerhard Richter." *The New York Times*, 18 Sep. 2020, pp. C1–2, https://www.nytimes.com/2020/09/18/arts/design/gerhard-richter-windows.html.

Higgins, Hannah. *Fluxus Experience*. University of California Press, 2003.

Joyce, James. *A Portrait of the Artist as a Young Man*. Viking Press, Penguin Books, 1966.

Koch, Gertrud. "The Richter-Scale of Blur." *October*, vol. 62, 1992, pp. 133–42, https://www.jstor.org/stable/778707.

Lacan, Jacques. "Joyce the Symptom II." *Autre Écrits "Joyce the Symptom,"* translated by Dan Collins, vol. 1976, 1975, http://apwonline.org/download/joyce-the-symptom-ii.pdf.

——. "On Psychoanalytic Discourse." *La Salmandra*, translated by Jack Stone, 1978, pp. 32–55, https://web.archive.org/web/20140729192754/http://web.missouri.edu/~stonej/t67894312xxxv.html.

——. *The Ethics of Psychoanalysis, 1959–1960, Book VII*. Edited by Jacques-Alain Miller, Translated by Dennis Porter, vol. 7, WW Norton, 1997.

——. *The Four Fundamental Concepts of Psychoanalysis*. Translated by Jacques-Alain Miller, WW Norton, 1998.

——. *The Sinthôme: The Seminar of Jacques Lacan, Book XXIII*. Translated by A. R Price, 1st edition, Polity, 2016.

Lacoue-Labarthe, Philippe. *Typography: Mimesis, Philosophy, Politics*. Edited by Christopher Fynsk, Stanford University Press, 1998.

Lane, Anthony, and Richard Brody. "Eyes Wide Open." *New Yorker*, vol. 94, no. 48, Feb. 2019, pp. 72–73.

Lister, Kat. "Composer-Pianist Max Richter: 'Creativity Is Activism.'" *The Guardian*, 2 Aug. 2021, https://www.theguardian.com/music/2021/aug/02/max-richter-album-exiles.

Mann, Jon. "When Joseph Beuys Locked Himself in a Room with a Live Coyote." *Artsy*, 3 Nov. 2017, https://www.artsy.net/article/artsy-editorial-joseph-beuys-locked-room-live-coyote.

Miller, Jacques-Alain. "Closing Remarks at the Rally of the Impossible Professions, against the False Promises of Security." *Hurly-Burly*, no. 1, May 2009, pp. 209–14, https://hal-univ-paris8.archives-ouvertes.fr/hal-00998504.

Nancy, Jean-Luc. *The Muses*. Stanford University Press, 1996.

Odell, Jenny. *How to Do Nothing: Resisting the Attention Economy*. Melville House, 2019.

Rancière, Jacques. *The Emancipated Spectator*. Translated by Gregory Elliott, Verso Books, 2011, p. 134.

Richter, Gerhard Nicolaus, et al. *Gerhard Richter – Text: Writings, Interviews and Letters, 1961–2007*. Thames & Hudson, 2009.

Richter, Max. *Memoryhouse*. CD, Deutsche Grammophon, 2009, https://www.maxrichtermusic.com/albums/memoryhouse/.

Saketopoulou, Avgi. "Trauma Lives Us: Affective Excess, Safe Spaces and the Erasure of Subjectivity." *Bully Bloggers*, vol. 6, 2014, http://web-facstaff.sas.upenn.edu/~cavitch/pdf-library/Saketopoulou_Trauma.pdf.

Schneiderman, Stuart. "The Boy Who Cried Wolf." *Lacanian Ink*, vol. 24/25, 2005, pp. 111–25.

Schreiber, Jürgen. "Das Geheimnis des Malers Gerhard Richter." *Der Tagesspiegel Online*, 22 Aug. 2004. *Tagesspiegel*, https://www.tagesspiegel.de/politik/das-geheimnis-des-malers-gerhard-richter/541096.html.

Sebald, W. G. *On the Natural History of Destruction*. Translated by Anthea Bell, Modern Library, 2004.

Sherer, Margaret. *A Network of Experience: Community Building and Social Restructuring in Fluxus*. Washington University, 2016, https://openscholarship.wustl.edu/cgi/viewcontent.cgi?&httpsredir=1&article=1720&context=art_sci_etds.

Silverman, Kaja. *Flesh of My Flesh*. Stanford University Press, 2009.

Storr, Robert, et al. *Gerhard Richter: Forty Years of Painting*. Museum of Modern Art, 2002.

Tallman, Susan. "The Master of Unknowing." *The New York Review of Books*, vol. 67, no. 8, May 2020, pp. 4–8, https://www.nybooks.com/articles/2020/05/14/gerhard-richter-master-unknowing/.

Thorn-Prikker, Jan. "ART: A Picture Is Worth 216 Newspaper Articles." *The New York Times*, 4 July 2004, p. 26, https://www.nytimes.com/2004/07/04/books/art-a-picture-is-worth-216-newspaper-articles.html.

Voigt, Kirsten Claudia. *Friedrich Nietzsche und Joseph Beuys: Das autopoietische Subjekt*. 1st edition, SCHIRMER/MOSEL VERLAG GMBH, 2016.

——. "The Great Reason of the Body: Friedrich Nietzsche, Joseph Beuys and the Art of Giving Meaning to Matter and Earth – Tate Papers." *Tate Papers*, Nov. 2021, https://www.tate.org.uk/research/publications/tate-papers/32/nietzsche-beuys-giving-meaning-matter-earth.

Žižek, Slavoj. *The Parallax View*. MIT Press, 2006.

Index

For Product Safety Concerns and Information please contact our EU
representative GPSR@taylorandfrancis.com
Taylor & Francis Verlag GmbH, Kaufingerstraße 24, 80331 München, Germany

www.ingramcontent.com/pod-product-compliance
Lightning Source LLC
Chambersburg PA
CBHW050653280326
41932CB00015B/2886